T0329956

Innovation Management

NEW HORIZONS IN INNOVATION MANAGEMENT

Books in the New Horizons in Innovation Management series make a significant contribution to the development of Innovation Studies. As this field has expanded dramatically in recent years, the series will provide an invaluable forum for the publication of high-quality works of scholarship and show the diversity of issues and practices around the world.

Global in its approach, it includes some of the best theoretical and empirical work with contributions to fundamental principles, rigorous evaluations of existing concepts and competing theories, historical surveys and future visions.

Titles in the series include:

Innovation Management

Perspectives from Strategy, Product, Process and Human Resources Research

Edited by

Vida Škudienė

ISM University of Management and Economics, Lithuania

Jason Li-Ying

Technical University of Denmark, Denmark

Fabian Bernhard

EDHEC Business School, France

NEW HORIZONS IN INNOVATION MANAGEMENT

EE **Edward Elgar**
PUBLISHING

Cheltenham, UK • Northampton, MA, USA

Published by
Edward Elgar Publishing Limited
The Lypiatts
15 Lansdown Road
Cheltenham
Glos GL50 2JA
UK

Edward Elgar Publishing, Inc.
William Pratt House
9 Dewey Court
Northampton
Massachusetts 01060
USA

A catalogue record for this book
is available from the British Library

Library of Congress Control Number: 2019952392

This book is available electronically in the **Elgar**online
Business subject collection
DOI 10.4337/9781789909814

ISBN 978 1 78990 980 7 (cased)
ISBN 978 1 78990 981 4 (eBook)

Printed and bound by CPI Group (UK) Ltd, Croydon, CR0 4YY

Contents

PART IV   PROCESS INNOVATION MANAGEMENT

PART V   HUMAN RESOURCE INNOVATION MANAGEMENT

PART VI   CASE STUDY

Figures

Tables

About the editors

Vida Škudienė is Professor in Management, Head of the MSc programme Innovation and Technology Management at ISM University of Management and Economics and serves as a visiting professor at Nagoya University of Commerce and Business, Japan. She conducted her PhD research at University of South Carolina, USA. Her research concentrates on organizational behaviour, innovation management, and relationship marketing. Professor Škudienė has presented her research at international conferences in France, Japan, Israel, USA (Hawaii, Chicago), Greece, Croatia, France, Spain, Norway, Jamaica, Sweden, Portugal and Italy (Boccioni) and published over 40 articles. She has taught and done research at EDHEC university in France, IPAM Instituto Portugues de Administracao de Marketing and Catholica University in Portugal, Zagreb School of Economics and Management in Croatia, Reykjavik University in Iceland, Aarhus University in Denmark, Salento University in Italy, and University of Northern Colorado, USA. Professor Škudienė is a member of editorial review boards of *Baltic Journal of Management, Business and Economics Journal* and *Organizations and Markets in Emerging Economies* and is a recipient of several research awards such as ISM Distinguished Scholar Award, Best Paper Award from Clute Institute, The International Academy of Business and Public Administration Disciplines and Marketing Management Association Awards, USA.

Jason Li-Ying is Professor in Corporate Entrepreneurship and Innovation and the director of research at the Centre for Technology Entrepreneurship, Technical University of Denmark. He has research interests in technology and innovation management, entrepreneurship in Big Science organizations, strategic management, and technology transfer. His work has been published in scientific journals such as *Long Range Planning, Journal of Product Innovation Management, Asia Pacific Journal of Management, Technovation, Technological Forecasting and Social Change, R&D Management, Journal of Knowledge Management, Journal of Technology Transfer*, and *Management and Organization Review*, among others. He is also a member of the journal ranking expert committee for the Danish Ministry of Education and Research. Besides his teaching and research excellence, he also serves as a board member at China-Denmark Innovation House and advisory board for FOM Technology Co. Ltd.

Fabian Bernhard is Associate Professor of Management and part of the Family Business Center at EDHEC Business School in Paris, Lille, and London. He is a research fellow for family business at the University of Mannheim in Germany and previously at Stetson University in Florida. Equipped with the insights from his own family's business, he worked for several years for a renowned financial consulting company in New York. In his academic work he specializes in the emotional dynamics in family businesses, the preparation of next generational leaders, and psychological attachment to the family business. His articles have been published in various academic and practitioner outlets as well as in the public media. He is a recipient of several honours and awards for his work on family businesses, such as The Best Dissertation Honorable Mention by FFI at Harvard. Since 2014 he has been serving on the editorial review boards of the *Family Business Review* and the *Journal of Family Business Strategy*. Since 2017 he has been a member of the Board of Directors of the Family Firm Institute in Boston.

Contributors

Vilte Auruskeviciene	ISM University of Management and Economics, Lithuania
Fabian Bernhard	EDHEC Business School, France
Ilona Buciuniene	ISM University of Management and Economics, Lithuania
Jin Chen	Tsinghua University, China
Alfredas Chmieliauskas	ISM University of Management and Economics, Lithuania
Suzanne L. Conner	Georgia Southwestern State University, USA
Gurram Gopal	Illinois Institute of Technology, USA
Kristina Grigorjevaite	ISM University of Management and Economics, Lithuania
Asta Klimaviciene	ISM University of Management and Economics, Lithuania
Jason Li-Ying	Technical University of Denmark, Denmark
Daniel Paulino Teixeira Lopes	Federal Center for Technological Education of Minas Gerais, Brazil
Tadao Onaka	Nagoya University of Commerce and Business, Japan
Egle Pilkauskaite	ISM University of Management and Economics, Lithuania
Sabina Senkevic	ISM University of Management and Economics, Lithuania
Sarunas Sereika	ISM University of Management and Economics, Lithuania
Saulius Simkonis	ISM University of Management and Economics, Lithuania
Vida Škudienė	ISM University of Management and Economics, Lithuania

Olga Stangej	ISM University of Management and Economics, Lithuania
Kenji Tadakuma	Nagoya University of Commerce and Business, Japan
Gintare Vezeliene	ISM University of Management and Economics, Lithuania
Yuandi Wang	Sichuan University, China
Rumintha Wickramasekera	Queensland University of Technology, Australia

PART I

Introduction

1. Innovation management: perspectives from strategy, product, process and human resource research

Vida Škudienė, Jason Li-Ying and Fabian Bernhard

INTRODUCTION

Innovations and the ways to manage them in organizational settings are undoubtedly a hot topic these days. This interest is not surprising as creating new ideas and continuously innovating are key to differentiation in a more and more competitive marketplace. Many companies see innovation as their best and sometimes only chance to acquire a competitive advantage in the market.

Accordingly, managers of various types of organizations, public or private, are eager to learn about the latest trends, but find it challenging to keep up-to-date with current management knowledge in terms of guiding principles and best practices. They seek to develop their competencies particularly in innovation management in order to meet more effectively the growing demands from a highly competitive contemporary market. However, the ability to innovate often involves simultaneously managing product, processes, people and strategy. This can be challenging. Therefore, understanding how to manage innovation from a strategic perspective and meanwhile remaining focused on best practices in product development, process change, and human resource management becomes extremely important for managers.

Students in management, economics, social science and engineering are also interested in learning about innovation. Many business schools have set up specific programmes or courses on how to deal with innovations in organizations. Classes on entrepreneurship and creativity are popular in STEM (science, technology, engineering and mathematics) universities. Incubators at universities flourish and are seen as the source of new ideas and innovative businesses. And finally, academics are also interested in an overview of the latest findings from cutting-edge research in innovation management.

Unsurprisingly the literature on these topics is abundant but finding one's way through the jungle of latest knowledge might be difficult. The present book tries to help students, academics, and practitioners by offering an up-to-date summary of innovation management with an integrated inner logic and a global perspective. In line with other scholars, we broadly define the concept of innovation as a new structure or management process, a policy, a new plan or programme, a new production process, or a new product or service produced in an organization. However, being different from many other volumes on the market, the present book examines innovation management through four unique perspectives – strategy, product, processes and people.

But why these four perspectives? How are they linked in terms of making sense of managing innovation? Consider Huawei Technologies Co. Ltd. (hereinafter Huawei), the Chinese multinational technology company, whose core businesses include telecommunications networks and equipment, and consumer electronics, including smartphones and laptops, headquartered in Shenzhen, Guangdong, China. Huawei made headline news in business and technology media a few years ago when it succeeded in the global 4G network market and became the world's second largest smartphone manufacturer behind Apple. Huawei is also taking a global leadership role in 5G wireless network technologies, as it holds the most 5G related patents and the largest market share of 5G network installation globally so far. Although Huawei could be criticized for using a copycat strategy during its early phase of business in the late 1980s and 1990s, after 30 years of development, there is no doubt that Huawei has become a global innovator. When asked how Huawei managed to succeed, according to a source from Huawei, the CEO of Huawei, Mr Zhengfei Ren, stated that:

> Huawei has developed and succeeded, first and foremost, thanks to the business environment, the sectors that rapidly and extensively demand technologies and value creation. We then managed to make an effective strategy that captured the opportunities embedded in the environment, and then following the strategy, we hired a lot of talents, whom we have made the best use of based on effective incentive schemes, so that these highly talented and highly motivated people were able to develop new products that make sense to the market. We also paid attention to how to make these new products, the process must be right. When the new products are right, and the processes of making them are right, we can sustain competitive advantage against competitors. We then bring the return from the market back to new waves of continuous research and development (R&D), and this full circle goes on and on and on . . .[1]

Mr Ren's view, more likely his management philosophy, on Huawei's success as such is perhaps the perfect answer to why we select strategy, product, processes and people as the four most critical aspects of innovation management to present to the readers. They are integrated parts of a coherent management logic as follows: the social, economic and political environments create potential business opportunities, which can only be grasped with an innovation strategy. Strategy further guides the direction of new product development by defining how radically new a product should be, what types of innovation are required to pull resources together and where the target market is. This usually is a journey of trial and error, which reflectively gives feedback to adapt the strategy. The process of reflective interaction between strategy and product innovation has a goal to 'get the right things'. In this process, technology is important but must serve the strategy and product innovation. Next, only getting the right things is not enough to achieve success – firms need to adopt new technology to increase efficiency and effectiveness. The process of innovation is about 'getting the things right'. Last but not least, and perhaps the most fundamental element in Mr Ren's mind, are the people, the human resources that drive innovation and meanwhile without losing control. Thus, human resource management (HRM) for innovation is about getting the right balance between control and incentive and about creating an innovative climate and culture.

The inner logic of innovation management that integrates the four critical aspects is illustrated in Figure 1.1 as an overall framework for this book, which is a collection of studies on each aspect. While understanding this integrated framework is important, readers who are interested in only a particular aspect can easily gain knowledge and insights by reading the respective chapter. The major questions addressed include: How to transform traditional human resource management by implementing innovative HRM systems? How to implement process and project innovation by integrating continuous improvement and business process re-engineering? How to manage the relationship between innovation performance and financial performance? What are the best management practices for a new product development? How to innovate through licensing? What can we learn from international industrial innovations experience?

OVERVIEW

This book offers new insights into the latest trends of innovation management in research and management. It consists of four parts that cover different perspectives and provide a holistic view across the key areas of innovation management. It illustrates the state of the art from the viewpoint of strategic innovation management, product innovation management, process innovation

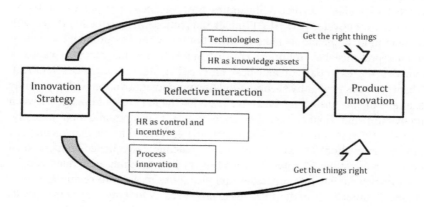

Figure 1.1   *Conceptual framework of the book*

management and human resource innovation management. Scholars from various countries in Europe (France, Denmark, Lithuania), Asia (China and Japan), and America (USA and Brazil) provide new understanding and research on the relevant topics, given their respective academic and practical backgrounds. They are experts in the field with knowledge on principles, strategies and applications in the specific area of innovation management.

The book addresses the four domains of the innovation management research, namely strategic, product, process and people. Readers are encouraged to look into the part that suits best their current needs or get inspiration by digging deeper into individual chapters. Management students at the master's level are offered a comprehensive overview on the topic that can stimulate the development of their innovation management skills. Academics can use this book to get a quick overview on the latest development in innovation management research and get inspired to seek new research directions. Practitioners, especially managers in large organizations, may also gain from reading this book, as it offers new insights for creating a sustainable innovation strategy to achieve competitive advantage in the long run. By offering an integrated framework with four key perspectives, this book can help practitioners to define and renew a winning innovation organization based on a sound understanding of the influential managerial elements.

After this introductory chapter, each part of the book focuses on a specific aspect of innovation management. Part II ('Innovation Management Strategy') provides insights into the strategic perspective. Chapters 2 and 3 put their emphasis on recent developments in the fast-moving Asian context. Chapter

2 highlights the importance of using technology licensing to innovate in the context of China. Chapter 3 illustrates how Japanese companies strategize in order to innovate. Part III ('Product Innovation Management') deals with product innovation and its management. For many readers product innovation often represents the prominent core of innovation management. Chapter 4 explains the essentials of and best practices in new product development. Chapter 5 goes further by shedding light on product innovation with a concrete example of soft furnishing. Next, we learn in Chapter 6 about linkage between innovation and financial performance in the telecommunication industry. Part IV ('Process Innovation Management') is devoted to the management of process innovation. The key theme is how to achieve excellence in operational process innovation. Chapter 7 gives answers by examining integrated continuous improvements into processes and also looks at ways to re-engineer processes. Chapter 8 illustrates innovation processes by looking at system analysts as an example. Part V ('Human Resource Innovation Management') comprises three chapters on HRM and its impact on innovation. Chapter 9 shows us the advantages and challenges of implementing an innovative electric HRM system. Chapter 10 examines the relationship between HR practices and innovation. Effective HR practices towards innovation are discussed through an analysis of data from Brazil in Latin America. Lastly, Chapter 11 offers a micro perspective by presenting an overview on the role of human emotions in innovative behaviours. A case study of UPS Lithuania is presented in Part VI and provides an opportunity for the reader to consider this company's innovative approach to strategic, process, employee motivation and compensation management areas.

In the following discussion, each of these parts is presented in more detail. We conclude with final observations on the innovation management research perspectives and their international research value for the reader.

Innovation Management Strategy

Innovation management builds upon understanding the context of internal and external capabilities, the ever-changing uncertainties of future technology developments and competitive challenges. In formulating innovation strategies, organizations and companies have to take into consideration interorganizational, national and international systems and resources. The fundamental debate in innovation management is based on two contrasting approaches toward corporate strategy: rational and incremental. The supporters of the rational strategy approach see it as a linear model of rational action: appraisal, determination, action and focus on the analysis with complete understanding of the internal and external factors before taking strategic decisions. In contrast, incrementalists argue that companies may receive only some information from their environment and therefore must adapt their innovation strategy in the light of new knowledge and information following a three-step procedure: make deliberate changes towards the objective, measure and evaluate these changes, and adjust (if necessary) the objective before deciding on the next change.

The corporate innovation strategy according to Teece and Pisano (1994) incorporates three elements: (1) competitive and national positions; (2) technological paths; and (3) organizational and managerial processes. The more recent research by Jaruzelski et al. (2011) suggests that there is no single optimum strategy for innovation and distinguishes three clusters of observable good practice-based strategy: technology drivers, need seekers, and market readers. Technology drivers focus on developing new technologies; need seekers aim to be first in the market and focus on identifying customer needs and product development; and market readers seek to be the first followers and focus mainly on process innovation.

Part II explores the decisions about what innovation path is relevant for companies as they inevitably involve issues of strategic perspective and tend to be different across industries and countries. For example the Chinese approach to innovation management is based on learning from multinational companies established by the developed countries. Chinese innovation management follows the market reader approach. By employing technology licensing, managers seek to access external resources and pursue tight collaboration with local partners. In this approach, Chinese take a unique path to develop innovation capabilities. In Chapter 2 ('Innovation management through technology licensing in China'), Li-Ying et al. argue that this kind of innovation strategy should be recognized by companies when strategic decisions are being made. The authors, based on the research of State Intellectual Property Office of China (SIPO) data, provide insights and examples of the Chinese management practices used to innovate effectively and claim that technology licensing is a unique and successful innovation strategy.

A lot of research into innovation management strategy has focused on technological paths in the automotive industry context. Michael Hobday (1995) analysed modernization development in East Asian countries and provided arguments about how companies in these countries succeeded in rapid learning and technological innovation. His conclusions are illustrated by the examples of Japanese and Korean firms. In Chapter 3 ('Innovation management: the Japanese way'), Tadakuma et al. discuss Japanese innovation management principles and provide a case study of Toyota Motor Corporation's innovation management. The authors explore insights into Japanese innovation management peculiarities referring to the company's social contribution, lifetime employment, decision making by consensus, sense of community and *Kaizen* perspectives. The impact of cultural mentality on the uniqueness of Japanese management style is discussed through the lens of work by Peter F. Drucker, Teresa Amabile and Clayton Christensen.

In the era of globalization, companies must constantly pursue innovation in order to advance in the competitive market. Never before has the world witnessed the rate of economic growth exemplified by contemporary China and Japan. This fact calls for consideration of Chinese and Japanese innovation management analysis. The two chapters in this part are devoted to the insights of Chinese and Japanese scientists and business representatives into the unique innovation strategy employed by these countries. By learning from these countries' experience, managers may develop an effective innovation strategy and successfully compete in the global market.

Product Innovation Management

Extant literature indicates that product innovation is the key factor for company sustainable competitive advantage and success (Atalay et al., 2013; Gunday et al., 2011; Jimenez and Sanz-Valle, 2011). Fauji and Utami (2013) indicated that product innovation in particular helps businesses improve their operations, processes and performance. Previous studies emphasize the importance of product innovation management that, if perceived by customers as resulting in higher product quality, can affect the intention to purchase the product (Fauji and Utami, 2013). According to Zhang et al. (2013) truly innovative products create value for customers, generate higher margins, and increase customer equity. However, for different product categories, different nationalities and different external as well as internal factors, the results may differ. Thus, it is imperative not only to take into consideration the promotional activities of innovative products but also to clearly demonstrate to customers that the company itself is innovative. The analyses of product innovation management provided by the researchers in Part III highlight the specifics of strategies and practices across countries and industry sections.

Chapter 4 ('Exploring best practices of new product development') by Suzanne Conner gives an overview of best practices in the New Product Development process from inception to success. According to the author, as new firms enter the market while others attempt to remain competitive in the increasingly crowded global business landscape, developing and introducing new products are often utilized as an attempt to gain market share or edge out the competition. Developing new products for any firm is more difficult than managing existing product lines due to uncertainties surrounding them. For firms, especially startups, that may not have the knowledge of how to develop new products successfully or how to bring them to market, this can be very difficult. By having a clear understanding of best practices in the new product development arena, the firm may increase its chances of initial and repeated success.

Chapter 5 ('Product design innovation and functional innovation effects on consumers' adoption of soft furniture') explores the effect of design innovation and functional innovation on consumers' purchase intention and willingness to pay for soft furniture products. Recent decades have changed the business environment substantially due to the progress of globalization and increased competition, which have affected and changed the basis for companies' success. As a result, to be successful, it is crucial to know the extent to which consumers perceive the company and its products as innovative and how this impacts consumer product adoption. Exploration of these aspects requires investigation of the overall design effect (form and function) of a product and its perception more widely, rather than a single aspect of a design. This chapter explores the effect of design innovation and functional innovation on consumers' purchase intention and willingness to pay for the soft furniture products.

Chapter 6 ('Innovation and financial performance in telecommunication companies') analyses the relationship between product innovation and financial performance in the European telecommunications industry. However, innovation cannot be a goal in itself. Innovation projects must serve companies' strategic goals and, ultimately, lead to value enhancement. Exploring the link between innovation and financial performance, this study focuses on financial measures that are commonly used by investors and financial analysts. Most of them are profitability ratios that can be calculated from the financial statements of a company, such as return on equity (one of the key financial ratios for shareholders), return on assets and operating margin. Successful product innovation management requires a strong market orientation providing high quality products consistent with customers' needs, with attractive price and innovative product features. The results may be useful for researchers and managers of firms operating in a similar industry in order to determine key performance indicators for both innovation and profitability measures.

Process Innovation Management

Process innovation is a key management lever that can drive enterprise growth through increased productivity and asset utilization. It enables firms to continuously lower operational costs and creates more investment opportunities. Part IV focuses on process innovation as a key lever for extracting sustainable competitive advantages that could lower operational expenses and enable firms to bring products to market faster.

Chapter 7 ('Implementing process innovation by integrating continuous improvement and business process re-engineering') describes how firms can achieve process innovation through a combination of continuous improvement

(CI) and business process re-engineering (BPR). While firms have often implemented CI in some functional areas, a comprehensive approach to CI is needed to drive process innovation. As better tools and methodologies become available firms can achieve significant operational improvement through the deployment of such tools. This adoption often results in a significant process restructuring, leading to the BPR approach. This chapter focuses on a range of process innovation activities and enables the development of a toolkit for process innovation, including Lean Six Sigma and the use of optimization tools and analytics.

Information Systems (IS) and Information Technology (IT) tools play a key role in driving process innovation and enable firms to achieve process excellence. Selection and deployment of appropriate IS can improve or break a company's operational processes, as evidenced by numerous high profile IS implementation failures. Traditionally, the process of IS development and deployment followed a Waterfall lifecycle where the entire process was split into a number of tasks that were performed serially. This caused significant delays and failures in deployment. Chapter 8 ('New role of systems analysts in Agile requirements engineering') explores Agile methodology, a new systems development and deployment process that focuses on continuous acceptance of changing functional requirements and delivery of small systems that can be rapidly tested, improved and deployed. The authors provide recommendations for the implementation of Agile methodology, focusing on the popular Scrum feature behind many Agile applications. Based on the current research, this chapter identifies the changes in knowledge and competencies required for system analysts to work effectively and collaborate successfully with various players in this new process framework.

The two topics in this part – the use of Agile methodology for rapid and successful implementation of modern IS and pursuing a combination of CI and business process restructuring – should be key tools in any business manager's toolkit for obtaining sustainable process innovation management benefits. These tools can play a major role in the more efficient use of resources and work towards a more sustainable economy.

Human Resource Innovation Management

In line with other organizational fields, human resource management has been subjected to rapid changes and the need to harness them as part of the strategic and tactical routine. Continuous technological development gives rise to multiple perspectives that affect human resource practice. Firstly, and perhaps most evidently, this trend results in subsequent technology- and internet-infused transformation of human resource management function, tools, methods and practices. Secondly, this shift calls for a reconceptualization of human resource inputs and outputs in the face of technologies, such as individual factors or broader phenomena. Part V covers three instances of the aforementioned transformation: innovative electronic human resource management value creation, the human resources management perspective on innovation, and the role of emotions in innovative and entrepreneurial behaviours.

The increasingly strategic role of human resource management and its subsequent evolution into electronic human resource management (or e-HRM) is evident in the vast number of companies that have adopted digital tools. Chapter 9 ('Transforming human resource management: innovative e-HRM value creation for multinational companies') presents an exploration of the transforming role of HRM and innovative value creation that is achieved through the employment of e-HRM practices. The chapter offers a body of insights accumulated through an empirical study conducted in multinational companies that are particularly sensitive to success and failures in HRM digitalization.

Chapter 10 ('Human resource management perspective on innovation') revisits two complex phenomena – innovation and human resource management. By drawing on the results of an empirical study conducted across 416 organizations in Brazil, the author explores the interplay between these phenomena. The chapter focuses on the alignment between the two: namely, how human resource management may be configured to yield different types of innovation, and how management innovations are embraced through multiple attributes. As a result, the study reveals the complexity of innovations from the perspective of human resource management, explores human resource management innovation and systematizes multiple innovation-related outcomes that stem from human resources.

Finally, the human side of innovations is inextricably linked with emotions that drive individuals involved in the ventures. Chapter 11 ('On the emotions that spark innovative and entrepreneurial behaviors in employees') explores the emotions that spark innovative and entrepreneurial behaviours. While this topic has attracted great interest across research and practice, the role of affect in entrepreneurial thinking and acting remains a nascent discipline. The author discusses the current developments in this field and guides us towards understanding the relation between affect and entrepreneurial cognition and behaviour. In this chapter, the author navigates between the different concepts of affect embedded in the notions of moods and emotions. The chapter outlines the key findings that will aid progress in addressing the role of positive and negative emotions, as well as the change of emotions in innovative and entrepreneurial cognition and behaviour.

Most business leaders and academics acknowledge the critical role that human resource management plays in the successful innovation management of organizations. New business models, industrial structures, and organizational systems require new ways of approaching and managing human resources. To deal with the challenges of these changes in line with rapid technological development and globalization, managers are forced to reconsider human resources as a basic building block in organizational frameworks designed for sustainable management of innovations. In order for the innovation framework to function sustainably, it is imperative that people effectively support the innovation aspirations. The insights of human resource management innovations present some basic human resource management tools that companies can use to develop innovation opportunities.

In Part VI, a case study of UPS Lithuania 'Choose your own salary' is presented. The company's innovative approaches to strategy, process, employee motivation and compensation management are explored. The discussion questions at the end of the case study refer to the relevant book chapters allowing the reader to compare the innovation management perspectives across the cultural and industrial lenses.

CONCLUSIONS

Innovation management is the management discipline that transforms creative ideas into market successes. While each case of innovation is contextualized, there are guiding principles and best practices for managers to follow, learn from, and adapt. This book suggests a conceptual framework that integrates strategy, product, process and human resource as four key and interrelated aspects of innovation management. Evidence and insights with a global scope are presented to readers who strive to find the most effective recipes to succeed in innovation.

Although the main takeaway from this book is that the winning strategy for innovation is to get the right things (product innovation) by getting the things right (process innovation) empowered by the right human resources, we must remind readers that there are more issues at stake in making such a winning strategy work. First of all, to grasp the business opportunities embedded in the environment by a sharp focus on the right product market and continuous adaptation of the strategy based on product-market feedback, a learning organization is needed. In other words, the capability of human capital to learn from fast-moving environments and turn uncertainty into knowledge is a key to the winning innovation strategy. A learning organization entails innovation leadership, effective and efficient decision making, risk-taking principles for project management, and an effective internal and external knowledge management system. Top management, mid-management, innovation officers, R&D managers, and even front-line sales personnel must be part of the learning organization to accumulate and share knowledge, to turn knowledge into valuable assets. A learning organization can only be built on an effective incentive and performance measurement system. A learning organization requires continuous investment in people, because any other kinds of investment, even in the latest technology and machinery, will eventually become a cost, but investment in people who are motivated to learn will eventually lead to a return.

Second, too much attention has been paid by practitioners to seeking new ideas (for instance, the concept of 'idea competition' is quite often used by many large organizations), while focus on value creation and value capture is often overlooked or downplayed. Value creation for the customers and supply chain put the market and the industry at the centre of a business's logic, instead of considering what technologies and ideas a firm has that it can introduce to unidentified potential customers. Firms that bear value creation in mind as the starting point of their business logic will find the translation from its innovation strategy to the right product innovation easy and natural. In addition, value capture is equally as important as value creation. If created value does not yield any rent to the innovating firm, then value is not captured. This, in turn, will cause a firm to lose resources and motivation to further innovate. Value capture needs good insight and execution on business models, pricing, intellectual property appropriation and learning from external partners. Keep in mind that value capture needs a process – innovative organizations need to invest in human capital to develop capabilities for value capture. Companies may not lack ideas, but they may lack capabilities to bring the ideas through the innovation process to hit the right market.

The third critical element, implicitly embedded in our innovation framework, is about external collaboration. From new product development to adopting new operational processes, to finding the right engineers and marketing people, it is more and more difficult for a firm to innovate alone. Open innovation has become a standard format for innovation, while knowledge inflow and outflow are often used for product and service innovations. Firms need to learn how to acquire external knowledge (either by acquiring technology or acquiring knowledgeable persons), and how to profit from letting others use the firm's internal knowledge. What is external to a firm may become an internal asset, as long as an innovating firm has the capability and motivation to learn. External collaboration will extend a firm's resource base to external partners' and reduce the cost of new product development, if coordination is efficient. Thus, the benefit of open innovation is dependent on a firm's capability of managing external collaboration, for which investment in human resources and operation process is crucial.

Overall, a learning organization that pays sufficient attention to value creation and value capture by collaborative innovation will find it easy to link strategy, product, process and human resources based on a coherent business logic that naturally hosts and fosters innovation. To conclude, we would like to remind our readers that this book offers the best practices at present, but the best practices in the future are yet to come and to be explored, tested and adopted by future entrepreneurs and innovators – who could well be YOU!

NOTE

1.   http://www.cghuawei.com/archives/11168.

REFERENCES

Atalay, M., N. Anafarta and F. Sarvan (2013), 'The relationship between innovation and firm performance: an empirical evidence from Turkish automotive supplier industry', *Procedia – Social and Behavioral Sciences*, 75, 226–235.

Fauji, M. and M. Utami (2013), 'How intellectual stimulation effects knowledge sharing, innovation and firm performance', *International Journal of Social Science and Humanity*, 3(4), 420–425.

Gunday, G., G. Ulusoy, K. Kilic and L. Alpkan (2011), 'Effects of innovation types on firm performance', *International Journal of Production Economics*, 133(2), 662–676.

Hobday, M. (1995), *Innovation in East Asia: The Challenge to Japan*, Cheltenham, UK and Northampton, MA, USA: Edward Elgar Publishing.

Jaruzelski, B., J. Loehr and R. Holman (2011), 'The Global Innovation 1000, Booz Allen Hamilton Annual Innovation Survey', *Strategy and Business*, 65. http://www.strategy-business.com/article/11404.

Jimenez, J.D. and R. Sanz-Valle (2011), 'Innovation, organizational learning and performance', *Journal of Business Research*, 64(4), 408–417.

Teece, D. and G. Pisano (1994), 'The dynamic capabilities of firms: an introduction', *Industrial and Corporate Change*, 3, 537–556.

Zhang, H., E. Ko and E. Lee (2013). 'Moderating effects of nationality and product category on the relationship between innovation and customer equity in Korea and China', *Journal of Product Innovation Management*, 30(1), 110–122.

PART II

Innovation management strategy

2. Innovation management through technology licensing in China

Jason Li-Ying, Yuandi Wang and Jin Chen

INTRODUCTION

Innovation does not necessarily mean inventing from scratch. Rather, innovation may be based on knowledge and technology developed by others. That is why Chinese companies are increasingly employing an open approach to accelerate their innovations (Williamson and Yin, 2014). In this open innovation process, many external knowledge sources can be used to develop innovative products or services. Chinese firms have done extraordinarily well in employing technology licensing to access these external sources. While the purpose of in-licensing technology is often for manufacturing, whether or not a company is able to innovate based on licensed technology is dependent on the nature of the licensed technology, the company's search strategy portfolio, and the company's enabling context, both internal and external. What's distinctive about the best performing Chinese companies in this respect is their balanced approach to technology search, tight collaboration with local partners, and unique ways of developing internal capabilities. Western competitors should take notice, regardless of whether they are involved in licensing relationships with Chinese companies or not.

INNOVATION THROUGH TECHNOLOGY LICENSING

Innovations based on in-licensed technologies are unique. On the one hand, they are original but not invented out of the blue; on the other hand, they are possible only when the knowledge within a company and the unknown elements outside of it can be integrated through an effective learning process. We spent more than four years researching the patterns of Chinese companies successfully innovating based on licensed technologies, using primary and secondary data (see "About the Research"). Using data from the State Intellectual Property Office (SIPO) covering the period 2000–2009, we found that the likelihood of a new patent application citing any of the filing company's previously in-licensed patents was positively associated with the company's total number of licensed patents in the previous period. This finding suggests that Chinese companies not only used licensed technologies for manufacturing, but also successfully applied them to further innovations (Li-Ying et al., 2013). On average, we found, a Chinese licensee company took about six years to learn from licensed technologies and generate its own technological innovations (Wang et al., 2014).

While as an overall trend, innovation through licensing is taking place among many successful Chinese companies, we found that innovation through licensing represents a unique path for these companies, placing significant demands on the companies' capabilities for searching, absorbing, (collaborative) learning, and re-creating knowledge.

What Kind of Technology?

Technologies differ in many aspects. First, they vary in terms of complexity – a complex technology is an applied system. Its components have multiple interactions and constitute a non-decomposable whole (Singh, 1997). A complex technology involves a merging of several diverse disciplines or a great number of interdependencies. Therefore, a complex technology could be difficult to transfer to and be learned by licensee companies. However, complex technologies are more difficult to imitate and to "invent around" competitors, so they in turn may help firms to build and sustain competitive advantage. Second, technologies have varying levels of generality. Technology generality refers to the extent to which knowledge required to develop one product can be applied to the development of another. General technologies are characterized by their potential for pervasive use in a broad array of industries and their technological dynamism. Third, technologies may be mature (old) or state of the art. Here the newness of the licensed technology is also relevant for future innovation.

Using data over 10 years after 2000, we found that the more complex and general technologies a Chinese company licensed in, the higher the likelihood that the company would generate new technological innovations (patents) in the near future (Wang et al., 2013). However, this positive association does not hold for technology newness. In fact, Chinese companies are still relying on mature technologies, with the longest average lag between the granting of a patent and its in-licensing being about 10 years, in the period 2005–2007. However, we see a tendency for the average age of in-licensed technologies to fall over the last five years, to an average of about three years. This suggests that Chinese licensees have gradually shifted their focus to newer technologies (Wang et al., 2015).

Balanced Search Strategy

External technology search is crucial for innovation because it provides firms with external sources of technology elements that can serve as strategic assets and compensate for gaps in the licensing firms' technical competencies. Conceptually, we can distinguish three distinctive dimensions for external technology search: technical, spatial and temporal (Li et al., 2008). The technical dimension measures the degree of similarity between the newly found knowledge and the company's existing knowledge base. Thus, it is a matter of substantial differences in technology. The spatial dimension refers to the physical space of the knowledge search. It matters because of the availability of common resources in a region and the sticky knowledge that resides in a geographical area where organizations have frequent interactions and joint practices, given the local institutions and culture. The third dimension is the temporal dimension, which examines the role of time in technology search. The time lag between emerging technological opportunities and the availability of complementary technologies requires that a firm explore technologies over time.

Most companies understand the importance of searching external technologies for innovation opportunities. However, when it comes to finding technologies of high innovation value to license, a balanced strategy is required. We found that the most successful Chinese companies primarily employed two unique search patterns (Li-Ying et al., 2014). In the first scenario, a licensee company is more likely to innovate based on licensed technologies when the in-licensed technology is technically familiar, relatively mature, and belongs to an owner that is geographically remote. In the second successful scenario, Chinese firms intending to unleash the innovation potential of unfamiliar in-licensed technical knowledge access mature technology from licensors who are geographically close. In contrast, licensing new and unfamiliar technology from geographically remote partners will inevitably fail to result in future innovation because it entails too many challenges in management; licensing mature and familiar technology from local neighbors is not effective either because there is too little novelty value a licensee company can draw upon. Thus, knowing what kinds of technology is not enough. Companies also must understand the importance of a balanced search strategy for future innovation.

Local Collaboration

Chinese licensee companies can exploit the advantage of tapping into the technologies developed by other firms, especially those in advanced economies, without having to replicate the entire technological trajectory. In this way, Chinese licensee companies may bypass the inertia that prevents some incumbent competitors from innovating in advanced economies. However, licensed technologies do not necessarily lead to new innovations. To innovate based on licensed technologies, it is often necessary for licensee companies to learn from other complementary knowledge agents in order to truly understand, absorb, transform, and reinvent the licensed technologies. Thus, it is crucial for licensee companies to invest in active collaboration with local knowledge partners, including universities, research institutes, and other industrial firms.

Companies that collaborate with many local partners are more likely to innovate based on licensed technologies than those having few such collaborations. We found that local knowledge partners help licensee companies learn about licensed technologies and adapt them to the local context, complement their insufficient absorptive capacity, and help reduce the transaction costs involved in technology licensing. Based on co-patenting data, we found that this facilitating role is most evident in partnerships with universities and slightly less evident in collaborations with other industrial firms (Wang and Li-Ying, 2015).

Local research institutes (other than universities), on the other hand, tend to supply new knowledge directly to licensee companies, but not facilitate innovations related to licensed technologies. This perhaps can be understood from two perspectives. First, according to the *China Science and Technology Statistics Data Book*, the shares of R&D expenditure of universities and industrial firms are increasing. However, as providers of complementary knowledge, research institutes are getting weaker. According to the *Nature Publishing Index* of the top 100 research-oriented institutions in China, about 80 percent are universities, including academies or colleges (see www.natureasia.com). Second, universities and research institutes conduct R&D differently. Since the economic reform in China, universities are mostly oriented towards basic research, while research institutes focus on industrial technology development and marketable applications of technology. However, Chinese research institutes are becoming more industrialized and commercialized. Thus, it is more risky for licensee companies to resort to complementary knowledge from research institutes, which are more likely than universities to "steal" the innovation opportunities represented by an in-licensed technology.

Furthermore, local collaborations need to be large not only in scale, but also in scope. A diversified group of local collaborators is more likely to provide complementary knowledge sources for the foreign technologies. A large scope of local collaborations also helps a licensee company verify the value of technological inputs from one partner by consulting another. Relevant complementary technologies within the local network may also be more effectively identified through a triangulation mechanism. Often, those firms that keep their options open by collaborating with various types of partners may learn from the licensed technology and further innovate more effectively than those with homogeneous collaboration networks.

What's in the Black Box? Internal Capability Development

While licensed technologies and knowledge from local collaborative partners are crucial external resources for future innovation, they by no means guarantee success. Our research found that it is equally important for licensee companies to actively invest in internal capability development. In other words, a strong absorptive capacity is the key (Cohen and Levinthal, 1990). These internal capabilities are reflected through a number of indicators, such as internal R&D, the scale of existing technology base, and the scope of complementary resources.

In the first place, internal R&D investments strengthen a firm's capabilities to recognize valuable licensing opportunities available outside its firm boundary, and receive, assimilate and eventually apply licensed technologies to new products that are aligned with local demand. Second, a large technology base provides a rich foundation on which a firm can recombine new knowledge elements to create innovation. Finally, a large scope of complementary resources increases the number of possible creative paths that are triggered by licensed technologies. Among these three indicators of internal capabilities, we found a large scope of complementary resources to be the most important.

While managers can trace these indicators of absorptive capacity and monitor the progress of internal capability development, they need to understand how exactly absorptive capacity can be formed and strengthened. Peering into the "black box" of a successful licensee company, our research revealed an inspiring development trajectory that entails three steps:

- Strengthening core competencies through strategic licensing.
- Consolidating core competencies through indigenous innovation.
- Extending core competencies through strategic diversification.

Strengthening core competencies through strategic licensing
First, it is crucial to clarify a firm's corporate strategy and identify strategically what technological knowledge is necessary to be in-licensed to strengthen the company's core competencies. Often, a licensee company has multiple business units, each with different core competencies. This scenario requires a higher level of strategic coordination with regard to technology licensing. Target technologies must be identified and acquired by the most relevant business units, and measures must be taken to ensure knowledge sharing across units.

Once relevant technologies are licensed, an internal learning process must be institutionalized and sufficient internal investment must be guaranteed to allow the firm to absorb the licensed technologies effectively. For instance, China Southern Railway (CSR) undertakes a unique process that includes *ossification*, *formalization* and *optimization*. Ossification simply requires CSR's personnel to rigidly and precisely replicate the licensor's practice without questioning the process. This step forces the company to learn precisely how the licensed technology functions. By doing so in a purely mechanical manner, CSR's R&D personnel are able to establish an ossified routine for operating the technology. After ossification, it is crucial to formalize the ossified routine through documentation (design, protocols, and other formats) in CSR's language of internal communication. This allows further knowledge dissemination and absorption within the company. After that, it is time for CSR to optimize some details of the licensed technology to make it work better with CSR's current technology systems. This is done through the interactive stages of product design and manufacturing, where detailed performance measures are implemented. However, this process might not be successful if the licensee does not make sufficient investment in the learning; CSR keeps the ratio of the cost of licensing to the investment in learning the licensed technology at about 1:3. In other words, for every RMB spent on license fee or royalty, CSR invests three RMB in the process of learning it.

Consolidating core competencies through indigenous innovation

Once the licensed technologies are fully understood, core competencies must be consolidated by being both lean and mean. When the licensed technology is integrated into the licensee's internal knowledge system, lean management becomes helpful to continuously formalize the use of licensed technology across every detail of design and manufacturing. Another advantage of employing lean management is that workers' productivity can be significantly increased and the tasks become less stressful, leaving workers more time to consider new ways of performing routine tasks. This becomes one of the seeds of indigenous innovation. Nevertheless, being lean is not enough; to innovate, the licensee company needs to be mean as well. One of the common traits shared by all Chinese licensee companies that succeed in innovation is that their R&D personnel are extremely hard working, often working overtime. For instance, during the four years after CSR licensed a major new technology from foreign partners, the company's R&D personnel seldom took weekends off, making Saturday a working day by default. They took just one day off during the New Year holiday period.

When consolidating its core competencies, a licensee company often finds its current knowledge base insufficient to deal with emerging challenges in developing indigenous technologies. The development of indigenous technologies is consistent with particular social and technological conditions specific to particular combinations of inputs determined by the local environment. Technologies developed by others, especially those in advanced economies, might not be directly applicable in the local context. Therefore, next to investing in their internal R&D departments, many companies relied on collaboration with universities and research institutes to compensate for missing competencies.

The development of indigenous technologies may also face both social and technical demands from foreign environments. For instance, when CSR's new high-speed train was introduced to foreign countries, CSR needed to learn both the social and technical requirements of the host country. In this context, consolidation of core competencies also requires the establishment of overseas R&D task forces employing local R&D talents. In short, solid consolidation of core competencies requires external collaboration in both local and foreign environments.

Another crucial element in the consolidation phase is branding. A strong brand both offers the licensee company advantages in marketing, and also supplies motivation for further innovation. The logic is simple: technologies invented by a company with a strong brand are more likely to be recognized as having high value. Therefore, for a licensee company, a stronger brand and innovation are two sides of the upward spiral, reinforcing each other.

Extending core competencies through strategic diversification

A consolidated base of core competencies lays the foundation for further innovation. In addition, as the licensed technologies may be developed over time into quite different product application trajectories, it is important for a licensee company to strategically diversify its technology base. Our research found that licensing a wide range of technologies may increase a licensee company's chance of making future innovation when the company has a high level of internal technological diversification.

Having access to a broad range of licensed technologies not only allows a company to benefit from the results of technology diversification; it also enables further technology diversification of a licensee company. When the licensed technologies are fully understood and consolidated, they can be extended to related technical areas, extending the company's core competencies. Meanwhile, a diversified technology base also creates more opportunities of application for licensed technologies to become new inventions in the future. A common and effective practice is to make the diversification gradual, starting from related technical areas.

Diversification needs to be strategic not only with respect to technical areas but also in terms of the pace of investment. When a licensee company diversifies to other technical areas, it is important to start with a moderate-scale investment instead of betting on only one horse. Many Chinese licensee companies in our research pointed out that there are a number of disadvantages if an initial investment in diversified technological areas related to licensed technologies is too large. First, it demands a much faster learning pace, which the licensee company might not able to sustain. Second, it may result in insufficient cash flow as it can take a long time to recoup the investment. In sum, strategic diversification means starting with technical areas related to the existing technology base of the company and a moderate scale of initial investment.

RESPONDING IN TWO BATTLEFIELDS: WITHIN AND OUTSIDE OF CHINA

Knowing how Chinese companies innovate through technology licensing, we see two ways to maintain competitive advantage for competing global companies. One is to replicate the best practices of successful Chinese licensee companies with respect to technology search strategy, collaboration with local partners, and continuous reinvention of core competencies. The other is to recoup the benefit of wisely designed partnerships by licensing out technologies to Chinese companies who understand the art of innovation through licensing.

The first approach requires systematic design and effective implementation of a technology search strategy that balances the search effort along the temporal, geographic, and technical dimensions. It also requires global companies to seek local R&D collaborators that help provide complementary knowledge. Finally, global companies must engage in a process of continuously reinventing their core competencies, following the path through strengthening, consolidating, and extending competencies in an accelerated manner as some Chinese counterparts do. This means global companies need to learn from Chinese licensee companies and do better than them. We believe that this approach is viable for global competitors because although our findings suggest these activities are the key to success in innovation through licensing, it is very hard for a single company to continuously do everything right. In fact, very few Chinese companies were able to effectively implement the entire strategy that we describe. Therefore, it is possible to gain competitive advantage by simply doing better than others, even if all are following the same recipe.

The second approach entails not only competition, but also cooperation; it is crucial for global companies to innovate both *for* and *with* China. Global companies feel the need to learn how to innovate for China simply because the Chinese market is too huge to ignore. They also desperately want to learn how to innovate from China because a large number of technological and market inputs originated in China can be transformed and integrated into the global market (Immelt et al., 2009).

Often, competitive advantage does not necessarily come from head-to-head competition. Instead, it may well come from cooperating with Chinese companies. One way is to strategically license technologies out to Chinese partners, knowing what they want and having a good anticipation of what they will do with the technologies afterwards. In this case, the global company needs to partner with a Chinese licensee firm that has a track record of successful innovation through licensing and a sound innovation strategy based on licensed technologies. As the likelihood of success in future innovation based on licensed technologies is relatively higher for a well-managed licensee firm, the global licensor company may recoup its investment in the licensed technologies through cross-licensing, co-patenting, and the majority holding of a joint venture. Cross-licensing entitles the global company to a waiver of licensing fees when using technology patented by the Chinese licensee company in the future. Co-patenting grants the global company the rights of patent holder if the Chinese licensee company invents new technology based on the technologies licensed previously from the global company. When a global company licenses its technologies to its own joint venture with a Chinese company, new technologies developed by the joint venture will be to the advantage of the global company, especially if it has retained a majority holding of shares in the joint venture.

CONCLUSIONS

Technology licensing has become an effective way towards innovation for many Chinese companies. Our research unveils the secrets about how they managed to succeed at innovating with licensed technology by focusing on what types of technologies they seek, how they balance their search strategy, how they find complementary knowledge through local collaboration, and how they integrate licensed technologies with internal knowledge bases through an effective learning process. For global companies and other under-performing Chinese companies operating in China and companies competing with Chinese products or service in global markets, it is worthwhile to learn from the Chinese best practices and respond with a viable strategy.

ABOUT THE RESEARCH

Technology licensing activities are visible, meaning that in most countries the firms involved in technology licensing can be identified and traced. The dataset used for this study was obtained from the State Intellectual Property Office of China (SIPO). Since 2001, SIPO has been required by legislation ("Regulations on Administration of Record Filing of Technology Licensing") to register technology licensing contracts within three months after they are signed by the licensor and licensee. Each technology transfer record registered at SIPO contains information on the licensor's name, the licensee's name, the licensed patent number and name, contract number and date, and license type (exclusive or nonexclusive). All licensees in the record are Chinese individuals or firms. So far, this dataset includes only licensing agreements that involve patented technology. The complete records for 2000–2013 are available to the public from the SIPO website (http://www.sipo.gov.cn/), covering a total of 103,119 patents licensed to Chinese licensees. Using the SIPO data, we have undertaken a series of studies on various research questions related to Chinese licensee companies during the last four years. The insights provided in this chapter are a synthesis of managerial implications based on the results of a number of relevant empirical studies, published and unpublished, which we have completed during the last two years. Meanwhile, to unveil the internal capability development of licensee companies inside the "black box," we also engaged in a number of face-to-face, open-structured interviews with Chinese licensee companies that were successful in innovating after licensing foreign technologies. With China Southern Railway (CSR), we conducted in-depth discussions about how they searched for new technologies to license, how they managed different types of technologies from different sources, and how they organized their internal routines and processes to absorb licensed technologies and eventually innovate independently. The researchers and the executives of CSR extensively exchanged their understanding on the entire "catch-up" process. The insights gained from discussions with CSR were cross-checked through interviews with executives of a number of leading Chinese licensee companies (see top ten licensee companies in Wang et al., 2015). We are convinced that the managerial insights we summarize in this chapter are highly representative for leading Chinese licensee companies with regard to their common approaches to innovation based on licensed technologies.

REFERENCES

Cohen, M.D. and D.A. Levinthal (1990), 'Absorptive capacity: a new perspective on learning and innovation', *Administrative Science Quarterly*, 35, 128–152.

Immelt, J.R., V. Govindarajan and C. Trimble (2009), 'How GE is disrupting itself', *Harvard Business Review*, 87(10), 56–65.

Li, Y., W. Vanhaverbeke and W. Schoenmakers (2008), 'Exploration and exploitation in innovation: reframing the interpretation', *Creativity and Innovation Management*, 17(2), 107–126.

Li-Ying, J., Y. Wang and S. Salomo (2014), 'An inquiry on external technology search through patent in-licensing and firms' technological innovations: evidence from China', *R&D Management*, 44(1), 53–74.

Li-Ying, J., Y. Wang, S. Salomo and W. Vanhaverbeke (2013), 'Have Chinese firms learnt from their prior technology in-licensing? An analysis based on patent citations', *Scientometrics*, 95(1), 183–195.

Singh, K. (1997), 'The impact of technological complexity and interfirm cooperation on business survival', *Academy of Management Journal*, 40(2), 339–367.

Wang, Y. and J. Li-Ying (2015), 'Licensing foreign technology and the moderating role of local R&D collaboration: extending the relational view', *Journal of Product Innovation Management*, 32(6), 997–1013.

Wang, Y., J. Li-Ying, J. Chen and Z. Lu (2015), 'Technology licensing in China', *Science and Public Policy*, 42(3), 293–299.

Wang, Y., N. Roijakkers and W. Vanhaverbeke (2014), 'How fast do Chinese firms learn and catch up? Evidence from patent citations', *Scientometrics*, 98(1), 743–761.

Wang, Y., Z. Zhou and J. Li-Ying (2013), 'The impact of licensed knowledge attributes on innovation performance of licensee firms: evidence from Chinese electronic industry', *Journal of Technology Transfer*, 38(5), 699–715.

Williamson, P. and E. Yin (2014), 'Accelerated innovation: the new challenge from China', *MIT Sloan Management Review*. http://sloanreview.mit.edu/article/accelerated-innovation-the-new-challenge-from-china/.

3. Innovation management: the Japanese way

Kenji Tadakuma, Tadao Onaka and Rumintha Wickramasekera

INTRODUCTION

Japan became the world's second largest (now the third largest) economy via rapid economic growth, recovering from the devastation of industries and infrastructure during World War II. This growth was driven by Japan's outstanding innovations mainly from the 1960s to the 1990s (Japan Institute of Invention and Innovation, 2016). However, in recent years innovations have stagnated compared to that earlier period in Japan (Onaka and Denscombe, 2015; Onaka et al., 2016). As an example, in aggregate-market-price ranking in the world, seven out of ten companies were Japanese in 1989, but there were no Japanese companies within the top ten in 2018. Toyota Motor Corporation barely ranked in the top 50 in 2018 (Iketomi et al., 2018). Apple's market capitalization and operating profit are about five times and three times higher respectively than those of Toyota. It is imperative that Japanese corporations learn from past success, return to the fundamental management principles for innovation and rebuild the power of innovation for future success. This chapter considers the question: 'How did Japanese companies after World War II produce a range of globally competitive innovations?'

In the next section we analyse the characteristics of Japanese management from the 1960s to the 1990s, a period that saw Japan produce many outstanding innovative products. The following section discusses the effectiveness of Japanese management and the drive for innovation in the light of current innovation management theories. Then, in order to understand Japanese management in depth, a case study of Toyota Motor Corporation is presented. This chapter emphasizes that the Toyota Production System (TPS) is not only a microscopic methodology used to increase productivity but also aims to incubate the innovation-oriented corporate culture reflecting its founder's philosophy. The six key managerial factors required to successfully implement innovations are presented by considering the Hybrid Vehicle Prius development case. Finally, we discuss our findings and the reasons why Japanese innovation management is not as successful as it once was.

JAPANESE MANAGEMENT IN THE POST-WORLD WAR II PERIOD

Japanese Innovation: Top Ten

What product comes to your mind when you think of Japanese innovation? Table 3.1 shows a range of outstanding Japanese innovations of the post-World War II era (Japan Institute of Invention and Innovation, 2016). Shinkansen opened the way to a new era of high-speed railway by changing the concept of rail travel, resulting in precise timetabling and superior safety developed by Japanese high-level engineering. Walkman of SONY was launched in 1979 and established a lifestyle in which people could enjoy listening to stereophonic music anywhere. Washlet, launched in 1990, provided the comfort of an electric toilet seat with a water spray feature for cleansing. A Nobel Prize winning invention – the blue light-emitting diode (LED) – started a new era of communication via fibre optics. Family Computer made by Nintendo may be the most famous among these innovations because it became a very familiar household product driving the video game market. Toyota Motor Corporation's success has demonstrated that its unorthodox innovation management system enabled the manufacture of highly reliable automobiles at the lowest cost and streamlined the new product development process. How did Japanese companies achieve this success? The aim of the following discussion is to answer this question and to shed light on what we can learn from Japanese experience.

Japanese Cultural Mentality

In order to better understand Japanese management style it is important to explain Japanese cultural mentality (Abbeglen, 2006; Hall, 1989; Nitobe, 1900; Uchida, 2009; Uchimura, 1908; Umesao, 1957). Abbeglen (2006) suggested that the main features of the Japanese management 'lifetime employment and social contract' are based on the Japanese deep sense of community. Japanese people's behaviour during disasters offers good examples of their sense of community and cooperative power: after the Great East Japan Earthquake in 2011 people waited in line to receive relief supplies without causing pandemonium; after another earthquake in Fukuoka city, damaged infrastructure was repaired within a week by people working in complete unity. A more recent example is the Japanese football team behaviour during the Football World Cup championship when they won praise around the world, not only for their

Table 3.1   *Japanese innovations: top ten in post-World War II period*

Product name	Innovator / Maker	Year	Brief overview
Endoscope	Olympus	Late 1940s	Fibre-optic tubular instrument for visualizing the interior of a hollow organ for diagnostic or therapeutic purposes
Instant noodles	Nisshin Food	1958 1971	Chicken ramen (1958) and Cup noodle (1971), the world's first instant noodles and the cup-type
Manga, Anime	Osamu Teduka	1963	TV broadcast animation and Manga
Shinkansen	Japanese National Railway	1964	Bullet train
Toyota Production System	Toyota Motor Corporation	1960s	Thorough elimination of 'Muda' 'Jidoka' automation with a human touch, Kanaban system etc.
Walkman	Sony	1979	Portable audio cassette players
Washlet	TOTO (now INAX)	1980	Electric toilet seats with water spray feature for cleansing
Family Computer (Famicom)	Nintendo	1983	Video game
Blue light-emitting diode (LED)	Nagoya University and Professor Nakamura Nichia	1989	Energy-efficient and environment-friendly light source
Hybrid vehicle	Toyota Motor Corporation	1997	A vehicle using two different forms of power – an electric motor and an internal combustion engine

prowess on the field, but also for their community mindedness in cleaning up after the events.

Kanzo Uchimura's *Representative Men of Japan*, written in 1908, describes the Japanese cultural mentality of 'self-sacrifice' as the pursuit of happiness for everyone beyond oneself and living virtuously with 'simplicity and frugality' (Uchimura, 1908). *Bushido: The Soul of Japan*, written by Inazo Nitobe in 1899, explains that the foundations of 'noblesse oblige' – the obligation of honourable, generous and responsible behaviour associated with Bushi-rank people – are the seven values of Rectitude, Courage, Benevolence, Politeness, Truthfulness, Honour and Loyalty (Nitobe, 1900). Nitobe (1900) claimed that any action based on the consideration of the balance between efforts and remuneration was contrary to the 'Bushi-do' outlook. Japanese believe that one should not count the return on efforts or investment and should not focus on what one can gain first. In societies pursuing rationality alone, people want to know how much will be earned by learning before they begin, and only if the earning is sufficient will people start learning (Uchida, 2009). In contrast, Japanese people are willing to learn from various sources and strive just for the sake of self-improvement (Uchida, 2009; Umesao, 1957). These ideas refer to deeply held beliefs and values of Japanese culture and serve as the basis for Japanese management style.

Japanese Management Characteristics

There are many research works focused on the study of Japanese company management (Abbeglen, 1958, 2006; Drucker, 1971; Hayes, 1981; Hiromoto, 1988; Howell and Sakurai, 1992; Imai, 1986; Itani, 2000; Porter et al., 2000). Abbeglen published *The Japanese Factory* in 1958. Drucker studied Japanese characteristic management in a review entitled 'What we can learn from Japanese management' in 1971. Hayes described Japanese factory productivity in 1981. In 2006, Abbeglen published a book related to Japanese management entitled *Twenty-First Century Japanese Management* which investigated the period from the 1990s to the beginning of the 2000s. These researchers attempted to unfold the Japanese management characteristics mainly focusing on 'social contribution', 'lifetime employment', 'decision making by consensus', 'sense of community' and 'continuous improvement (Kaizen)' principles.

- **Social contribution.** The social contribution principle is clearly represented in Japanese companies' mottoes and philosophy. Various Japanese companies' mottoes and philosophy over the years emphasize Japanese status and company social contribution: 'Always be faithful to your duties, thereby contributing to the company and to the overall good', 'Create food to serve society', 'Reconstruct Japan and elevate the nation's culture through dynamic technological and manufacturing activities', 'Service and Trust', 'Strong aspiration to create high quality, world famous products' (OLYMPUS, 1919; TOYOTA, 1935; SONY, 1946; NICHIA, 1956; NISSIN FOODS, 1958; TOTO, 1962).
- **Lifetime employment.** Employees accepted job rotations within a company because lifetime employment gave them income stability and job security (Abbeglen, 2006). Employees grew and kept learning in the company on the basis of security provided by the company. Lifetime employment could be compared to a social contract and a promise to work together to secure jobs and payment for all employees in the company. The sense of value on the basis of lifetime employment was a sense of community, continuity and group solidarity.
- **Decision making by consensus.** In Japan, the importance of consensus in managerial decision making enabled companies to bring major changes. Reaching a final decision by consensus took longer than that by top-down

imposition. However, once the decision was made, the implementation was very efficient and fast.

- **Sense of community.** Japanese companies considered stakeholders, such as customers, partners, employees and owners, to be communities bound together by a common destiny. Employees were considered the main stakeholders for Japanese managers.
- **Continuous improvement (Kaizen).** Japanese companies implemented Kaizen motivational practices for continuous improvement. The target on quality was 'zero defects' through striving for quality systematically and thoroughly.

In the post-World War II period, Japanese management and Japanese cultural mentality were inextricably linked in the overall framework of Japanese innovation management style. Japanese cultural power was a foundation of management that enabled companies to facilitate and sustain the commitment of their people to create and innovate. Japanese built learning organizations that focused on the cultural values of social contribution, continuous improvement, sense of consensus and community.

JAPANESE INNOVATION MANAGEMENT CULTURE IN THE LIGHT OF CURRENT INNOVATION MANAGEMENT THEORIES

In this section we further examine Japanese management culture in the light of innovation management theories propounded by Peter Drucker, Teresa Amabile, Clayton Christensen and other researchers (Amabile, 1998; Anthony, 2014; Blank, 2013; Brown, 2009; Christensen, 1997; Christensen and Raynor, 2003; Christensen et al., 2004; Drucker, 2002; Dyer et al., 2011; Mauya, 2012; Onyemah et al., 2013; Osterwalder and Pigneur, 2010; Owens and Fernandez, 2014; Ries, 2011).

Peter Drucker (2002) claims that innovation opportunity arises due to seven factors. Four such factors exist within a company or industry: unexpected occurrences, incongruities, process needs, and industry and market change. Three additional factors exist outside a company in its social and intellectual environment: democratic changes, changes in perception, and new knowledge. He also emphasizes that innovation is both conceptual and perceptual: would-be innovators must also go out and look, ask and listen. Successful innovators use both the right and left sides of their brains. Innovation, according to him, is work rather than genius. It requires knowledge, ingenuity, focus and hard work. If diligence, persistence and commitment are lacking, talent, ingenuity, and knowledge are of no avail. In line with Drucker's analysis, Japanese management style recognizes that diligence, persistence and commitment are important innovation drivers. Japanese corporations create environment, atmosphere and spirituality to cultivate the mentality that enables employees to create and innovate.

According to Teresa Amabile (1998) the three components of creativity are 'expertise', 'creative thinking skill' and 'motivation'. An inner passion to solve the problem at hand leads to solutions far more creative than do external rewards, such as money. She considers that this component, called intrinsic motivation, is the one that can be most immediately influenced by the work environment. The enjoyment of seeing, searching and contribution is a source of internal motivation. One of the Japanese management characteristics is 'lifetime employment.' Lifetime employment provides job security and income stability. So employees' physiological, safety and social belonging needs are satisfied (Maslow, 1943). Lifetime employment also allows cultivating employees' contribution mind and loyalty to the company. Japanese management creates a corporate culture that is likely to cultivate 'the enjoyment of seeing and searching' where high-rank needs, self-actualization and the contribution mind enhance the intrinsic motivation to innovate.

Clayton Christensen (Christensen, 1997; Christensen and Raynor, 2003; Christensen et al., 2004; Dyer et al., 2011) developed the RPV (Resources, Processes, Values) theory referring to the requirements that are essential for companies to succeed: having enough management resources and assets, processes and values is essential for successful company innovation management. According to Christensen, a sustaining innovation provides a high-end product and service greater than the customer needs. He claims that Disruptive Innovation delivers more-suitable functionality and good usability at a lower price (Christensen and Raynor, 2003). The disruptive innovation moves upmarket delivering the performances that mainstream customers of existing markets require. Then, the mainstream customers start shifting to disruptive innovation offerings in volume. Why do 'excellent enterprises' and 'big corporations' conducting sustaining innovation fail? It is difficult to invest enough resources to small or non-existent markets because of lower gross margins, smaller target markets and simpler products and services that may not appear as attractive as existing solutions when compared against traditional performance metrics. Values and processes of conventional mainstream organization are not applicable for disruptive innovation. Innovators, according to Christensen, have the superiority of 'Associating', 'Observing', 'Experimenting', 'Questioning' and 'Networking'. According to Christensen's RPV theory (Christensen and Raynor, 2003), values provide adequate priority for business. The values of Japanese organizations are based on their founders' vision and defined by the company's motto and management principles. Japanese management features, such as decision making by consensus and commitment to lifetime employment, are based on the value of consensus, social contribution and sense of community. To generate an innovation based on the disruptive innovation theory the organization needs to market a product to smaller markets and develop low-cost, simple, small and usable products. Japanese corporations draw upon a strong social contribution philosophy according to which the in-house innovator has a strong contribution mind and is motivated to implement an idea.

Lean start-up is a methodology aimed at creating successful new business ventures (Anthony, 2014; Blank, 2013; Brown, 2009; Mauya, 2012; Onyemah et al., 2013; Osterwalder and Pigneur, 2010; Owens and Fernandez, 2014; Ries, 2011). Lean start-up is named after the Toyota Production System (Ono, 1978) that was developed by Taiichi Ono (Ries, 2011). Lean manufacturing is another name for the Toyota Production System (TPS), a production system that embodies the philosophy of 'the complete elimination of all waste' in all aspects of production in pursuit of the most efficient methods. TPS can be flexible to small volume production in great varieties. Lean start-up is lean manufacturing applied to starting a business. At the heart of the lean start-up is the Kaizen mind striving for the highest quality in Japanese management. The innovations shown in Table 3.1 were iterated by Kaizen (continuous improvement) based on Japanese companies' vision and philosophy and Japanese cultural mentality making prototypes repeatedly.

To summarize this section, Figure 3.1 shows the relationship between Japanese management and innovation methodology in the light of the current innovation management theories. Japanese companies develop 'expertise' on the basis of 'learning with an open mind', 'creative thinking skill' and 'continuous improvement' (Kaizen) following Japanese mentality. According to Maslow (1943) lifetime employment can cultivate intrinsic motivation after satisfying low-rank needs. Culture and environment are likely to produce 'creativity' comprehensively. Japanese management culture represents company founders' vision and philosophy and is defined as social contribution through Kaizen activity iterating the cycle of lean start-up.

TOYOTA MOTOR CORPORATION CASE

In order to understand better the relationship between Japanese management and innovation, we examine the case of Toyota management with the Toyota Production System (TPS) and Hybrid Vehicle Prius development examples. As stated above, TPS is a production system that is grounded in the philosophy of 'the complete elimination of all waste' imbuing all aspects of production in pursuit of the most efficient methods (Ono, 1978; TOYOTA, 1950; Womack et al., 1990). The two main frames of TPS are 'Just in Time' (JIT) and 'Jido-ka'. They incorporate 'leveling' – operation efficiency improvement, 'visualization', 'Andon', 'five why' – iteration of 'why' to find the true reason,

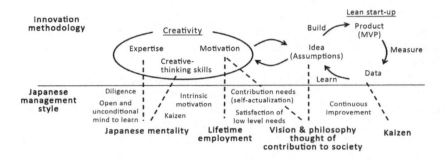

Figure 3.1   Relationship between Japanese management style and current innovation theories

and 'Genchi-genbutsu' – hands-on experience to think about problems and challenges based on onsite facts. The way of thinking is based on a solution to overcome difficulties that exist onsite. 'Poka-yoke' is foolproofing management so as not to produce a defective product by an error or a mistake. 'Seven Muda (wastes)' is based on the principle that wastes must be removed from manufacturing process, transport, inventory, motion, waiting, over-processing, overproduction and defects.

'Toyota Business Practice' (TBP) is represented by the Eight Step Problem Solving 'A3 report': one-page reports in accordance with eight step problem solving, used for documenting and reporting (Goldsmith, 2014; Shook, 2009). 'Kaizen' is continuous improvement – always better than now (Imai, 1986; Narusawa et al., 2009). 'Ji-kotei-kanketsu' is own-process completion: the way of thinking to realize a system, condition and environment thoroughly that can only make a good product and do good work scientifically (Sasaki, 2015). Toyota implements original management thinking and methodology. TPS covers Toyota quality and productivity, Kaizen and 'Ji-kotei-kanketsu'. All these systems are implemented at the same time and work as a pair of wheels, overseeing the whole process not just a part of it.

As mentioned above, TPS comprises 'Just in Time' and 'Jido-ka'. 'Jido-ka' can be defined as 'automation with a human touch' for manufacturing high-quality products, in order not to produce defective goods. The 'Andon problem display board' communicates abnormalities. When a problem arises, the person in line pulls the string, the 'Andon', to stop machines. The line manager checks the problem display board to find the place where the problem arose. Then the line manager visits the place and removes the cause of the problem. After that the improvements are incorporated into the standard workflow. Good products can be produced by the daily improvements based on the 'Jido-ka' concept (Ono, 1978; TOYOTA, 1950). 'Just in time' is a philosophy of complete elimination of waste for productivity improvement. 'Just in time' means making 'only what is needed, when it is needed and in the amount needed'. In TPS a unique production control method called the 'Kanban system' plays an integral role. The operator from the next process goes to the preceding process with 'Kanban' to retrieve the necessary parts when they are needed and in the amount needed. The 'Kanban' system ideally controls the entire value chain from the supplier to the end consumer (Ono, 1978; TOYOTA, 1950). Many companies have tried, but few, if any, have been able to duplicate the success of Toyota Production System (Kanno, 2014, 2018; Okamura, 2004; Spear, 2004; Spear and Bowen, 1999; Staats and Upton, 2011; Takeuchi et al., 2008). Why have many corporations failed to introduce TPS? Spear and Bowen (1999) explained that Toyota's success lies in the fact that TPS is used not just for 'tools and tactics' but also in continuous experiments, to solve problems by workers and managers, and to create a system that is constantly improving the company. Kanno (2018) stated that it is important for onsite workers to be motivated and willing to 'perform a good job'. It is difficult to introduce TPS because workers generally see the job as an 'assigned task' and 'trouble shooting or irregularity handling is the boss's job'. That is for successful introduction to TPS, a key component is a system able to judge and facilitate initiatives by onsite workers. Tanaka, who was ex-general manager of Toyota, insisted that there should not be prescriptive rules for TPS. This is a continuous process and does not mean appointing a person who is good at TPS. Top management has to take it seriously and continue to follow TPS all day and every day.

Figure 3.2 illustrates the important points to introduce TPS by using the framework of McKinsey 7S factors. The 'Kanban' system (System), 'Production potential' (Skill), 'Genchi-Genbutsu' (Style), 'Kaizen' (Staff) and 'Elimination of Muda' (Shared Value) are driving forces to introduce TPS correctly. Onsite workers are expected to work without prompting and actively because according to Kaizen, workers onsite have to work proactively. For onsite workers to act proactively, a behavioural guideline and a system are provided.

The reasons for TPS introduction failure are related to these components' implementation: introduction of just the 'Kanban' system as a tool or not immersing 'Elimination of Muda' as a shared value. It can be considered that TPS is an innovation regarding the change of corporate culture. It is difficult to introduce TPS if companies' culture is not aligned with TPS philosophy. A strong will on the part of top management and perseverance in introducing TPS are needed. The introduction of TPS must be well understood and all the

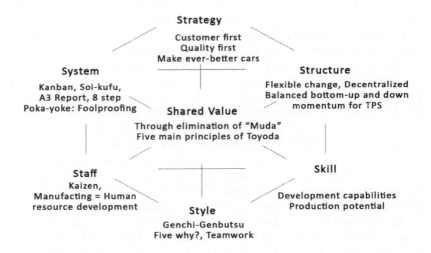

Strategy
Customer first
Quality first
Make ever-better cars

System
Kanban, Soi-kufu,
A3 Report, 8 step
Poka-yoke: Foolproofing

Shared Value
Through elimination of "Muda"
Five main principles of Toyoda

Structure
Flexible change, Decentralized
Balanced bottom-up and down
momentum for TPS

Staff
Kaizen,
Manufacting = Human
resource development

Style
Genchi-Genbutsu
Five why?, Teamwork

Skill
Development capabilities
Production potential

*Figure 3.2   Consideration of Toyota production system based on
McKinsey 7S framework*

processes need to be involved, taking time and having authority to implement the system. In the case of Toyota, the success of the company is due to the introduction of TPS and making persistent efforts for innovation regarding corporate culture to enhance the power of expansion and integration (Takeuchi et al., 2008).

'Just in Time' and 'Jido-ka' systems were developed by Taiichi Ono referring to the founder's, Kiichiro Toyoda, and his father's, Sakichi Toyoda, teaching (Ono, 1978). Taiichi Ono (1978) came up with the 'Jido-ka' concept from the philosophy and practice of Sakichi. The Toyoda automatic loom stopped when the string was cut or ran out, and not only in high-speed operation. That is the basis of Jido-ka – automation with a human touch. The 'five why' basic principles, which Taiichi referred to repeatedly, also derived from Sakichi. 'Just in Time' was originated from Kiichiro's idea. In those days Kiichiro thought thoroughly about how Japanese automobile production could surpass the American method (Ono, 1978). Through the strong influence of the founder's philosophy, Taiichi Ono succeeded in the realization of TPS. The founder's vision and philosophy are the source of TPS. The 'five main principles of Toyoda' (TOYOTA, 1935) are the fundamental philosophy of management even today (Onaka, 2017; TOYOTA, 2018a): always be faithful to your duties, thereby contributing to the company and to the overall good;

always be studious and creative, striving to stay ahead of the times; always be practical and avoid frivolousness; strive to build a homelike atmosphere at work that is warm and friendly; have respect for spiritual matters and remember to be grateful at all times.

Hybrid Prius Development

Toyota's first hybrid vehicle development dates back to 1968. There were no secondary or rechargeable batteries at that time to meet the performance requirements for a hybrid vehicle. The project was discontinued at the beginning of the 1980s (TOYOTA, 1997). Figure 3.3 shows the first Prius development outline. The development started from 1993 (TOYOTA, 2017). At first the G21 Project was launched as means to promote technological development with Project General Manager Uchiyamada as the leader. The G21 Project efforts began by finding ways to achieve a ground-breaking improvement in fuel efficiency that would lead the way in the twenty-first century. Uchiyamada was the leader of the experiment evaluation division in charge of noise and vibration. When chosen as project leader of G21, he was the manager of human resources in the Engineering Administration Division and knew the engineers with appropriate skills very well (Nonaka et al., 2010). The G21 Project set a target of raising fuel efficiency performance to 1.5 times the level of conventional engines. However, in a top-down move, the executive vice president for research and development rejected this target and ordered the higher target of a double improvement. The development team set an L/O (Line Off) target for 1999. But the top management decided to accelerate the project and aim for release in 1997, two years ahead of the original plan. At the end of 1995 the prototype could run only 500 metres. Launching a production vehicle in two years was not an easy task. Although there were many technical difficulties and challenges, Toyota managed to overcome them successfully (TOYOTA, 2017). The press conference to unveil the Prius was held on 14 October 1997 in Tokyo. The biggest accomplishment of the team was 28 kilometres per litre. The team had kept their promise to deliver double the fuel efficiency of a similar gasoline engine car. What was more, the price was even lower than the media had reported in March 1997 (TOYOTA, 2017).

Six Key Factors of Hybrid Prius Development Success

The six key success factors of management innovation were defined during the Hybrid Prius development: raising high aspiration with a clear guiding principle; an almost impossible top-down outlook goal and entrustment to middle

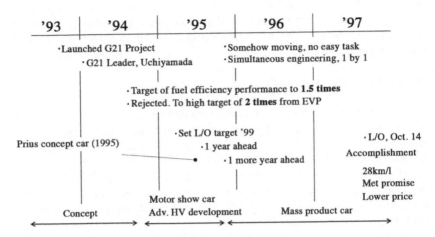

Figure 3.3   First Prius development outline

Note: L/O is an abbreviation of 'Line Off' which means 'launching the product'.

management and engineers; zero-based thinking and talent matching; obeya activity; basic culture; and continuous R&D.

- **Raising high aspiration with a clear guiding principle.** Providing clear guiding principles for the development team is a minimum requirement for the team to work proactively. When any member joins a newly established project team, the member's performance rating is conducted by his or her previous organization. In such a case, it is natural that the new member will avoid doing anything that will undermine the department where they worked previously. But to produce an innovation, the team has to overcome sectionalism and raise high aspirations among team members. For that purpose, the principle 'not to be a profitable member for the ex-department' was declared. In addition, the urgency and value of innovation were discussed seriously and positively among team members. Other principles defined were 'Engineering discussion should be done beyond and regardless of position and age', 'Not only criticism but also proposal is important', 'Speed', 'Sharing information', 'Think thoroughly' and 'Organize own idea in one step above position'.
- **Almost impossible top-down outlook goal and entrustment to middle management and engineers.** In a top-down move, Wada, the executive vice president (EVP) for research and development, ordered the high target of a two-fold improvement in fuel efficiency, despite the original target being 1.5 times the level of that of conventional engines. Uchiyamada

selected the Hybrid system to reach the target of fuel efficiency performance. The challenges were 'High cost' and 'Still infant technology' at that time. In addition, Wada emphasized that if that was not possible, the project would be axed (TOYOTA, 1997). At first, Uchiyamada planned to launch both gasoline and HV vehicles to fill a deficiency of the hybrid cost by selling gasoline vehicles. However, Chairman Toyoda directed to 'develop only the Hybrid vehicle' (TOYOTA, 2017). Furthermore, President Okuda decided to accelerate the project by a year and aim for release in 1997. That left only approximately two years from the official start of the development to launch. This was too short to develop new mass product cars under normal circumstance. The development period of Japanese carmakers in the 1980s was 42 months; however, the period for Prius was much shorter (Clark and Fujimoto, 1991). As mentioned above, the plan was implemented in a strong-willed top-down approach. On the other hand, the decision making over hardware details was conducted by Uchiyamada (Chunichi Shimbun-sha, 2015). EVP Wada focused on the broader perspective and instructed CE (Chief Engineer) Uchiyamada to 'Do it absolutely'. This strong top-down direction enhanced the 'must do' motivation among the development team. Entrustment to middle management enabled faster decision making and made it easier to promote companywide progress, such as establishment of business reform organization and collaboration with Panasonic and the introduction of 3D virtual assembly technology. Takeuchi et al. (2008) claimed that such a high and near-unattainable target – an 'impossible goal' – worked at Toyota because Toyota's senior executives pushed the development team to break free from established routine. This practice went back to Toyota's origins. EVP Wada said 'I asked for two times improvement, then as a result, the team achieved one-point-five times. I would not call one-point-five times at the first stage an adequate target'. In addition, when Chairman Toyoda ordered the development of only the Hybrid vehicle, he said, 'If I didn't say this, you [Uchiyamada] would concentrate on "Only Gasoline vehicles development after all"' (Chunichi Shimbun-sha, 2015). This mentality of Toyota's top management was consistent. The characteristics of decision making were 'Cutting off the team's retreat' and 'Challenge purposely' for the 'almost impossible outlook goal'. However, the 'almost impossible goal' could not be achieved without entrustment to middle managers and engineers. The planning division worked hard with few holidays. In the case of the Prius development, when performance criteria were not satisfied, the engineers worked seven days a week to meet the deadline (Chunichi Shimbun-sha, 2015; Nonaka et al., 2010; TOYOTA, 2017). Such dedicated engineers were supporting Toyota's manufacturing excellence. How can they be so tough? Generally the following five reasons can be given:

'Elite pride', 'Delegation of product planning and marketing', 'Fame of attracting people's attention', 'Understanding and control of whole development process', 'Joy of realizing customers are pleased with the product', 'Contribution to social infrastructure' and 'Trust for Toyota's executives succeeding and embodying their founder's five main principles declaring social contribution with technology innovation and respect to employees'.

Toyota's vision is not only selling cars to customers and competing with competitors but also continuing to evolve high-quality cars for today's society (Chunichi Shimbun-sha, 2015; Emori, 2014; Ono, 1978; Sano, 2015; Suzuki, 2014; Toyoda, 2015; TOYOTA, 1966, 1992). It can be understood from the development of the Prius, MIRAI and Corolla. The G21 Project started from the opportunity to contribute to twenty-first century energy and environment challenges and not just to produce a status symbol or quality form of transportation. As chairman Eiji Toyoda said at the time, 'Toyota has to provide contributable products for customers and society'. MIRAI is the world's first mass-produced fuel cell vehicle that achieves zero CO_2 emissions, which is a major contribution in terms of the environment. This is not only a zero CO_2 emissions product but also represents a paradigm shift, including infrastructure, in terms of energy diversification (Sano, 2015; Suzuki, 2014). The Corolla was first launched in 1966. It led to a new era of private car ownership in Japan. Project General Manager Hasegawa conveyed his passion to his next-generation development team at the time: 'Corolla for all mankind's welfare and happiness' (TOYOTA, 1966). Thus, Toyota sought to establish a new era for society by producing and developing high-quality cars for the modern world.

- **Zero-based thinking and talent matching.** 'Zero-based thinking and talent matching' were enabled through CE Uchiyamada's distinctive development approach. Firstly, he did not have experience in planning and had to implement everything from zero-based thinking. The zero-based thinking played a vital role in changing established and routine forms of development. Secondly, Uchiyamada's previous experience was with the Engineering Administration Division in which he worked for human resource and organization management. He therefore was well placed to find professional engineers suitable for the G21 Project team.
- **Obeya activity.** 'Obeya' means 'Large room'. In obeya activity the main members and representatives of each department gather in the same place and discuss the development. At first, Uchiyamada selected engineers from each department who had experience, were tolerant of others' opinions and focused on the total optimization of the whole car system. Then,

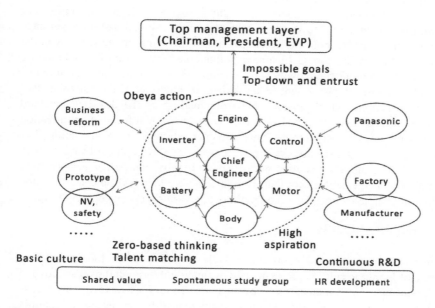

Figure 3.4   Hybrid Prius innovation management system

Uchiyamada defined and shared with the G21 team a 'Code of Conduct' related to setting the higher goal and not being profit-inducing representatives to their own departments. This management style helped to solve problems in the early phases and develop successful collaboration. It also enabled the team to think about the total optimization and simultaneous engineering. Furthermore, by gathering all the departments' representatives in the same place and sharing ideas, obeya activity enabled quick decision making.

- **Basic culture.** Toyota's shared value was cultivated by earnest and sincere education on the basis of the 'five main principles of Toyoda' (TOYOTA, 1935). According to these values, Toyota encourages spontaneous informal study groups. In recent years Nissan's informal activity developed 'Note e-power' in a shorter period than that of normal car development (Katayama, 2018). This shows that informal activity is effective for efficient development.
- **Continuous R&D.** The research and development (R&D) of hybrid technology started 20 years ago in small steps. Toyota is innovating constantly and broadly, studying biotechnology and nuclear fusion (Suto, 2016; TOYOTA, 2018b) as well as further developing TPS.

Figure 3.4 shows the Hybrid Prius innovation management system. At first, Uchiyamada was selected as a Chief Engineer. He had to implement 'zero-based thinking' to the development because he had had no experience in the planning division. He conducted 'talent matching' by networking at the administration division. Uchiyamada defined the 'High aspiration and guiding principle' to work proactively for the team. 'Basic culture' and 'Continuous R&D' brought improvement of the hybrid technology. The team conducted 'Obeya action', which enabled the front loading of the development, and collaboration beyond the walls between each department for total optimization and simultaneous engineering. This also enabled quick decision making. The setting of an 'almost impossible goal' pushed the development team to break free from established routine performance. Finally, the policy of entrusting middle management meant that Toyota was able to market the world's first hybrid vehicle in advance of competitors in a very short development term.

CONCLUSIONS

In this chapter Japanese management style was analysed by looking into the role of Japanese cultural mentality and evaluating it through the perspective of current innovation management theories. The Toyota Motor Corporation case was discussed to exemplify Japanese management by discussing thoroughly Toyota's Management System and the Hybrid Prius innovation management system. We have seen that Japanese cultural mentality and the corporate founder's philosophy served as the basis to produce outstanding innovations through fundamental Japanese management principles. However, we may ask why Japanese corporations, which once brought abundant innovations into being, are not as successful these days. The answer to this question lies in the explanation for why many other companies have failed to implement the Toyota Management System. The reason is that corporations are not able to perceive and recognize that the Toyota Management System is not only a mechanical system, pursuing scientific management, but also a human system, exploring sustainable evolution. We must understand that innovation can be realized only by human beings who are treated with respect and through a development process that is sustainable and not by human resources whose sole function is to maximize investors' returns in the short term. Without supreme respect for organizational members the innovation cannot be expected. In other words, only never-ending respect to employees aiming at self-realization through social contribution can sustain the foundation for innovation. Unfortunately many Japanese corporations have chosen to be the best investors' property after they welcomed and introduced American management standards at the end of the twentieth century. They want to become excellent students of the US standard. Now would be a good time to test whether a more humanistic approach in corporations could be adopted once again. It would be a test of whether we could replace the management foundation of large enterprises, which currently enshrines diminishing respect for employees as human beings, with the fundamental management principle of respecting human beings exploring sustainable evolution of innovation with pride and desire for social contribution. As long as corporate managements expect innovation, they have to face the reality that there is only one way to nurture the source, the people: with supreme respect and priority.

Japanese companies realize that an era of profound transformation that could happen once in a century is needed to overcome the stagnation of innovation. With that in mind, Japanese companies have taken up the challenge to once again become leaders in innovation. For example, Toyota Motor Corporation's recovery from the severe difficulties it faced in the aftermath of the global financial crisis, the large-scale recall of cars around the world, the Great East Japan Earthquake, flooding in Thailand, and other issues has transformed Toyota from a car-making firm into a mobility company. Toyota now provides a suite of services related to transportation globally. As highlighted above, Toyota has focused intensely on crisis response. In 2019 Toyota achieved sales in excess of 30 billion yen for the first time in Japan (TOYOTA, 2019). It keeps growing in a sustainable and evolutionary manner. Toyota strives to undergo a 'complete redesign' toward the future as a mobility company. Moreover Toyota has struggled to retrieve the 'essence that makes Toyota, Toyota', that is, the 'Toyota Production System' and 'refining costs'. This philosophy based on 'back to origin' and 'unshakeable foundations' (TOYOTA, 2019) is the key to Japanese innovation management success.

REFERENCES

Abbeglen, J.C. (1958), *The Japanese Factory: Aspects of its Social Organization*, Glencoe, IL: Free Press.

Abbeglen, J.C. (2006), *Twenty-First Century Japanese Management: New Systems, Lasting Values*, Basingstoke: Palgrave Macmillan.

Amabile, T. (1998), 'How to kill creativity', *Harvard Business Review* (September–October).

Anthony, S.D. (2014), *The First Mile: A Launch Manual for Getting Great Ideas into the Market*, Boston, MA: Harvard Business Review Press.

Blank, S. (2013), 'Why the lean start-up changes everything', *Harvard Business Review* (May).

Brown, T. (2009), *Change by Design: How Design Thinking Transforms Organizations and Inspires Innovation*, New York: Harper Business.

Christensen, C.M. (1997), *The Innovator's Dilemma: When New Technologies Cause Great Firms to Fail*, Boston, MA: Harvard Business School Press.

Christensen, C.M., S.D. Anthony and E.A. Roth (2004), *Seeing What's Next: Using the Theories of Innovation to Predict Industry Change*, Boston, MA: Harvard Business Review Press.

Christensen, C.M. and M.E. Raynor (2003), *The Innovator's Solution: Creating and Sustaining Successful Growth*, Boston, MA: Harvard Business Review Press.

Chunichi Shimbun-sha (2015), *Past, Present and Future: The Genealogy of Toyota* (in Japanese), Aichi: Chunichi Shimbun-sha Inc.

Clark, K.B. and T. Fujimoto (1991), *Product Development Performance: Strategy, Organization, and Management in the World Auto Industry*, Boston, MA: Harvard Business School Press.

Drucker, P.F. (1971), 'What we can learn from Japanese management', *Harvard Business Review* (March).

Drucker, P.F. (2002), 'The discipline of innovation', *Harvard Business Review* (August).

Dyer, J., H. Gregersen and C.M. Christensen (2011), *The Innovator's DNA: Mastering the Five Skills of Disruptive Innovators*, Boston, MA: Harvard Business Review Press.

Emori, T. (2014), 'Special interview with Akio Toyoda & Hiroshi Tsukakoshi' (in Japanese), *PHP Matsushita Konosuke Juku*, 21(January–February), PHP Institute, Kyoto.

Goldsmith, R.H. (2014), *Toyota's 8-Steps to Problem Solving*, Createspace Independent Publishers.

Hall, E.T. (1989), *Beyond Culture*, New York: Anchor Books.

Hayes, R.H. (1981), 'Why Japanese factories work', *Harvard Business Review* (July).

Hiromoto, T (1988), 'Another hidden edge: Japanese management accounting', *Harvard Business Review* (July–August), 22–25.

Howell, R. and M. Sakurai (1992), 'Management accounting (and other) lessons from the Japanese', *Management Accounting* (December), 28–34.

Iketomi, H., Y. Katatae and K. Fukazawa (2018), 'Heisei era economic history' (in Japanese), *Weekly Diamond*, 32(106), 28–59, Tokyo: Diamond Inc.

Imai, M (1986), *Kaizen: The Key to Japan's Competitive Success*, New York: McGraw-Hill.

Itani, H (2000), *Japanese Corporate Governance* (in Japanese), Tokyo: Nikkei Publishing Inc.

Japan Institute of Invention and Innovation (2016), 'Innovation top ten of Japan' (in Japanese), accessed June 23, 2019 at http://koueki.jiii.or.jp/innovation100/innovation_list.php?age=topten.

Kanno, H. (2014), *Learning from Failure of Management* (in Japanese), Tokyo: Nikkei Publishing Inc.

Kanno, H. (2018), 'Not succeed to imitate Toyota Production System' (in Japanese), *President*, Japan, President Inc. (June), accessed 23 June 2019 at https://president.jp/articles/-/25566.

Katayama, O. (2018), 'Management of huge organization', interview with Ikujiro Nonaka, Honorary Professor of Hitotsubashi University (in Japanese), accessed 23 June 2019 at https://biz-journal.jp/2018/07/post_24131_2.html.

Maslow, A.H. (1943), 'A theory of human motivation', *Psychological Review*, 50(4), 370–396.

Mauya, A. (2012), *Running Lean: Iterate from Plan A to a Plan that Works*, Sebastopol, CA: O'Reilly Media.

Narusawa, T., J. Shook and J. Womack (2009), *Kaizen Express: Fundamentals for Your Lean Journey*, Boston, MA: Lean Enterprises Institute Inc.

NICHIA (1956), 'Corporate philosophy', accessed 23 June 2019 at http://www.nichia.co.jp/en/about_nichia/company.html.

NISSIN FOODS (1958), 'Enduring values', accessed 23 June 2019 at https://www.nissin.com/en_jp/about/values/.

Nitobe, I. (1900), *Bushido: The Soul of Japan – The History of the Intercourse between the U.S. and Japan*, reprinted (2005), Kyoto: PHP Institute.

Nonaka, I., R. Toyama and T. Hirata (2010), *Managing Flow: The Dynamic Theory of the Knowledge-Based Firm* (in Japanese), Tokyo: Toyo Keizai Inc.

Okamura, T. (2004), 'Succeeded and failed company on introduction of TPS' (in Japanese), in *Logistics Business (LOGI-BIZ)*, Tokyo: Rhinos Publications Inc., vol. 4, accessed 23 June 2019 at https://magazine.logi-biz.com/pdf-read.php?id=378.

OLYMPUS (1919), 'The founding of Olympus and the spirit of creation', accessed 23 June 2019 at https://www.olympus-global.com/company/milestones/founding.html.

Onaka, T. (2017), *Toyoda Kiichiro and the Heirs* (in Japanese), Chiba: Global Management Networks Co.

Onaka, T. and N. Denscombe (2015), *Corporate Sustainability Governance*, Chiba: Global Management Networks Co.

Onaka, T., N. Denscombe and M. Ungerer (2016), *Bushido AI Programming*, Chiba: Global Management Networks Co.

Ono, T. (1978), *Toyota Production System* (in Japanese), Tokyo: Diamond Inc.

Onyemah, V., M.R. Pesquera and A. Ali (2013), 'What entrepreneurs get wrong', *Harvard Business Review* (May).

Osterwalder, A. and Y. Pigneur (2010), *Business Model Generation: A Handbook for Visionaries, Game Changers, and Challengers*, Hoboken, NJ: John Wiley.

Owens, T. and O. Fernandez (2014), *The Lean Enterprise: How Corporations Can Innovate Like Startups*, Hoboken, NJ: John Wiley.

Porter, M.E., M. Sakakibara and H. Takeuchi (2000), Can Japan Compete?, Basingstoke: Macmillan.

Ries, E. (2011), *The Lean Startup*, New York: Crown Publishing.

Sano, H. (2015), *The Story of Project MIRAI: Interview with Toyota Engineers of MIRAI Project* (in Japanese), All of Toyota, MIRAI, Japan: San-Ei Shobo Publishing Co.

Sasaki, S. (2015), *Toyota's Ji-Kotei-Kanketsu: Own-Process Completion* (in Japanese), Tokyo: Diamond Inc.

Shook, J. (2009), 'Toyota's secret: A3 report', *MIT Sloan Management Review* (July).

SONY (1946), 'The founding prospectus in 1946', accessed 23 June 2019 at https://www.sony.net/SonyInfo/CorporateInfo/History/.

Spear, S. (2004), 'Learning to lead at Toyota', *Harvard Business Review* (May).

Spear, S. and H.K. Bowen (1999), 'Decoding the DNA of the Toyota production system', *Harvard Business Review* (September–October), 97–106.

Staats, B. and D.M. Upton (2011), 'Lean knowledge work', *Harvard Business Review* (October).

Suto, H. (2016), 'Joint research of nuclear fusion fuel for high efficient heating with Toyota' (in Japanese), accessed 23 June 2019 at https://news.mynavi.jp/article/20160726-a284/.

Suzuki, T. (2014), 'Interview with Satoshi Ogiso (Present Executive Vice President of Toyota)' (in Japanese), Toyota MIRAI, Tokyo: Kotsu Times SHA Co.

Takeuchi, H., E. Osono and N. Shimizu (2008), 'The contradictions that drive Toyota's success', *Harvard Business Review* (December).

TOTO (1962), 'Company mottos in 1962', accessed 23 June 2019 at
https://jp.toto.com/en/company/profile/philosophy/group/index.htm#slogan.

Toyoda, S. (2015), *Step by Step with Belief for the Future* (in Japanese), Tokyo: Nikkei Publishing Inc.

TOYOTA (1935), 'Five main principles', accessed 23 June 2019 at
https://www.toyotaglobal.com/company/vision_philosophy/guiding_principles.html.

TOYOTA (1950), 'Toyota production system', accessed 23 June 2019 at
https://www.toyotaglobal.com/company/vision_philosophy/toyota_production_system/.

TOYOTA (1966), 'Philosophy of Corolla' (in Japanese), accessed 23 June 2019 at
https://toyota.jp/information/philosophy/corolla/history/index.html.

TOYOTA (1992), 'Guiding principles at Toyota', accessed 23 June 2019 at
https://global.toyota/en/company/vision-and-philosophy/guiding-principles/.

TOYOTA (1997), 'Prius development completed in approximately two years', accessed 23 June 2019 at http://www.toyotaglobal.com/company/history_of_toyota/75years/text/leaping_forward_as_a_global_corporation/chapter4/section8/item1_a.html.

TOYOTA (2017), 'The story behind the birth of the Prius, part 1', accessed 23 June 2019 at https://newsroom.toyota.co.jp/en/prius20th/challenge/birth/01/.

TOYOTA (2018a), *Annual Report 2018*, accessed 23 June 2019 at
https://www.toyotaglobal.com/pages/contents/investors/ir_library/annual/pdf/2018/annual_report_2018_fie.pdf.

TOYOTA (2018b), *Sustainability Data Book 2018*, accessed 23 June 2019 at https://global.toyota/en/sustainability/report/sdb/.

TOYOTA (2019), 'May 8, 2019 FY2019 Financial Results', accessed 23 June 2019 at https://global.toyota/en/ir/presentation/.

Uchida, T. (2009), *Henkyo-sei* (in Japanese), Tokyo: Shinchosha Publishing Co.

Uchimura, K. (1908), *Representative Men of Japan*, reprinted (2013), Avery Morrow's Printing and Bagels.

Umesao, T. (1957), *An Ecological View of History: Japanese Civilization in the World Context* (Japanese Society Series), reprinted (2003), Melbourne: Trans Pacific Press.

Womack, J.P., D.T. Jones and D. Roos (1990), *The Machine that Changed the World*, New York: Simon & Schuster.

PART III

Product innovation management

4. Exploring best practices of new product development

Suzanne L. Conner

INTRODUCTION

As new firms enter the market while others attempt to remain competitive in the increasingly crowded global-business landscape, developing and introducing new products is often utilized as an attempt to gain market share or edge out the competition. New product development (NPD) is "the transformation of a market opportunity into a product available for sale" (Krishnan and Ulrich, 2001, p. 1). In other words, it is creating new value for the customer. Developing new products for any firm is more difficult than managing existing product lines due to uncertainties surrounding them. For firms, especially startups, that may not have the knowledge of how to develop new products successfully or how to bring them to market, this can be increasingly difficult. By having a clear understanding of best practices in the NPD arena, the firm may increase its chances of initial and repeated success. This chapter gives an overview of key best practices in the NPD process from inception to success. The perspective taken is of developing not just a product with incremental improvements but also one that could be considered a breakthrough new product or at the least, a substantial improvement.

THE FOUNDATION

Just as in building a house, a company must have a solid foundation in order to support NPD. A few key elements to look at in order to determine whether or not a firm may be successful are discussed below such as firm culture, capabilities and knowledge; the author of the chapter believes that most companies would struggle to do well, if not fail, in NPD if these areas were misaligned.

Firm Culture

The organizational culture of a firm is the "complex set of values, beliefs, assumptions and symbols that define the way in which a firm conducts its business" (Barney, 1986, p. 657). This culture will impact policies as well as decision making and, if embraced by employees, will guide their behavior. In order to develop new, innovative products, the firm must have a culture that supports the employees involved (Berson et al., 2008). Employees must feel management support (Chandler et al., 2000; Henard and Szymanski, 2001), that they can take risks without fear of repercussions (Manso, 2017), and that there are incentives to innovate (Chandler et al., 2000; Manso, 2017). In the absence of these firm traits, employees are more likely to play it safe and only minimal, incremental innovations, if any, may take place. Therefore, top management must support innovation.

The culture of the firm not only affects employees and their innovation, it also influences the relationship with suppliers. Due to the need to reduce costs, many companies are now outsourcing aspects of product development in order to be competitive in the market. Research by Belassi et al. (2017, p. 195) demonstrated that in the realm of new product development, organizations with "a culture that is results oriented, open, and long-term oriented are in the best position to form cooperative buyer–supplier relationships." While organizational culture affects innovation and new product development, successful innovation also requires strategic fit and other firm competencies.

Firm Capabilities

According to the Product Development and Management Association's 2012 Comparative Performance Assessment Study, about 25 out of every 100 ideas are actually commercialized with about 15 of those considered successful (Markham and Lee, 2013). Due to the risk of failure, before or after launch, many firms shy away from new product development yet research has demonstrated that innovativeness is positively related to short-term financial outcomes and overall firm value (Pauwels et al., 2004; Sorescu and Spanjol, 2008). In order to screen out products likely to fail while increasing the rate of product success in the market, the firm must have the following key capabilities: industry knowledge, customer knowledge, and competitor knowledge.

In order to be successful with NPD, firms must have a set of capabilities in order not only to launch and succeed with new products, but also to screen out before the expense of development and launch those that will likely fail. Even though companies may cooperate with other firms for aspects of their product innovation, therefore potentially decreasing the need for capabilities in the areas to follow due to complementary skill sets, we will address what this author believes are the key factors that enable the company to function independently and exploit those existing capabilities.

Industry Knowledge

Organizations that have extensive knowledge in one area of industry are, generally, best suited to continue in that, or a relatively parallel industry, for NPD. Not only does this reduce risk, but the rest of the organization's capabilities are not being stretched too far in terms of manufacturing requirements, market research, research and development (R&D), channel development, and so forth. Over time, firms that are actively involved in NPD are likely to not only gain knowledge from external sources (for example suppliers) in the industry, but also from other units/departments within the organization itself (for example marketing and sales) through interactions in the NPD process. In fact, Yang et al. (2017) demonstrated that in high-tech firms an increased depth and breadth of knowledge in an industry greatly added to a firm's new product success, yet having broad knowledge with a shallow depth of knowledge negatively impacted new product success. Therefore, in terms of developing successful products, most firms should attempt to develop products in their current sphere of expertise.

Competitor Knowledge

Market-based learning has been determined to be a source of sustainable competitive advantage (Hult, 1998; Slater and Narver, 1995). All firms should have information on their competitors that can be used as benchmarks to compare their products and/or processes with those in competition in the industry. According to Doyle (1996, p. 51), benchmarking "compares customer satisfaction with the products, services, and relationships of the company with those of key competitors."

If done well, one can determine where one's firm is now, and where one wants to be relative to others. Benchmarking is not a process that is done once, and then filed away; it is something that should be an ongoing process and entails not only finding the gaps, but also producing plans to close those gaps.

Customer Knowledge

Knowing what customers want and their purchase behaviors leads to market advantage (Li and Calantone, 1998). Not only is this for current customers, but non-customers as well. Current customer needs can be accumulated through salespeople in the field; analysis of customer usage data; customer complaints and inquiries; surveys; and focus groups.

In order to find out what non-customers desire, salespeople in the field possess a wealth of knowledge as they have first-hand experience as to why customers do not adopt the company's current products. Market research, though time consuming and often expensive, can, if the correct questions are asked and the right people are reached, give big picture results. Surveys, whether they are administered on paper or online are often utilized; however, it is important they are well-constructed and will actually garner the information one is seeking without being overly taxing for the respondent.

PLANNING FOR INNOVATION

Cross-Functional Teams

Developing products that will satisfy consumers' needs, meet the financial goals of the firm, and can be produced through the firm's manufacturing capabilities is extremely difficult if the product is created in a silo. R&D may come up with the most technologically advanced gizmo of the year, but customers may not want it. Manufacturing may have just produced ten thousand units of a new product with plenty of inputs to create tens of thousands more, when marketing figures out that customers won't pay enough for it to cover the pricing requirements of the product. Therefore, companies that are successful with NPD, utilize cross-functional teams (CFTs) to leverage interorganizational knowledge.

CFTs are charged with management and coordination of the NPD project (Griffin and Hauser, 1992) and generally comprised of representatives from manufacturing, engineering, R&D, marketing, finance, human resources, and other functional areas as deemed necessary. Of course, these requirements vary based on the level of innovativeness of the product or the newness of the product to the company. For example, where the team has marching orders to develop a new-to-the-world product (one that has not existed in the past) or it is beyond the firm's current capability (for example a car manufacturer wants to enter the athletic wear market), which is high risk, utilizing a full CFT is likely. If manufacturing is only adding a new color to the product line that is considered low risk, it is likely not necessary to bring the entire team together; only the members whose functional areas would be affected by the change may be brought in as needed and the remaining team members would be informed of key issues.

There are many ways to structure these CFTs in terms of commitment to the NPD team. Some companies may have the CFT team working on projects together full time while others may have the team come together only when there is a need. As may be seen, there is a lot of flexibility in creating CFTs based on the culture, strategies, goals and resources of the organization as well as the newness of the product. Also, the stage of new product development generally impacts which functions should be interacting (Olson et al., 2001); in most projects, it is not beneficial, or financially wise, to have all of the team members actively involved at every stage but it is a good idea to keep everyone informed of the current status of the project. In fact, a study by Kong et al. (2015), explored the effects of marketing–manufacturing integration at each stage of NPD with various results in regard to speed to market, cost reduction and market performance.

There are other factors that a firm needs to consider when developing CFTs such as: the personalities of the team members and how they will work together; the criteria that will be used to review their performance (for example based on milestones, goals); how they will be rewarded (for example individually or as a group) and what for; as well as the term of the CFT (for example whether they will remain as a team across multiple projects or just one). There are different schools of thought on each of these, and approaches that may fit one company better than another, but this author believes strongly that rewards should not be based solely on the market success of the new product due to the fact that there are many things out of the team's control within the firm and the external landscape.

Another factor to consider in this area is the product champion. This person, from the CFT, is the cheerleader for the product, and should have a good relationship with the decision makers in order to fight for the product when management may want to terminate the process. They should be able to use influence (Howell and Shea, 2001; Markham, 1998) and are likely to be involved in the entire process.

Rules of the Road

As with building a house or driving a car, there are rules that are to be followed for a successful outcome; in NPD, there is no difference. While there are companies that have successfully introduced products without utilizing a formal strategy, utilizing one keeps management and those involved in development focused on the goal. Having a written strategy will also help scope-creep from setting in; at various points throughout the NPD, these rules of the road should be referred to frequently in order to make sure the team, and the product being developed, is on the right track. This document, often called a Product Innovation Charter (PIC), is generally created by senior management and, among other things, should include why a new product is sought (for example declining market share, management direction, a new technology or material), the objectives and goals for what the product will accomplish, and any specific information that should be adhered to such as time-to-market, cost, quality, and other considerations the NPD team must take into account. While the content and name of PICs vary from company to company and are not used by all, the PIC does seem to impact new product performance positively (Bart and Pujari, 2007).

PRODUCT DEVELOPMENT

Opportunity Identification

Opportunities for new products can be found in myriad ways. In this example, we will look at it from the perspective of an existing company. This author believes that opportunities can be found by:

- Salespeople. Front-line salespeople have direct contact with customers and may have developed relationships with them. Through ordinary sales calls, salespeople can garner information on what the customer is not happy with, the needs they have, and/or what types of products may be of benefit to them. In order for this to work, salespeople must desire and have a means to share this information.
- Suppliers. Suppliers that have provided inputs for existing products may know of new materials that could create efficiencies or changes in existing products, or create new products.
- Customer service. Customer service is typically where customers go in order to solve a problem. By keeping accurate records of customer complaints and praise, the company can utilize this information for ideas on how to improve the existing products or create new products. However, since this is generally a large amount of data, the company must have a plan in place for reviewing and acting upon the information gathered.
- Lead users/nonusers. Lead users are great sources of new product ideas, especially if the new product is in the same realm as products they already use. It is likely that through consistent use of a particular product, these customers have had thoughts of what they wish the product would do, or of other additional products that would make their life easier. Nonusers, if they are accessible, may provide information on why they are not using a particular company's products and may offer insights into what they are seeking. These groups are generally most helpful when doing iterations of a product, not for new-to-the-world types of products.
- Brainstorming. If NPD teams have been created, brainstorming can be a fruitful way of developing new concepts and ideas, especially if the NPD team have been working together, feel comfortable, and are willing to be open as well as nonjudgmental.

Regardless of how the opportunities are found, there are generally many pieces of information that need to be sifted through. In order to choose the opportunities that have the best chance of success, they need to be chosen carefully through product selection.

Product Selection

Screening new product ideas generally entails deciding whether or not the new product would: fit with the firm's current capabilities and strategy, be technically feasible, be what customers would want, offer market opportunities, and perform well financially. This list may vary based on the firm involved and the guidelines set forth by management, but in general, these are the key issues most often assessed. At this point, the roadmap needs to be checked again to make sure the current product ideas will meet those guidelines. In the beginning, there may be many products being considered for development.

Throughout the development of a new product, from idea conception to final product, it is beneficial to utilize some version of a stage-gate process (SGP). Utilizing an SGP means that at various, predetermined places during development, the project is evaluated to determine whether the must-meet criteria have been met; if they haven't, the project is killed in order to save resources for other potential projects (Cooper et al., 2002). This author believes that should-meet criteria should also be included in order to help prioritize focus for the remaining projects and that the criteria should be both quantitative and qualitative in nature.

Others utilize a system that is more flexible and allows customer inputs at each stage of the process and therefore can lead to development of products that customers actually want. In this way, customers are involved from the idea stage through the launch phase and are shown the potential product, including its form and features, throughout those stages. This is good when one has established customers and can get useful feedback from them; however, this can also be risky as each customer may want something different and be unhappy if the final product isn't exactly what they were asking for. This author believes that combining the two approaches may be ideal in particular situations and for certain products since the intent and company goals are kept in mind while including more customer feedback, therefore creating a win-win situation for all involved as long as expectations are managed.

Concept Design and Product Feedback

Whether customers are involved throughout the process, or in later stages of development, it is important their feedback on the new product is gathered. Often this is done once an idea is formed in order to see if the concept is something customers may adopt and often consumers have valuable ideas that can add to the product. If one chooses to wait until the prototype phase of development, it is useful to assess the product, whether in a virtual form, a rough prototype or an almost-completed functional product, to see if there are any issues with its form and function. Prototype testing is most effective if the prototype can be tested in the situation and conditions in which it would be used, especially for closer-to-launch products. However, it is also important to note that in markets that are rapidly changing, getting customer input during the ideation stage and launch stage may be preferable to during the development portion due to delays in launch which may lead to decreased financial performance (Chang and Taylor, 2016). In fact, labeling products as 'customer-ideated' often enables a company to increase the markup on that product and in the food and electronics sectors, customers perceive the product as higher quality (Nishikawa et al., 2017). Also, when making the decision whether or not to involve customers, especially earlier in the development phase, one must consider the potential that one's idea could be leaked to another firm who may develop it before one's own firm has the opportunity. Where one has a technology, process, or material that would be difficult to copy, the risk is less, but it is still something to consider.

Quality Function Deployment

Developing any product requires tradeoffs, often in terms of quality, function, and design especially since most products are created under budgetary and other constraints. In order to get the best overall product, this author believes that utilizing the Quality Function Deployment (QFD) tool allows translation of customer requirements into products that improve satisfaction in the end. This tool demonstrates how tradeoffs affect components of the product and how making tradeoffs in different areas will affect the benefits the customer is seeking. For more information on, and training in, QFD, the QFD Institute is a great resource (QFD Institute).

Tracking

Tracking of ideas, successes and failures is an important aspect of NPD. Ideas may be good, but the idea could have been before its time or the company may not have the financial or technical resources to act on it. At a later time, resources or the market may change and the old idea could be successfully brought to life. Ideas that were deemed failures at any stage of NPD should also be kept. That way, if the idea ever surfaces again, time will not be wasted on it again and there is the potential to learn from past mistakes.

Post-launch it is also important to track the performance of new products. Before the launch, goals should be set and performance measured against them. Contingency (aka what-if) plans should also be formalized in case the product is not performing as well as expected. In order to do so, it is important to not only have performance goals set, but a good idea of what could go wrong in terms of: customer expectations, adoption of the product, a competitor launching a similar product, salespeople not performing as projected, etc. Plans regarding how to mitigate those problems and at what point action would be taken also need to be determined.

CONCLUSIONS

NPD is an exciting area to work in, offering rewards and challenges that others may not be exposed to. Unfortunately, it's also not a one-size-fits-all venture and therefore the approaches that work for one company may not work for another; multinational organizations will have the resources to do things differently than a local business owner. From whatever standpoint one approaches NPD, utilizing the guidelines above as best practices should alleviate some of the pitfalls associated with it and set one's organization on a firm footing for success.

REFERENCES

Barney, J.B. (1986), 'Organization culture: can it be a source of sustained competitive advantage?', *Academy of Management Review*, 11(3), 656–665.
Bart, C. and A. Pujari (2007), 'The performance impact of content and process in product innovation charters', *Journal of Product Innovation Management*, 24(1), 3–19.
Belassi, W., M. Cocosila and A.Z. Kondra (2017), 'The effects of organizational culture on buyer–supplier relationships in new product development', *International Journal of Business & Management Science*, 72(2), 195–218.
Berson, Y., S. Oreg and T. Dvir (2008), 'CEO values, organizational culture and firm outcomes', *Journal of Organizational Behavior*, 29(5), 615–633.
Chandler, G.N., C. Keller and D.W. Lyon (2000), 'Unraveling the determinants and consequences of an innovation-supportive organizational culture', *Entrepreneurship Theory and Practice*, 25(1), 59–76.
Chang, W. and S.A. Taylor (2016), 'The effectiveness of customer participation in new product development: a meta-analysis', *Journal of Marketing*, 80(1), 47–64.
Cooper, R.G., S.J. Edgett and E.J. Kleinschmidt (2002), 'Optimizing the stage-gate process: what best-practice companies do', *Research Technology Management*, 45(5), 21–27.
Doyle, P. (1996), *Marketing Management and Strategy*, London: Prentice Hall.
Griffin, A. and J.R. Hauser (1992), 'Patterns of communication among marketing, engineering, and manufacturing: a comparison between two new product teams', *Management Science*, 38(3), 360–373.

Henard, D.H. and D.M. Szymanski (2001), 'Why some new products are more success-ful than others', *Journal of Marketing Research*, 38, 362–375.

Howell, J.M. and C.M. Shea (2001), 'Individual differences, environmental scanning, innovation framing, and champion behavior: key predictors of project performance', *Journal of Product Innovation Management*, 18(1), 15–27.

Hult, G.T. (1998), 'Managing the international strategic sourcing process as a market-driven organizational learning system', *Decision Sciences*, 29(1), 193–216.

Kong, T., G. Li, T. Feng and L. Sun (2015), 'Effects of marketing–manufacturing inte-gration across stages of new product development on performance', *International Journal of Production Research*, 53(8), 269–284.

Krishnan, V. and K. Ulrich (2001), 'Product development decisions: a review of the literature', *Management Science*, 47(1), 1–21.

Li, T. and R.J. Calantone (1998), 'The impact of market knowledge competence on new product advantage: conceptualization and empirical examination', *Journal of Marketing*, 62(4), 13–29.

Manso, G. (2017), 'Creating incentives for innovation', *California Management Review*, 60(1), 18–32.

Markham, S.K. (1998), 'A longitudinal examination of how champions influence others to support their projects', *Journal of Product Innovation Management*, 15(6), 490–504.

Markham, S.K. and H. Lee (2013), 'Product Development and Management Association's 2012 Comparative Performance Assessment Study', *Journal of Product Innovation Management*, 30(3), 408–429.

Nishikawa, H., M. Schreier, C. Fuchs and S. Ogawa (2017), 'The value of marketing crowdsourced new products as such: evidence from two randomized field experi-ments', *Journal of Marketing Research*, 54, 525–539.

Olson, E.M., O.C. Walker, Jr., R.W. Ruekert and J.M. Bonner (2001), 'Patterns of cooperation during new product development among marketing, operations, and R&D: implications for project performance', *Journal of Product Innovation Management*, 18(4), 258–271.

Pauwels, K., J. Silva-Risso, S. Srinivasan and D.M. Hanssens (2004), 'New products, sales promotions and firm value: the case of the automobile industry', *Journal of Marketing*, 68(4), 142–156.

QFD Institute. Qfdi.org, last accessed September 17, 2018.

Slater, S. and J.C. Narver (1995), 'Market orientation and the learning organization', *Journal of Marketing*, 59 (July), 63–74.

Sorescu, A.B. and J. Spanjol (2008), 'Innovation's effect on firm value and risk: insights from consumer packaged goods', *Journal of Marketing*, 72(2), 114–132.

Yang, D., L. Jin and S. Sheng (2017), 'The effect of knowledge breadth and depth on new product performance', *International Journal of Market Research*, 59(4), 517–536.

5. Product design innovation and functional innovation effects on consumers' adoption of soft furniture

Vilte Auruskeviciene and Sabina Senkevic

INTRODUCTION

Recent decades have changed the business environment substantially due to globalization and competition, which have affected and changed the basis for companies' success. Innovation has become a key element for achievement and competitiveness (Kaplan, 2009). Product innovation, as Hanaysha (2016) stated, has become a key factor in driving companies' performance and growth; however, it is successful only when consumers adopt these products (Hetet et al., 2014). According to Bartels and Reinders (2011), most of the failures regarding innovations happen due to poor understanding of consumers and their expectations. At the very heart of successful product innovation is the knowledge of how consumers perceive the company and its products as being innovative and how this perception impacts innovative product adoption.

Li et al. (2015) believe that the adoption intentions for new products are driven by product usefulness and originality. From consumers' point of view, usefulness is related to function, whereas originality is related to design. This raises an issue of examining how, in particular, product innovativeness is perceived from usefulness and originality perspectives. In this study, we explore what effect product innovativeness, from the usefulness and originality perspectives, has on consumers' adoption of soft furniture products.

The Lithuanian soft furniture market was chosen for study due to a number of reasons. First of all, Lithuania is known for high-quality furniture production, which is constantly increasing and, according to the Lithuanian Department of Statistics, has increased by more than 18 per cent from 2010 until 2018. Second, although a lot of resources are being invested by the furniture-producing companies for product development, failure rates are huge (up to 60 per cent). Finally, design and functionality are important features determining consumers' decision to adopt not only in the furniture-products category but in many other categories such as automobiles, telecommunications, TVs, watches, washing machines, etc.

So far innovation studies have focused on extensive debates of 'market pull' merits versus 'technology push' merits for the explanation of failure (or success) of new products. However, limited research has been done at the nexus of product design and function innovation, and their effects on new product adoption. This study is an initial attempt to address the issue and test the effect of design innovation and functional innovation on consumers' purchase intention and willingness to pay for soft furniture products.

PRODUCT INNOVATIVENESS AND ITS ADOPTION

Generally, innovation is defined as idea, practice, product, or any other adoption of a change that is new to the market. Product innovation, by many researchers, is understood as the main strategic factor for company success and survival (Gunday et al., 2011; Jimenez and Sanz-Valle, 2011). Thus, an innovative product is the outcome of successful development and adoption of a new idea. Product innovation is considered to be the main driver of company performance and operations, to improve organizational growth, increase market share, increase the loyalty of existing consumers, and attract new consumers (Forsman, 2011; Fuji and Utami, 2013).

However, the success of a new product in the market is predetermined by consumers' willingness to adopt it. Consumer adoption is defined by the cognitive (purchase intention and willingness to pay) and behavioural intentions (adoption) steps (Mathur, 1999). According to the Theory of Reasoned Action (TRA), consumer attitude impacts intention that, in turn, impacts action/adoption (Fishbein and Ajzen, 1975). Prior research also suggests that perceptions of level of innovation and the attitudes toward innovation are key predictors of innovative product success (Montoya-Weiss and Calantone, 1994). Hence, perceived product innovativeness by consumers is likely to impact purchase intention and willingness to pay.

THE ROLE OF DESIGN AND FUNCTIONAL INNOVATIONS

A product transcends design and functional, or utilitarian, features inform the consumer about why one product is better than other products. According to Townsend et al. (2013) product design is the first approach between the product and consumer, which enables an individual to evaluate product features, benefits, and value. Product design is related to an individual's perceptions about it and motivates them either to accept or reject it (Townsend et al., 2013). Consumers evaluate product design through shapes, proportions, sizes or volume, packaging, and its newness. It is important to note that product design plays a crucial role and is a key factor of a brand strategy; therefore, it is not surprising that a lot of resources are usually invested into product improvement and brand performance (Townsend et al., 2013). Rindova and Petkova (2007) claim that product design is related to colours, materials used, shapes and proportions. What is more, design has a strong impact on consumers' perception since it provides visual cues, which enable interpretation, and stimulate consumers' cognitions and emotions. As a result, individuals are able to assess the value of a new product (Rindova and Petkova, 2007).

Still, product function is often more important to consumers and it is their primary yardstick to evaluate a product. Most commonly it is not good if a product looks very nice but is not able to execute its task. Product function is related to a component design that fulfils the purpose of the product, and as a consequence, provides utility for the consumer. Functional characteristics enable individuals to use the product more efficiently and comfortably, and therefore to satisfy their particular needs and wants; as a result, function solves consumption-related needs (Townsend et al., 2013). To consumers, differently than to manufacturers, product design creates the first (positive or negative) impression and, if this impression is strong, it determines their decision to purchase the product. However, a consumer repurchases the product only if both product features – design and function – assessments are positive.

Products can be new to the market, new to the company, and new to a consumer. The benefits of design and function of a new product extend even beyond a consumer's needs and expectations, as the company can offer design and functions of a product consumers do not yet know they want. Thus, spending resources on product design and functionality can improve company performance (Marsili and Salter, 2006). This study examines how functional and design innovations moderate the relationship between consumers' perceived product innovativeness and their attitude toward the product as well as the link between consumers' perceived product innovativeness and its adoption: purchase intention and willingness to pay.

DEVELOPMENT OF THE CONCEPTUAL MODEL

As Fishbein and Ajzen (1975) explained, an individual's behaviour can be determined by his or her intentions and they define two main determinants of intention: (1) a personal determinant – attitude toward the behaviour, and (2) a social determinant – subjective norm. Fu and Elliott (2013) believe that attitude toward the behaviour and subjective norms have positive influences on behavioural intention but are determined differently. The attitudinal impact arises from the individual's own beliefs with regard to the possible outcomes of a behaviour, and his/her evaluation of particular outcomes (Fu and Elliott,

2013). In contrast, the normative impact comes from the individual's perception of his/her significant others' beliefs, and his/her own willingness to accept these beliefs (Fu and Elliott, 2013). Moreover, Fu and Elliott (2013) suggest, when purchasing a new product, it is very common that individuals tend to ask for others' opinions and take into account their beliefs about particular product adoption. This facilitates the enhancement of consumers' motivation. For this reason, from the innovative product perspective, the attitudinal route is directly related to the new product, while the normative route is indirectly related to the new product via other individuals' evaluation of the new product. As a result, both of these routes are predicted to have positive effects on behavioural intention (Fishbein and Ajzen, 1975). Fu and Elliott (2013) treat consumers' purchase intention as a behavioural intention. Additionally, in this research an individual's willingness to pay was included and related to a behavioural intention as well. Moreover, as the TRA considers that behavioural intention is a mediator between attitude, subjective norm, and actual behaviour, it was assumed to have a similar effect on purchase intention and willingness to pay. Hence, the research hypotheses are as following:

H1a: Consumers' attitude toward a product has a direct positive impact on their intention to purchase the product.

H1b: Consumers' attitude toward a product has a direct positive impact on their willingness to pay for the product.

H2a: Subjective norms are positively related to consumers' intention to purchase the product.

H2b: Subjective norms are positively related to consumers' willingness to pay for the product.

Perceived product innovativeness indicates the extent to which individuals consider new products as having novel and unique attributes and features in comparison with other products in the same product category (Fu and Elliott, 2013). Li et al. (2015) revealed that even small, novel changes in the product are positively received by consumers and have a considerable effect on consumers' adoption intentions. In addition, the research done by Fu and Elliott (2013) suggests that perceived innovativeness positively and strongly impacts a consumer's intention to purchase a new product. Moreover, Lafferty and Goldsmith (2004) argue that perceived innovativeness improves consumers' motivation and consequently, simplifies the adoption process. Fu and Elliot (2013) also explain that individuals are more willing to receive the information about a new product and, as a consequence, their attitude regarding the product will influence their behavioural intention. It is possible that it can have a similar effect on an individual's willingness to pay for the product. For this reason, the following research hypotheses were identified:

H3a: Consumers' perceived product innovativeness has a direct impact on their intention to purchase the product.

H3b: Consumers' perceived product innovativeness has a direct impact on their willingness to pay for the product.

As mentioned before, perceived product innovativeness explains the degree to which individuals consider a new product as being superior due to unique attributes and features compared with other products of the same category (Fu and Elliot, 2013). Thus, it is believed that it may vary based on the type of innovation itself (i.e. design innovation versus functional innovation). Therefore, it is possible that the type of innovation can have a moderating effect on the relationship between the perceived product innovativeness and attitude toward the product; the perceived product innovativeness and purchase intention, as well as perceived product innovativeness and willingness to pay. For this reason, the next hypotheses, regarding an individual's attitude toward the product, intention to purchase the product and willingness to pay for the product, were formulated:

H4: The type of innovation (design innovation versus functional innovation) moderates the relation between consumers' perceived product innovativeness and their attitude toward the product.

H5a: The type of innovation moderates the relation between consumers' perceived product innovativeness and their intention to purchase the product.

H5b: The type of innovation moderates the relation between consumers' perceived product innovativeness and their willingness to pay for the product.

METHODOLOGY

This study was based on the TRA and relevant literature to investigate the effect of design innovation and functional innovation on consumers' purchase intention and willingness to pay for the soft furniture products. The quantitative research method was selected in order to perform the empirical research. A structured questionnaire was employed to gather field data.

All items were measured using the 7-point Likert scale, ranging from 1 – 'strongly disagree' to 7 – 'strongly agree'. The research instrument was adapted from prior studies. *Perceived product innovativeness* scale was adapted from Fu et al. (2008), and Fort-Rioche and Ackermann (2013). *Attitude, Subjective norm, Purchase intention,* and *Willingness to pay* scales were adapted from Fu and Elliott (2013). *Type of product innovation* was manipulated using three different stimuli: a picture with design innovation, a picture with functional innovation, and a picture with the standard product. Each picture was shown to respondents randomly, one picture per person. Each picture corresponded to the particular type of product innovation. The questionnaire included 22 statements and was available in two languages: English and Lithuanian. Since in this research the Lithuanian market was analysed, the questionnaire was distributed in Lithuanian to get more accurate results.

RESULTS

The total number of research participants who answered questionnaires was 238: 70.5 per cent of whom were women and 29.5 per cent men. Most of the participants (59.5 per cent) were 25 to 34 years old. The minority belonged to the 55–64 age range. The respondents' monthly income before taxes ranged from 501–1000 EUR to 1001–1500 EUR, which corresponds to 23.3 per cent and 26.7 per cent of respondents respectively. Referring to the purchase frequency of soft furniture products, the majority of participants had last bought such a product 2–5 years ago, while 19.9 per cent of the respondents had never bought any furniture product.

As Table 5.1 shows, participants from the first group would like to pay 0–499 EUR and 500–999 EUR for a design-innovation product, which corresponds to 45.3 per cent and 33.3 per cent of the respondents, respectively. Whereas for the functional-innovation product, participants from the second group were ready to spend 0–499 EUR and 500–999 EUR, which is 37.9 per cent and 31.0 per cent, respectively. Conversely, for the standard product, individuals from the third group would pay 0–499 EUR and 500–999 EUR as well; that comprises 38.4 per cent and 35.6 per cent of the respondents, respectively. Most of the respondents would spend no more than 499 EUR for the soft furniture product.

However, some individuals were ready to spend the largest amount of money – more than 2,500 EUR, on the functional-innovation product (4.6 per cent), and the standard product (1.4 per cent), whereas no one was willing to spend this amount for the design-innovation product.

Since in this research several types of product innovation are analysed in relation to the soft furniture products, it was interesting to explore the opinions of potential customers regarding three different kinds of products: those that

Table 5.1   *Willingness to pay depending on the product*

Factor	Value (EUR)	Design innovation	Functional innovation	Standard product
Willingness to pay	0–499	45.3%	37.9%	38.4%
	500–999	33.3%	31.0%	35.6%
	1,000–1,499	10.7%	16.1%	15.1%
	1,500–1,999	4.0%	6.9%	8.2%
	2,000–2,499	6.7%	3.4%	1.4%
	2,500+	–	4.6%	1.4%

have integrated functional innovation, those that represent the design innovation category, and the standard product. From the research results, it can be seen that individuals saw the products as being innovative, trendy and fashionable, with corresponding mean values for functional $M = 5.28$ and design $M = 5.26$ products. It was not surprising that the standard product was evaluated lower, with the value $M = 3.77$, meaning that standard products are less innovative, less trendy, and do not create a new product category for consumers. Moreover, regarding innovation perception it seems that whether an individual looks at functional product innovation or at design product innovation, he or she perceives them at the same level of innovativeness.

Regarding the respondents' attitude toward the products, functional-innovation and standard products were assessed more positively, and more favourably, with the values of $M = 5.06$ and $M = 5.12$, respectively. However, individuals' attitudes toward design-innovation products were a bit lower, possessing the value of $M = 4.45$. The subjective norm was much higher for the standard product ($M = 3.88$), than for functional-innovation ($M = 3.04$) and design-innovation products ($M = 2.54$). This is explained by the fact that individuals believe that their friends, and other people important to them, would want them and expect them to have a standard soft furniture product more than one with design or functional innovation.

Regarding purchase intentions, respondents were more likely to buy the product with the integrated functional innovation ($M = 5.28$) than the standard product ($M = 4.24$), or the product with design innovation ($M = 2.69$). Concerning individuals' willingness to pay for these products, it was identified, on average, that the amount in Euros they would pay for the soft furniture product would be approximately 786 EUR for the functional-innovation product, 607 EUR for the design-innovation product, and 655 EUR for the standard product. Consequently, it can be stated that potential customers value functional innovation the most, and are ready to spend the largest amount of money for it. The main findings of this research are:

- Individuals possess a more positive attitude toward functional-innovation products and the standard product, whereas design innovation is a bit less valued in the soft furniture product category.
- Individuals possess much higher purchase intentions and are more willing to spend their money for the functional-innovation soft furniture product than for the standard soft furniture product or the one with an innovative design.
- Hypothesis H1a was supported: consumers' attitudes toward a product have a direct positive impact on their intention to purchase the soft furniture product.
- Hypothesis H1b was rejected: consumers' attitudes toward a product do not affect their willingness to pay for the soft furniture product.
- Hypotheses H2a and H2b were supported since there is statistical evidence that subjective norm is positively related to consumers' intention to purchase the soft furniture product and their willingness to pay for the soft furniture product.
- There is statistical evidence that perceived product innovativeness has a direct but negative impact on consumers' intention to purchase the soft furniture product, thus Hypothesis H3b was rejected as it was justified statistically that perceived product innovativeness does not have a direct positive impact on consumers' willingness to pay for the soft furniture product.
- It was found statistically that the functional innovation strengthens the relationship between consumers' perceived product innovativeness and their attitude toward the soft furniture product, thus Hypothesis H4 was supported.
- Hypothesis H5a was supported. The functional innovations strengthen the relationship between consumers' perceived product innovativeness and their intention to purchase the soft furniture product, whereas design innovation does not.
- It was found that the type of innovation does not affect the relationship between consumers' perceived product innovativeness and their willingness to pay for the soft furniture product.

DISCUSSION

The aim of this study was to explore the effects of perceived product-design innovation and functional innovation on consumers' adoption of soft furniture products in the Lithuanian market. The relationship between perceived product innovativeness and consumers' adoption was examined taking into account the moderating effects of design and functional innovation. The direct relationships of attitude, subjective norm, and perceived product innovativeness on consumers' adoption and the moderating effect of design and functional innovations on the relationship between perceived product innovativeness and attitude were examined.

Responses from 238 research participants disclosed that perceived product innovativeness does not only influence consumers' intention to purchase directly but this relationship can be strengthened by functional innovation in the soft furniture product category. A similar relationship was found in Fu and Elliot's (2013) study, which disclosed that perceived product innovativeness positively impacts consumers' purchase intentions. However, in the current study, it was identified that perceived product innovation has a direct negative effect on consumers' intention to purchase the product. Thus, the more a soft furniture product is perceived as innovative, the lower an individual's intention to purchase this product; this is not surprising as individuals are more inclined to choose classical/standard furniture. Regarding consumers' willingness to pay, Hwang et al. (2016) explain that consumers are willing to pay for the products if they perceive benefits. However, in this study it was found that perceived product innovativeness does not affect consumers' willingness to pay for the product.

In the literature, there is evidence confirming that the form and function of a product affect an individual's beliefs about and preferences regarding the product (Townsend et al., 2013). In this study it was identified that individuals perceive functional innovation and design innovation at the same level of innovativeness. In addition, the moderating effect of the different types of innovation was recognized.

Regarding the type of innovation, it was found that consumers are more likely to adopt the functional-innovation soft furniture product than a design-innovation furniture product. This is not surprising as individuals relate the beauty of the design to the aesthetic standards they have in mind, whereas innovative products usually do not correspond with the existing standards, so individuals are less happy with the physical attractiveness of innovative products (Verganti, 2009). In general, innovation has a positive impact on consumers' adoption of the soft furniture products, in terms of purchase intentions, but the relationship depends on the type of innovation. The reasons for what actually drives such consumer thinking can be found in the literature. Perceived innovativeness might go along with an individual's desire to be exceptional and the desire for exclusivity during the launch of new products (Fu and Elliot, 2013). Tian et al. (2001) explain that individuals' need for uniqueness explains their choice and desire through the adoption, utilization, and disposition of the products. Nevertheless, it is important to mention, in this study it was identified that the type of innovation does not influence consumers' willingness to pay for the product, which might be affected by consumers' incapability to evaluate a real product's benefits and unique values (Fadzline et al., 2014).

Regarding the attitude and subjective norm, this study confirms the main TRA relationships, since attitude and subjective norm were both positively related to individual's purchase intention. Similar relationships were investigated in the research by Fu and Elliot (2013), where attitude and subjective norm both affect intention to purchase the product. This shows that attitudinal influence arises from a person's own beliefs and is directly related to new product adoption, thus people are more motivated by themselves to buy a soft furniture product. This finding goes along with the research of Rogers (2003) and Venkatesh et al. (2003) that suggest that attitudes are formed based on the perception of innovative characteristics. Thus, these perceptions enable an individual to develop positive or negative feelings about the behaviour and, consequently, positive or negative attitudes are being converted into adoption or rejection.

In contrast, the subjective norm, which according to TRA is tied in with the normative route, is related to new product adoption through other individuals' evaluation of the product: friends, family members, and important others (Fu and Elliot, 2013). This suggests that important others can influence individuals to adopt the soft furniture product. As research findings showed, an individual's friends or other people that are important to them would expect and want him or her to adopt the soft furniture product. To be more precise with the particular product category, from the design innovation and functional innovation perspective, it was identified that customers' internal preferences are associated with products with an integrated functional innovation as well as the standard product. This study indicates that the type of innovation strengthens the relationship between consumers' perceived product innovativeness and their attitude toward the soft furniture product and provides statistical evidence that functional innovation strengthens the relationship between consumers' perceived product innovativeness and their intention to purchase the soft furniture product, whereas design innovation does not.

MANAGERIAL IMPLICATIONS

The recommendations for practitioners are evident: it is worth investing in new product development as this creates opportunities to enhance customer intention to purchase more products. Moreover, Henard and Dacin (2010) believe product innovations might not only strengthen a firm's reputation but also increase consumers' motivation and enthusiasm toward the firm's products and lead to new product sales. From the soft furniture market perspective, individuals are more willing to buy the product when they perceive it as being innovative, depending on the type of innovation. To be more precise, the research results showed that consumers value functional aspects of new products much more than design aspects. Therefore, firms should invest more in functional innovation, which is characterized by 'structural and technological features' (Townsend et al., 2013) and such products must enable individuals to use them in a more efficient and comfortable way (Townsend et al., 2013).

These research results align with prior research confirming that product design is one of the key factors of an effective brand strategy (Townsend et al., 2013). According to Kaplan (2009), firms should exploit marketing communications, which allow making potential consumers feel that a particular product is innovative. Thus, the main message about the product should reflect its innovativeness. What is more important, according to Fadzline et al. (2014), is that customers are more willing to pay for a product that possesses a set of unique values. By the same token, as the literature review showed, one of the main attributes of innovative product adoption is the relative advantage, which enables customer to perceive the innovation as better than the product it replaces (Rogers, 2003). In addition, Ho and Wu (2011) suggest that consumers are more likely to adopt a product that possesses greater relative advantages. As a result, the main marketing message should highlight the product's unique features, functionality, benefits, advantages and other superiorities, which distinguish it from the others and, consequently, not only contribute to an individual's perception of the product's innovativeness, but also lead to augmented adoption of these products among consumers (Fu and Elliot, 2013). As a consequence, all of these components would facilitate the process of creating a strong brand, enabling the firm to achieve a differentiated position in the market; the company would also be able to decrease risk and improve future profits (Townsend et al., 2013).

CONCLUSIONS

The review of the literature has shown that consumers' intentions have been studied widely in the innovation management field; however, little attention has been given to exploring what effect design innovation and functional innovation has on consumers' adoption of soft furniture products in terms of purchase intentions and willingness to pay. Thus, the aim of this research was to investigate if design innovation and functional innovation have an impact on consumers' purchase intention and willingness to pay for soft furniture products. This study contributes to existing literature by providing insights into the importance of product innovativeness types, design and functionality, and their role in consumers' innovative product adoption, specifically willingness to pay and purchase intention.

The findings of this study have shown that in the soft furniture product category individuals perceive functional innovation and design innovation at the same level of innovativeness; however, individuals possess much higher purchase intention and are more willing to spend their money for the functionally innovative soft furniture product rather than for the standard soft furniture product or the one with innovative design. Furthermore, it was found that the perceived product innovativeness has a direct but negative impact on consumers' intention to purchase the soft furniture product but does not influence consumers' willingness to pay for the product. The identified moderating effect of innovation type (design and function) showed that functional innovation may strengthen the relationship between consumers' perceived product innovativeness and intention to purchase the soft furniture product, whereas design innovation does not. Another important finding is that the type of innovation does not influence consumers' willingness to pay for the product. What is more, the functional and design innovation strengthen the relationship between a consumer's perceived product innovativeness and his or her attitude toward the soft furniture product. In addition, it was identified that the consumers' attitude toward a product has a direct positive impact on their intention to purchase a soft furniture product, but does not influence their willingness to pay. It was confirmed that the opinion of important others influences consumers' intention to purchase and their willingness to pay for the soft furniture product. Hypothesis H5b was rejected.

The results of this study are important to managers and companies operating in the soft furniture industry. First of all, companies should invest in new product development and focus mainly on functional innovation aspects characterized by structural and technological features, as this would enhance consumer perception of innovativeness, and increase adoption of the soft furniture products in terms of purchase intentions. Moreover, firms should focus on marketing communications and spread the message of product innovativeness, highlighting its main benefits, relative advantages, and unique values for consumers. We propose that following this guidance will increase customers' adoption of the soft furniture products and enable companies to perform much better in terms of profitability, growth and competitive advantage, compared to companies that do not exploit innovation.

REFERENCES

Bartels, J. and M. Reinders (2011), 'Consumer innovativeness and its correlates: a propositional inventory for future research', *Journal of Business Research*, 64(6), 601–609.

Fadzline, P., N.M. Nor and S.J.A.N.S. Mohmad (2014), 'The mediating effect of design innovation between brand distinctiveness and brand performance: evidence from furniture manufacturing firms in Malaysia', *Social and Behavioral Sciences*, 130, 333–339.

Fishbein, M. and I. Ajzen (1975), *Belief, Attitude, Intention, and Behavior: An Introduction to Theory and Research*, Reading, MA: Addison-Wesley.

Forsman, H. (2011), 'Innovation capacity and innovation development in small enterprises: a comparison between the manufacturing and service sectors', *Research Policy*, 40(5), 739–750.

Fort-Rioche, L. and C.L. Ackermann (2013), 'Consumer innovativeness, perceived innovation and attitude towards "neo-retro" product design', *European Journal of Innovation Management*, 16(4), 495–516.

Fu, F.Q. and M.T. Elliott (2013), 'The moderating effect of perceived product innovativeness and product knowledge on new product adoption: an integrated model', *Journal of Marketing Theory and Practice*, 21(3), 257–272.

Fu, F.Q., E. Jones and W. Bolander (2008), 'Product innovativeness, customer newness, and new product performance: a time-lagged examination of the impact of salesperson selling intentions on new product performance', *Journal of Personal Selling & Sales Management*, 28(4), 351–364.

Fuji, M. and M. Utami (2013), 'How intellectual stimulation effects knowledge sharing, innovation and firm performance', *International Journal of Social Science and Humanity*, 3(4), 420–425.

Gunday, G., G. Ulusoy, K. Kilic and L. Alpkan (2011), 'Effects of innovation types on firm performance', *International Journal of Production Economics*, 133(2), 662–676.

Hanaysha, J. (2016), 'The importance of product innovation in driving brand success: an empirical study on automotive industry', *American Journal of Economics and Business Administrations*, 8(1), 35–43.

Henard, D.H. and P.A. Dacin (2010), 'Reputation for product innovation: its impact on consumers', *Journal of Product Innovation Management*, 27(3), 321–335.

Hetet, B., J. Moutot and J. Mathieu (2014), 'A better understanding of consumer's perception of an innovative brand through perceived novelty', Nantes: Audencia Ecole de Management, 1–10.

Ho, C.H., and W. Wu (2011), 'Role of innovativeness of consumer in relationship between perceived attributes of new products and intention to adopt', *International Journal of Electronic Business Management*, 9(3), 258–266.

Hwang, J., K. Lee and T.N. Lin (2016), 'Ingredient labeling and health claims influencing consumer perception, purchase intentions, and willingness to pay', *Journal of Foodservice Business Research*, 19(4), 352–367.

Jimenez, J.D. and R. Sanz-Valle (2011), 'Innovation, organizational learning and performance', *Journal of Business Research*, 64(4), 408–417.

Kaplan, M. (2009), 'The relationship between perceived innovativeness and emotional product responses: a brand oriented approach', *Innovative Marketing*, 5(1), 39–47.

Lafferty, B.A. and R.E. Goldsmith (2004), 'How influential are corporate credibility and endorser attractiveness when innovators react to advertisements for a new high-technology product?', *Corporate Reputation Review*, 7(1), 24–36.

Li, G., R. Zhang and C. Wang (2015), 'The role of product originality, usefulness and motivated consumer innovativeness in new product adoption intentions', *Journal of Product Innovation Management*, 32(2), 214–223.

Marsili, O. and A. Salter (2006), 'The dark matter of innovation: design and innovative performance in Dutch manufacturing', *Technology Analysis & Strategic Management*, 18(15), 515–534.

Mathur, A. (1999), 'Adoption of technological innovations by the elderly: a consumer socialization perspective', *Journal of Marketing Management*, 9(3), 21–35.

Montoya-Weiss, M. and R. Calantone (1994), 'Determinants of new product performance: a review and meta-analysis', *Journal of Product Innovation Management*, 11(5), 397–417.

Morris, M.G. and V. Venkatesh (2000), 'Age differences in technology adoption decisions: implications for a changing work force', *Personnel Psychology*, 53(2), 375–403.

Rindova, V.P. and A.P. Petkova (2007), 'When is a new thing a good thing? Technological change, product form design, and perceptions of value for product innovations', *Organization Science*, 18(2), 217–232.

Rogers, E.R. (2003), *Diffusion of Innovations* (5th ed.), New York: Free Press.

Tian, K.T., W.O. Bearden and G.L. Hunter (2001), 'Consumers' need for uniqueness: scale development and validation', *Journal of Consumer Research*, 28(1), 50–66.

Townsend, J.D., K. Wooseong, M.M. Montoya and R.J. Calantone (2013), 'Brand-specific design effects: form and function', *Journal of Product Innovation Management*, 30(5), 994–1008.

Venkatesh, V., M.G. Morris, G.B. Davis and F.D. Davis (2003), 'User acceptance of information technology: toward a unified view', *MIS Quarterly: Management Information Systems*, 27(3), 425–478.

Verganti, R. (2009), *Design-Driven Innovation: Changing the Rules of Competition by Radically Innovating What Things Mean*, Boston, MA: Harvard Business Press.

6. Innovation and financial performance in telecommunication companies

Asta Klimaviciene and Sarunas Sereika

INTRODUCTION

Shareholders invest in companies expecting that the value of their investment will increase over time. Therefore, while other strategic goals may exist, the ultimate goal of a for-profit company is shareholder value maximization. It is important for companies to prioritize decisions that result in value enhancement. As companies operate in an environment that is dynamic and constantly changing, they must innovate in order to keep ahead of their competitors. Otherwise they risk a decrease in revenues or insufficient reduction in their costs which may lead to lower profits and, ultimately, to lower company value.

The telecommunications industry, which is the focus of this study, is an example of an area where innovation is paramount. The PwC study by El-Darwiche et al. (2017) reports declining revenues and profitability in this industry in the last decade. The authors suggest that telecommunication companies must either consolidate or innovate. They operate in an environment of rapid technological change. Companies must keep developing innovative products and solutions in order to sustain their market share. According to Lee (2003), one of the key characteristics of the telecommunications sector is very high fixed costs. This acts as an entry barrier for new companies. However, existing companies in the industry face intensifying competition, which results in decreasing revenues. In order to keep the same level of profitability, they need to search for cost reduction opportunities. Investment in innovation can help companies reduce their fixed costs.

Innovation cannot be a goal in itself. Innovation projects must serve a company's strategic goals and, ultimately, lead to its value enhancement. While innovation can take many forms, this study focuses on product innovation. The preference is given to measures of outputs that are externally observable and may be directly compared among different telecommunication companies, such as patents and trademarks. Exploring the link between innovation and financial performance, this study focuses on financial measures, which are

72

commonly used by investors and financial analysts. These include profitability ratios, such as return on equity (ROE), which is one of the key financial ratios for shareholders, return on assets (ROA), and operating margin. Since this study analyses publicly listed telecommunication companies, earnings per share (EPS) is also examined.

The link between innovation and financial performance has been explored in academic literature (such as Artz et al., 2010; Ernst, 2001; Hall et al., 2005; Greenhalgh and Rogers, 2007; Krasnikov et al., 2009; Neuhäusler et al., 2011; Sandner and Block, 2011; Shane and Klock, 1997). Most studies cover companies from multiple industries. However, Aas and Pedersen (2011) suggest that this relationship is industry-dependent. Therefore, it is important to explore this research question on an industry level. A few studies focus on a specific industry, such as manufacturing (Czarnitzki and Kraft, 2010; Zahra and Das, 1993), pharmaceuticals (Roberts, 1999; Sorescu et al., 2003), personal computers (Bayus et al., 2003) and food machinery (Bigliardi, 2013).

The telecommunications industry, despite its importance for the global economy, is relatively underexplored in academic literature in terms of the links between innovation and financial performance. For example, Bigliardi et al. (2012) explore the telecommunications industry in Italy, but their focus is on approaches to open innovation. The authors use qualitative case study methods and do not address financial performance measures. The aim of this study is to determine the relationship between product innovation and financial performance in the European telecommunications industry. The results may be useful for managers of firms operating in a similar industry in order to determine key performance indicators for both innovation and profitability measures.

RESEARCH BACKGROUND

Innovation is a concept that can be explored in different dimensions. Gopalakrishnan and Damanpour (1997) suggest three groups of innovation dimensions: the stage of innovation process (generation and adoption), the level of analysis (industry, organization, sub-unit, or innovation level), and the type of innovation (product or process, radical or incremental, technical or administrative). They conclude, 'innovation is a complex construct'. In very broad terms it can be defined as 'something new'. Therefore, it is important to define innovation in the context of a research study and be careful when discussing results in the light of prior literature to ensure the comparability of innovation measures.

Wang and Ahmed (2004) suggest categorizing innovation measures on five dimensions: behavioural, market, process, product and strategic innovativeness. This study focuses on product innovativeness, which can be defined as the perception of the product as new, original, unique or radical (Henard and Szymanski, 2001).

Consistent with previous literature, innovation performance measures are based on the 'Oslo Manual' guidelines (OECD and Eurostat, 2005). It is widely used as a source of information for innovativeness evaluations. The 'Oslo Manual' suggests two types of innovation measurement approaches: broad company analysis including all innovation types, or a narrow analysis examining a specific innovation area. This study employs the latter method, focusing on product innovation.

Product innovation can be determined using two main approaches: internal information or external publicly available information. Internal information is usually gathered via surveys or interviews. Since the companies examined in this study are listed on stock markets, external information that is publicly available is much more detailed than for private companies. Therefore, this study employs product innovation proxies that can be gathered from publicly available data.

Acs et al. (2002) define three categories of innovation indicators: measures of inputs into technological process (R&D expenditures), intermediate output (number of inventions or patents) and a direct measure of innovation output. The latter category is not considered in this study, since telecommunication companies are service providers, which makes the direct measurement of innovation output somewhat subjective.

R&D expenditure is a common measure of innovation input. Its relationship with financial performance is examined by Shane and Klock (1997), Hall et al. (2005), Greenhalgh and Rogers (2007), Artz et al. (2010) and Sandner and Block (2011). The number of patents is another common measure of company's innovation performance. Patents were employed in Ernst (2001), Greenhalgh and Rogers (2006), Artz et al. (2010), Czarnitzki and Kraft (2010), Neuhäusler et al. (2011) and Sandner and Block (2011). The disadvantage of this approach is that some patents may describe ideas that are not necessarily feasible to develop, and therefore may not have resulted in product innovation. On the other hand, Pavitt (1982) suggests that the focus on patenting activities may underestimate innovation performance in large firms.

Miles (2000) argues that innovativeness indicators such as R&D expenditures or the number of patents issued are inaccurate for service sector companies. Alternative and more appropriate indicators in this case are trademarks (Mendonça et al., 2004). Patent protection is not always available for telecommunication companies. In such cases trademarks indicate better performance related to innovations (Paallysaho and Kuusisto, 2008; Schmoch, 2003). While trademarks seem to be poor indicators of internal, organizational, process-based innovations, they are useful when measuring product innovations (Gotsch and Hipp, 2011). Trademarks have been used as innovation output measures by Greenhalgh and Rogers (2007), Krasnikov et al. (2009) and Sandner and Block (2011).

Financial performance of a company can be measured using different approaches. One option is to use indicators from financial statements, such as total assets or revenues. The disadvantage of using absolute values is that it is difficult to compare them across different companies. Very few studies on innovation and performance employ absolute values; for example, Griffiths et al. (2005) use net profit before tax. Financial ratios, which are relative measures of financial performance, are commonly employed.

Since this study examines the relationship between innovation and financial performance, it is important to identify financial variables that are the most closely linked to product innovation. Some literature uses Tobin's q ratio to measure financial performance (Greenhalgh and Rogers, 2007; Hall et al., 2005; Neuhäusler et al., 2011; Sandner and Block, 2011; Shane and Klock, 1997). Tobin's q is the ratio between the market value of the company and the balance sheet value of its assets. Ernst (2001) and Artz et al. (2010) measure sales growth; however, such an approach focuses on only one potential effect of product innovation (increase in sales revenues) while ignoring the potential decrease in costs. Krasnikov et al. (2009) and Artz et al. (2010) use ROA as one of their financial performance measures to capture company profitability.

While innovation is a widely researched topic in management literature, a meta-analysis by Walker (2004) identified only 30 publications from 1981–2003 which were quantitative studies exploring the relationship between innovation and company performance. Only 19 of these studies utilized efficiency as a dependent variable, expressed in financial performance measure ROE or ROA. Walker (2004) noted that while innovation has a positive effect on financial performance, the impact is larger for company effectiveness (for example, measured by market share).

Most studies have documented a positive impact of innovation performance on companies' financial performance. Geroski and Machin (1993) examine large publicly listed UK companies. Their findings suggest that innovations have a positive effect on profitability, and that indirect effects relating to spillovers and lower sensitivity to business cycles have a much larger impact than direct effects. Roberts (1999) finds that product innovation in the US pharmaceutical industry leads to persistently higher profitability enabling companies to outperform competitors. Bayus et al. (2003) focus on 16 large publicly traded companies from the personal computer industry. They document a positive effect of new product introductions on various financial performance measures (asset growth, ROA, ROE). Jansen et al. (2006) distinguish between exploratory innovation and exploitative innovation. They find that both types of innovation are beneficial to financial performance depending on whether the company operates in a dynamic or a competitive environment. Govindarajan and Kopalle (2005) explore three different categories of innovations: disruptive, radical, and competency-destroying innovations, and find that only disruptive innovations are positively associated with financial performance. Kostopoulos et al. (2011) study companies from the manufacturing and services sector in Greece and find that financial performance (measured by return on sales and ROA) is positively related to innovation performance (measured by proportion of sales from innovative products or services). Bigliardi (2013) documents a positive relationship for small and medium enterprises from the food machinery industry.

Some studies report contradictory results. Sorescu et al. (2003) focus on radical innovations in pharmaceutical companies. Their results are somewhat inconclusive: an increase in a company's market value relative to an introduction of an innovative product depends on various company-specific characteristics. Kemp et al. (2003) examine small and medium enterprises from the Netherlands. Their innovation output variable is the proportion of new products or services in total sale revenues. It is found to be positively related with growth in turnover, but there is no significant impact on profits. Results reported by Aas and Pedersen (2011) suggest that the relationship between innovation and performance may be industry-dependent: they find that service innovation in Norwegian companies has a positive effect on financial performance in the manufacturing sector, but not in the service sector. Artz et al. (2010) find that the number of patents is negatively related with sales growth and ROA. This result is in contrast with most of the literature. The authors argue that it may be due to strategic patenting, where 'firms are using patents as strategic weapons' (Artz et al., 2010, p. 736). Gok and Peker (2017) document a negative link between innovation and financial performance but find that introducing a market performance measure in the model as mediator inverses the result.

Empirical research results may be dependent on specific measures of innovation and financial performance. Table 6.1 presents a summary of previous literature that is the most closely related to this study with respect to measurements of innovation performance (patents and trademarks) and financial performance.

Most studies focusing on patents document a positive effect on financial performance. However, there are some exceptions: Artz et al. (2010) find a negative effect, while Shane and Klock (1997) and Neuhäusler et al. (2011) report insignificant results. Research using trademarks as an innovation measure documents a positive effect on financial performance irrespective of the measure used. The main hypothesis of this study is that innovation performance has an impact on financial performance of telecommunication companies. Based on a literature review, the expected effect on profitability should be positive for both patents and trademarks as innovation measures.

Table 6.1   *Research foundation summary*

Study	Innovation performance	Financial performance	Documented effect
Artz et al. (2010)	R&D expenditures, patents, new product announcements	ROA Sales growth	Negative for patents, positive for other measures
Neuhäusler et al. (2011)	Patents	Tobin's q ROI	Insignificant
Czarnitzki and Kraft (2010)	Patents	Return on sales (categorical)	Positive
Ernst (2001)	Patents	Sales growth	Positive
Sandner and Block (2011)	R&D, patents, trademarks	Tobin's q, market value	Positive for trademarks
Krasnikov et al. (2009)	Trademarks	Cash flows, Tobin's q, ROA, stock returns	Positive
Greenhalgh and Rogers (2007)	R&D, trademarks	Tobin's q	Positive
Griffiths et al. (2005)	Patents, trademarks	Net profit before tax	Positive (greater for patents)
Hall et al. (2005)	R&D, patents	Tobin's q	Positive
Shane and Klock (1997)	R&D, patents	Tobin's q	Insignificant for patents

THE CHOICE OF VARIABLES

Consistent with previous literature (Acs et al., 2002; Artz et al., 2010; Neuhäusler et al., 2011) three product innovation measures are considered: research and development (R&D) expenditure, patents, and trademarks. The *Oslo Manual* (OECD and Eurostat, 2005) suggests that for service companies it may be difficult to differentiate between R&D expenditure and other innovation activities. Therefore, it would not be appropriate to use this measure as a proxy for innovation performance. Since R&D expenditure represents costs of a company, the immediate influence on financial performance is negative. R&D expenditures are part of operating expenses. Therefore, they directly reduce its operating profit as well as net profit. If R&D expenditure leads to innovative products, it should be reflected in financial results of a company in future periods. However, not all R&D expenditure results in innovative products. Large amounts of money spent on R&D may even indicate inefficient use of resources without generating desired innovative outcomes. In addition, R&D expenditures do not cover all sources of technological changes in a company. For example, a company may acquire another company with innovative products. This will not be reflected in R&D expenditures. Since it would be difficult to evaluate direct results of R&D expenditure on the financial performance of telecommunication companies, this variable is deemed to be too 'noisy' and is not analysed in this study.

Two intermediate innovation outputs are tested empirically: the number of patent applications, and the number of trademark registrations per company in a given year.

Commonly used measures of financial performance are Tobin's q and profitability ratios (see Table 6.A.2). A potential problem with Tobin's q as a measure of financial performance is that it includes market capitalization. Therefore, this measure is sensitive to stock price fluctuations. Griffiths et al. (2005) argue against market value as a financial performance measure while studying the effect of innovations. Product innovation is a long-term process, while the stock price fluctuates daily. It is not expected that a registration of a patent application or trademark will be immediately reflected in the stock price. Therefore, market capitalization is used as a control variable in this study rather than a direct financial performance measure.

Given the focus of the study on telecommunication companies, financial performance measures relating to profitability are chosen. Successful innovation activities should lead to either an increase in revenues or a reduction in costs. The profitability of a company will increase if it increases revenues while keeping costs constant, or if its revenues remain constant but costs decrease.

Following Karlsson et al. (2001) who also study telecommunication companies, this study focuses on three profitability ratios: operating margin, ROA and ROE. Operating margin is chosen because product innovation relates to main operations of a company. It is a ratio between operating profit and sales revenues. It shows the profitability of the main operations of the company. In addition to this measure, the study will also use other main financial performance measures that are related to profitability: ROE, ROA and EPS. ROE shows the profitability of the capital invested by shareholders of the company. It is a ratio between net profit and shareholders' equity. ROA measures the profitability of the company's assets: net profit earned by each Euro of total assets. Since telecommunication companies need large long-term investments in fixed assets, ROA is an important profitability measure for this industry. Some previous literature has used ROA as a financial performance measure (Artz et al., 2010; Krasnikov et al., 2009), therefore using this variable will facilitate the comparison of results. Finally, EPS is a measure that is commonly used to evaluate the financial performance of publicly listed companies. This ratio shows the net profit attributed to an owner of one share of a company.

Product innovation is a long-term process. It is not expected that innovation performance will be contemporaneously reflected in financial results of a company. The *Oslo Manual* (OECD and Eurostat, 2005) indicates that a time delay exists between the occurrence of innovation and its effect on company's performance. Damanpour and Evan (1984) were the first to address the problem of 'organizational lag' in this context in the academic literature. A critical review by Walker (2004) suggests that a short-term effect of innovations on organizational performance may be negative. Therefore, due to organizational inertia it is important to build lags into the model. The main problem is to determine the length of the lags. While it is possible to experiment with different lags, it may lead to empirical data-mining. Previous literature has used lags ranging from one year (Bayus et al., 2003) to five years (Neuhäusler et al., 2011). The consensus seems to suggest employing a medium-term lag of two to three years (Artz et al., 2010; Ernst, 2001). Ernst (2001) found that European patent applications affect financial performance with a three-year lag. Since this study also uses data on European patents, the time delay effect is acknowledged by using a three-year lag of innovation performance measure.

Financial performance measures are dependent variables in this study. In order to analyse the effect of innovation performance measures on these variables, a model is augmented by control variables. Walker (2004) stresses the importance of including internal and external control variables to avoid measuring noise by the simplistic assumption that 'innovation matters to extremes'. In this study proxies for financial performance are measures of profitability. Therefore, the model needs to be augmented by main factors of profitability. No adjustments for sector are made, as all companies are from the same industry. Profitability depends on economic and business cycles. Therefore, to control for global profitability drivers this study includes changes in GDP of the European Union as a control variable.

Profitability is closely related to risk, which depends on the financing structure of the company. This study employs two financial risk measures as control variables: debt ratio and financial leverage. Both ratios measure the relative indebtedness of the company: the proportion of total assets that are financed by either total liabilities (debt ratio), or long-term financial liabilities (financial leverage).

The model will examine the effect of innovation performance on financial performance while controlling for internal and external factors of profitability. As described in this section, the following variables will be used as proxies: number of patents and trademarks for innovation performance (independent variables) and operating margin, ROE, ROA and EPS for financial performance (dependent variables).

DATA AND DESCRIPTIVE STATISTICS

This study focuses on telecommunications industry companies that provide cellular connectivity, mobile data, cable and other services. Since companies in

Table 6.2   *Descriptive statistics of panel data variables*

Variable	Mean	Median	Min	Max
Revenues USD, B	43.2	39.7	6.50	90.5
Total assets USD, B	95.8	100.1	8.6	252.0
Capitalization USD, B	51.9	46.1	8.9	155.3
EPS	1.6	1.3	−11.2	36.0
Gross margin, %	57.3	57.0	26.3	90.7
Operating margin, %	14.8	16.2	−48.0	29.9
Net profit margin, %	7.9	9.0	−74.7	22.0
ROE, %	18.9	15.7	−21.1	84.9
ROA, %	5.1	5.0	−15.4	46.6
Leverage	1.7	1.5	0.0	10.8
Debt ratio, %	38.6	39.8	1.5	62.3
Patent applications	72	39	0	2,880
Trademarks	181	23	0	1,616

different countries may operate under different regulatory conditions, the data sample was constructed from publicly listed companies which are registered and operate in European Economic Area (EEA) or Switzerland. Companies operating under similar economic, social, legal and technological conditions form a more homogeneous sample. The data sample covers 12 European telecommunications industry companies headquartered in nine countries (a full list is provided in Appendix Table 6.A.1). The data period is from 2006 to 2016. Information on patent applications is collected from the 2.3.6 edition of the cumulative database of European Patent Office. Trademark registrations are retrieved from World Intellectual Property Organization (WIPO) global brand database.

While most financial variables are available at quarterly frequency, those relating to innovations, namely patent applications and trademarks, are reported on a yearly basis. Therefore, the data frequency used for empirical analysis is annual. Detailed explanations of variables are provided in Appendix Table 6.A.2. Since the data sample has company and time dimensions, econometric methods appropriate for panel data analysis are employed. A summary of descriptive statistics is provided in Table 6.2.

Telecommunication companies analysed in this study are relatively large. On average their annual revenues are approximately 40 billion USD, the balance sheet value of total assets is around 100 billion USD, while their market capitalization is centered around 50 billion USD. However, these companies are not homogeneous in terms of size.

The average earnings per share (EPS) is 1.58, but there is a lot of variability both across companies and over time, with the minimum value of −11.2 and the maximum of 36.

The gross margin of companies in the sample is on average 57 per cent, ranging from a minimum of 26 per cent to a maximum of over 90 per cent. Since telecommunication companies belong to the service sector, such high levels of gross margins are not surprising. Operating margins, which represent the profitability of the main business of the company and incorporate all operating expenses, are on average 15 per cent. While most companies have been generating operating profits throughout the sample period, there are several companies with negative operating margins in a particular year. The extreme case is Vodafone, which had operating losses in 4 out of 11 years. Net profit margins are on average around 8 per cent, but there is a lot of variation in this profitability measure.

ROE is on average around 19 per cent, while ROA is 5 per cent. Both measures demonstrate large variations which are explored later in this section. The average debt ratio is 39 per cent, meaning that European telecommunication companies finance less than half of their assets by liabilities. This financial risk measure differs by company and by year, and ranges from 1.5 per cent to 62 per cent.

The number of patent applications and trademarks vary substantially by year and by company. Most telecommunication companies are active in registering their innovations every year. Based on absolute numbers, the companies that consistently file the most patent applications are BT Group, Deutsche Telekom and Vodafone. The leading company in terms of trademark registrations is BT Group. Since a lot of variables demonstrate significant changes over time, descriptive statistics for each year are presented for further analysis in Table 6.3.

The telecommunications industry was in decline from 2006 to 2016. Market capitalization of the sample companies declined from an average of 72.5 billion in 2006 to 40.7 billion in 2016, representing a decrease of over 40 per cent. This implies that market participants regard the prospects of telecommunication companies more pessimistically. . . . Revenues of telecommunication companies increased in 2007–8, while the global financial crisis led to a −17 per cent decrease in 2009. The period from 2011 to 2015 is marked by decreasing revenues, with a modest increase of 2 per cent in 2016. The analysis of change in total assets reveals that on average companies did not invest in their assets during 2011–15.

While revenues and total assets were declining, companies managed to retain their margins. The average gross margin has been in the range of 56–60 per cent. Operating margins have fluctuated more: they were around 18–19 per cent in 2008–10, and then dropped to 12–14 per cent in 2011–16. This

Table 6.3   Mean values of cross-sectional data for each year

Averages p.a.	'06	'07	'08	'09	'10	'11	'12	'13	'14	'15	'16
ROA, %	5.7	7.3	6.3	5.1	6.8	4.7	3.2	3.4	7.1	3.2	3.3
ROE, %	22.5	27.5	24.9	21.4	26.5	16.8	14.6	11.1	19.4	9.8	15.0
Change in revenues	n.a.	13%	8%	-17%	10%	-3%	-9%	-7%	0%	-9%	2%
Change in total assets	n.a.	7%	-1%	0%	3%	-3%	-4%	0%	-8%	-8%	2%
Capitalization, B	72.5	89.9	63.8	55.0	50.1	42.6	37.7	45.3	46.4	44.1	40.7
EPS	0.28	1.60	2.02	1.61	2.18	1.18	1.42	0.95	4.28	1.17	0.73
Gross margin, %	42.6	58.2	58.1	60.1	56.6	56.7	55.9	56.0	59.4	57.2	57.8
Operating margin, %	12.2	16.6	19.8	18.1	19.5	13.6	11.9	13	13.7	12.5	14.3
Net profit margin, %	4.1	10.8	12.0	9.3	13.8	8.3	5.8	6.3	5.3	6.5	6.2
D/A, %	37.9	38.4	41.3	41.2	39.2	40.4	37.7	37.7	34.8	36.8	35.9
Patent applications	59	60	72	66	64	61	57	57	72	71	87
Trademarks	240	265	289	157	122	133	133	143	120	133	115

shows that companies did not manage to reduce their operating costs to match the decline in revenues. A similar trend is evident in net profit margins, which were in the range of 9–13 per cent during 2007–10 and dropped to 5–6 per cent in 2012–16.

The most important financial ratio for shareholders is ROE, since it measures the return on their invested capital. It has declined from over 20 per cent in 2006–10 to 10–15 per cent in 2012–16. Year 2014 was an exception with ROE of 19.4 per cent. A significant decrease in average ROE is consistent with decreasing market capitalization of telecommunication companies. ROA has been declining from 5–7 per cent during 2006–10 to an average of 3 per cent in 2012–16. Year 2014 is an exception with ROA of 7.1 per cent. However, this is mostly due to an 8 per cent decrease in average total assets. While assets declined at a similar rate in 2015, ROA dropped by more than 50 per cent.

The average number of patent applications per company during 2006–16 fluctuated from 57 to 87 per year. The number of trademark registrations was the highest during 2006–8. There was a sharp decrease of over 45 per cent in 2009 which may be attributed to the global financial crisis and subsequent cost savings. Trademark registrations continued to decline until 2014. The average for 2016 was 115, which is less than half of pre-crisis levels. The decrease in trademark registrations may also be attributed to consolidation activities in the telecommunications industry, such as mergers and acquisitions and efforts to establish a single brand over wider geographical areas.

Table 6.4   Correlation coefficients

Panel A

	ROA	ROE	Gross margin	Operating margin	Net profit margin	Patents	Trademarks
ROA	1.0						
ROE	0.8	1.0					
Gross margin	0.1	0.4	1.0				
Operating margin	0.4	0.4	0.3	1.0			
Net profit margin	0.6	0.6	0.2	0.9	1.0		
Patents	-0.3	-0.4	-0.6	-0.4	-0.3	1.0	
Trademarks	-0.0	-0.1	-0.2	-0.2	-0.1	0.2	1.0

Panel B

	Revenues	Total assets	Capitalization	Patents	Trademarks
Revenues	1.0				
Total assets	0.9	1.0			
Capitalization	0.8	0.8	1.0		
Patents	0.3	0.4	0.2	1.0	
Trademarks	0.2	0.0	0.1	0.5	1.0

DATA ANALYSIS

The relationship between innovation and financial performance is first examined via correlation analysis (Table 6.4).

Financial variables are naturally highly correlated among themselves. For example, the correlation coefficient between ROA and ROE is 0.8, while that of operating margin and net profit margin is 0.9. Correlations between absolute financial variables are also high: 0.9 for revenues and total assets, and 0.8 between market capitalization and both revenues and total assets. There is a modest correlation between innovation performance variables: 0.5 for patent applications and trademarks.

The relationship of interest in this study is between innovation and financial performance measures. Contemporaneous correlations between patent applications and financial ratios are negative, ranging between −0.3 for ROA and net profit margin to −0.6 for gross margin. This is somewhat expected, as patent applications are expensive. The more patent applications a company files in a given year, the higher their operating expenses, and thus the lower

Table 6.5   Summary of empirical research results

Financial performance measure	Patent applications	Trademarks
Return on assets (ROA)	Positive, highly statistically significant	Insignificant
Return on equity (ROE)	Positive, highly statistically significant	Insignificant
Operating margin	Negative, highly statistically significant	Insignificant
Earnings per share (EPS)	Insignificant	Insignificant

their profits and profitability ratios. Contemporaneous correlations between patent applications and absolute financial measures are small but positive (0.2–0.4). This implies that companies file more patent applications in years when their revenues, total assets, and market capitalization are increasing. In contrast, contemporaneous correlations between trademark registrations and financial variables are close to zero.

Panel data regression is conducted using financial performance measures as dependent variables, and innovation variables as independent variables. Four models are estimated for selected profitability measures: ROA, ROE, operating margin, and EPS. Each model includes patents and trademarks as product innovation performance measures and selected internal and external control variables (as described previously). Innovation variables are included in a model with a three-year time lag. Table 6.5 presents the key results from panel regression analysis.

Results reveal a significant difference between the importance of patent applications and trademark registrations on financial performance of European telecommunication companies. This study has found no effect of trademarks on any of the financial performance proxies (ROA, ROE, operating margin, and EPS). The relationship between patent applications and financial performance, however, seems to depend on the chosen financial variable. No relationship is documented between EPS and patent applications. Patent applications seem to have a negative effect on operating margin. This result is somewhat surprising, given that patent application data is lagged by three years, consistent with the previous literature (Artz et al., 2010; Ernst, 2001).

Patent applications have a positive relationship with both ROA, which is an important profitability measure for companies with a large amount of fixed assets, and ROE, which measures the profitability of investments by the company's shareholders.

DISCUSSION

The results of empirical analysis suggest that the impact of innovation performance on financial performance depends on specific measures. Therefore, results should be compared with previous studies which used patent applications and trademarks as intermediate outputs of product innovation activities.

Panel regression results indicate the relationship between the number of patents and certain financial performance measures. Patent applications tend to have a positive effect on the profitability of a telecommunication company in terms of both ROE and ROA. Such a result is consistent with findings by Ernst (2001), Griffiths et al. (2005), Czarnitzki and Kraft (2010) and Hall et al. (2005). The study which is the most related in terms of innovation and financial performance measures is Artz et al. (2010) who find a negative effect of patents on ROA. The industry effect documented by Aas and Pedersen (2011) may explain the difference of results. Artz et al. (2010) examine 35 industries rather than focusing on a single industry. Moreover, this study examines telecommunication companies that are among the largest in the sector. MacDonald (2004) argues that patenting has an effect only on large companies.

The absence of relationship between the number of trademark registrations and financial performance measures contradicts findings from previous literature. Griffiths et al. (2005), Greenhalgh and Rogers (2007), Krasnikov et al. (2009) and Sandner and Block (2011) report a positive effect of trademarks on financial performance. This study does not find a significant effect. The average number of trademark applications per telecommunication company during 2009–16 is approximately half the number during 2006–8. Since this study used GDP change as a control variable, the results cannot be explained by changes in overall economic environment. Results by Krasnikov et al. (2009) are most directly comparable since they use trademarks as a proxy for innovation, and ROA as one of their financial performance measures. However, their sample includes 108 US firms from multiple industries over the period 1995–2005, which may explain the differences in results. The registration of trademarks in the telecommunications industry in Europe may not be always directly linked to innovations, especially in the case of creating single brands during consolidation processes.

MANAGERIAL IMPLICATIONS

The data employed in this study show that the number of patent applications started to increase towards the end of the sample period. The largest average number of patent applications per company (87) occurs in 2016, which is the last year in the sample. The telecommunications service sector is characterized by decreasing revenues, total assets, and market capitalization. The increase in the average number of patent applications may indicate that managers of these companies view patenting activities positively, believing that increasing innovation via this route will help move their companies out of stagnation and enhance financial performance.

Results indicate that telecommunications sector companies in Europe may expect an increase in financial performance (as measured by ROA and ROE) from patent applications but not necessarily from trademark registrations. Companies and their shareholders should not expect a quick effect. An investment not only in terms of money but also in terms of time is required. An increase in patenting activities by telecommunication companies is expected to enhance financial performance measures in the medium term.

LIMITATIONS

This study focuses on large companies from the telecommunications industry that operate in Europe. Therefore, results may not apply to companies from other sectors, other geographical regions, or to small and medium companies. The relatively narrow focus is intentional in order to ensure a homogeneous sample of companies operating in similar conditions.

This study uses external innovation performance indicators. Admittedly, the numbers of patent applications and trademark registrations cover only a limited proportion of innovation activities. They cannot be expected to represent the overall innovation policy of a company. Moreover, patents and trademarks are measures of outputs of innovative activities. It is not evident how many resources, including human capital, were dedicated to developing this output.

Another limitation of this study is that all innovation performance measures are treated equally. In practice, some patent applications or trademark registrations are more important than others. It would be recommended to use a weighted number of patents. However, it is not clear how to assign weights to each patent under calculation using objective criteria. One option would be to collect the number of citations per patent and use it as a proxy of relative importance. This approach was not considered, as it would have its own limitations, as some citations may be more significant than others. Also, the accumulation of citations requires time, so the absolute number will underestimate the importance of more recent citations (Hall et al., 2005).

CONCLUSIONS

This study examines the relationship between innovation and financial performance in large European telecommunication companies. Previous literature tends to document a positive relationship. However, results depend on specific measures used as proxies for innovation and organizational performance and tend to vary by industry.

Production innovation output measures chosen for this study are the number of patent applications and trademark registrations. Their relationship with four profitability measures is explored: operating margin, ROA, ROE, and EPS.

The main finding is that patents have a positive impact on ROA and ROE, while the effect on operating margin is negative. No significant relationship between trademarks and profitability measures is detected. The results for patent applications are broadly consistent with prior studies, while the absence of relationship between trademarks and profitability is somewhat surprising. A closer comparison of findings reveals that differences can be attributed to specific data samples, especially the focus on one industry versus multi-industry studies.

The suggestion for future research is to address the potential industry-dependent effects when exploring the links between innovation and financial performance. This can be achieved by at least two approaches. First, subsequent studies may focus on individual industries, such as this study. The alternative approach of multi-industry studies is to ensure that controls for industry are included in models.

REFERENCES

Aas, T.H. and P.E. Pedersen (2011), 'The impact of service innovation on firm-level financial performance', *The Service Industries Journal*, 31(13), 2071–2090.

Acs, Z.J., L. Anselin and A. Varga (2002), 'Patents and innovation counts as measures of regional production of new knowledge', *Research Policy*, 31(7), 1069–1085.

Artz, K.W., P.M. Norman, D.E. Hatfield and L.B. Cardinal (2010), 'A longitudinal study of the impact of R&D, patents, and product innovation on firm performance', *Journal of Product Innovation Management*, 27(5), 725–740.

Bayus, B.L., G. Erickson and R. Jacobson (2003), 'The financial rewards of new product introductions in the personal computer industry', *Management Science*, 49(2), 197–210.

Bigliardi, B. (2013), 'The effect of innovation on financial performance: a research study involving SMEs', *Innovation*, 15(2), 245–255.

Bigliardi, B., A.I. Dormio and F. Galati (2012), 'The adoption of open innovation within the telecommunication industry', *European Journal of Innovation Management*, 15(1), 27–54.

Czarnitzki, D. and K. Kraft (2010), 'On the profitability of innovative assets', *Applied Economics*, 42(15), 1941–1953.

Damanpour, F. and W.M. Evan (1984), 'Organizational innovation and performance: the problem of "organizational lag"', *Administrative Science Quarterly*, 29(3), 392–409.

El-Darwiche, B., P. Peladeau, C. Rupp and F. Groene (2017), '2017 telecommunications trends: aspiring to digital simplicity and clarity in strategic identity', *Strategy&*, PwC.

Ernst, H. (2001), 'Patent applications and subsequent changes of performance: evidence from time-series cross-section analyses on the firm level', *Research Policy*, 30(1), 143–157.

Geroski, P. and S. Machin (1993), 'The profitability of innovating firms', *RAND Journal of Economics*, 24(2), 198–211.

Gok, O. and S. Peker (2017), 'Understanding the links among innovation performance, market performance and financial performance', *Review of Managerial Science*, 11(3), 605–631.

Gopalakrishnan, S. and F. Damanpour (1997), 'A review of innovation research in economics, sociology and technology management', *Omega*, 25(1), 15–28.

Gotsch, M. and C. Hipp (2011), 'Measurement of innovation activities in the knowledge-intensive services industry: a trademark approach', *The Service Industries Journal*, 32(13), 2167–2184.

Govindarajan, V. and P.K. Kopalle (2005), 'Disruptiveness of innovations: measurement and an assessment of reliability and validity', *Strategic Management Journal*, 27(2), 189–199.

Greenhalgh, C. and M. Rogers (2006), 'The value of innovation: the interaction of competition, R&D and IP', *Research Policy*, 35(4), 562–580.

Greenhalgh, C. and M. Rogers (2007), 'Trade marks and performance in UK firms: evidence of Schumpeterian competition through innovation'. *SIEPR Discussion Paper No. 06-34*.

Griffiths, W.E., P.H. Jensen and E. Webster (2005), 'The effects on firm profits of the stock of intellectual property rights', *Intellectual Property Research Institute of Australia Working Paper No. 05/05*.

Hall, B.H., A. Jaffe and M. Trajtenberg (2005), 'Market value and patent citations', *The RAND Journal of Economics*, 36(1), 16–38.

Henard, D.H. and D.M. Szymanski (2001), 'Why some new products are more successful than others', *Journal of Marketing Research*, 38(3), 362–375.

Jansen, J.J.P., F.A.J. Van Den Bosch and H.W. Volberda (2006), 'Exploratory innovation, exploitative innovation, and performance: effects on organizational antecedents and environmental moderators', *Management Science*, 52(11), 1661–1674.

Karlsson, J., B. Back, H. Vanharanta and A. Visa (2001), 'Financial benchmarking of telecommunications companies', *Turku Centre for Computer Science TUCS Technical Report No 395*.

Kemp, R.G.M., M. Folkeringa, J.P.J. de Jong and E.F.M. Wubben (2003), 'Innovation and firm performance: differences between small and medium-sized firms', *SCALES-paper N200213*.

Kostopoulos, K., A. Papalexandris, M. Papachroni and G. Ioannou (2011), 'Absorptive capacity, innovation, and financial performance', *Journal of Business Research*, 64(12), 1335–1343.

Krasnikov, A., S. Mishra and D. Orozco (2009), 'Evaluating the financial impact of branding using trademarks: a framework and empirical evidence', *Journal of Marketing*, 73(6), 154–166.

Lee, S. (2003), 'Indicators for the assessment of telecommunications competition', *OECD Working Party on Telecommunication and Information Services Policies DSTI/ICCP/TISP(2001)6/FINAL*.

MacDonald, S. (2004), 'When means become ends: considering the impact of patent strategy on innovation', *Information Economics and Policy*, 16(1), 135–158.

Mendonça, S., T.S. Pereira and M. Godinho (2004), 'Trademarks as an indicator of innovation and industrial change', *LEM Working Paper Series, No. 2004/15*.

Miles, I. (2000), 'Services innovation: coming of age in the knowledge-based economy', *International Journal of Innovation Management*, 4(4), 371–389.

Neuhäusler, P., R. Frietsch, T. Schubert and K. Blind (2011), 'Patents and the financial performance of firms: an analysis based on stock market data', *Fraunhofer ISI Discussion Papers Innovation Systems and Policy Analysis, 28*.

OECD and Eurostat (2005), *Oslo Manual: Guidelines for Collecting and Interpreting Innovation Data* (3rd ed.), Paris: OECD Publishing.

Paallysaho, S. and J. Kuusisto (2008), 'Intellectual property protection as a key driver of service innovation: an analysis of innovative KIBS businesses in Finland and the UK', *International Journal of Services Technology and Management*, 9(3/4), 268–284.

Pavitt, K. (1982), 'R&D, patenting and innovative activities: a statistical exploration', *Research Policy*, 11(1), 33–51.

Roberts, P.W. (1999), 'Product innovation, product-market competition and persistent profitability in the U.S. pharmaceutical industry', *Strategic Management Journal*, 20(7), 655–670.

Sandner, P.G. and J. Block (2011), 'The market value of R&D, patents, and trademarks', *Research Policy*, 40(7), 969–985.

Schmoch, U. (2003), 'Service marks as novel innovation indicator', *Research Evaluation*, 12(2), 149–156.

Shane, H. and M. Klock (1997), 'The relation between patent citations and Tobin's Q in the semiconductor industry', *Review of Quantitative Finance & Accounting*, 9(2), 131–146.

Sorescu, A.B., R.K. Chandy and J.C. Prabhu (2003), 'Sources and financial consequences of radical innovation: insights from pharmaceuticals', *Journal of Marketing*, 67(4), 82–102.

Walker, R.M. (2004), 'Innovation and organisational performance: evidence and a research agenda', *Advanced Institute of Management Research Paper No. 002*.

Wang, C.L. and P.K. Ahmed (2004), 'The development and validation of the organisational innovativeness construct using confirmatory factor analysis', *European Journal of Innovation Management*, 7(4), 303–313.

Zahra, S.A. and S.R. Das (1993), 'Innovation strategy and financial performance in manufacturing companies: an empirical study', *Production and Operations Management*, 2(1), 15–37.

APPENDIX

Table 6.A.1   List of companies

Company	Country (headquarters)
SFR (owned by Altice)	France
Belgacom-Proximus	Belgium
BT Group	UK
Deutsche Telekom	Germany
KPN	Netherlands
Orange	France
Swisscom	Switzerland
Telecom Italia	Italy
Telefonica	Spain
Telenor	Norway
Telia	Sweden
Vodafone	UK

Table 6.A.2   *Description of variables*

Variable	Explanation
Dependent variables (financial performance)	
Return on assets (ROA)	ROA = Trailing 12 month net income / average of the previous five quarters of total assets
Return on equity (ROE)	ROE = trailing 12 month net income / average of past five quarters of book value of shareholder's equity
Earnings per share (EPS)	Normalized EPS = normalized net income / average diluted shares outstanding
Operating margin	Operating margin = operating income / net sales
Independent variables (innovation performance)	
Number of patents	Number of patent applications by each company for each year from 2006 to 2016. Data source: EUIPO
Number of trademarks	Number of trademark applications by each company for each year from 2006 to 2016. Data source: WIPO
Control variables (financial)	
Revenues	Annual revenues from financial reports (income statements)
Capitalization	Market capitalization at the end of the year Market capitalization = number of shares outstanding × price
Total assets	Annual revenues from financial reports (balance sheets)
Debt ratio	Debt ratio = total liabilities / total assets
Financial leverage	(Long-term debt + current portion of long-term debt) / total assets
Control variables (external)	
EU GDP growth	Annual growth in gross domestic product of the European Union

PART IV

Process innovation management

7. Implementing process innovation by integrating continuous improvement and business process re-engineering

Gurram Gopal and Egle Pilkauskaite

INTRODUCTION

Firms today are under tremendous pressure to innovate in order to meet or exceed customers' changing expectations and compete globally. Rapid advances in technology are enabling many firms to enter new industries and compete successfully against entrenched firms. Companies like Netflix are partnering with other firms like Amazon in certain domains and competing with the same firms in other areas. While new product introductions have traditionally been regarded as the primary drivers of competitive advantage, operational process innovation is gaining more importance as a key driver of success in the marketplace. The ability to manage disruptive marketplace changes while focusing on operational excellence is becoming recognized as the key enabler of future success. Companies are shifting towards process-centric management in order to adjust to continuous changes in business requirements, decreased product lifecycles and to keep up with the pressure of rising costs in the market (Neubauer, 2009). A company realizes its strategic outcomes by developing a process-centric approach and focusing on operational excellence (Aparecida da Silva et al., 2012). Process innovation has become one of the most relevant drivers for business change projects, especially in the Business Process Management (BPM) field as the interrelation of process management and innovation has been a key discussion topic in various organizations (Recker, 2014). So, enterprises are trying to develop a process-centric organizational approach as they strive to improve their performance by implementing both radical and incremental innovations.

Any type of operational process innovation chosen by a firm depends on its tactical and strategic goals. Incremental process innovations are implemented by using a Continuous Improvement (CI) approach including techniques to incrementally improve and maintain existing business process performance and quality (Harmon, 2007). Companies opt for a Business Process Re-engineering (BPR) approach to use information technology (IT) advances and radically redesign current business process and benefit from significant improvements in key operational measures – process cost, lead time and quality (Hammer and Champy, 2006). Thus, CI and BPR approaches bring different results depending on the specific strategic position and direction of the company.

Recent academic literature and business leaders are focusing on an integrated strategy of CI and BPR. Implementation of process innovation in the core business process by using a combination of CI and BPR approaches may bring more sustainable results to a company as CI initiatives build a base for more radical process innovations and maintain process orientation in the enterprise (Harrington, 1995). In addition, an integrated strategy of incremental CI and radical innovation may result in more significant gains in performance since gains in customer satisfaction, productivity and technological advantage may be much greater than if these approaches are established separately (Terziovski, 2002).

The following sections explain business processes and business process management and offer practical tools for process innovation along with insights into key enablers for successful implementation.

BUSINESS PROCESS OVERVIEW

Definition of a Business Process

A business process can be viewed as a structured sequence of elements that are interrelated and cross-functional boundaries within the organization (McKay and Radnor, 1998). As an example, a customer support and service process is described as 'all the activities involved in making it easy for customers to reach the right parties within the company and receive quick and satisfactory service, answers and resolutions of the problem' (Kotler, 2000). Armistead and Machin (1997) organize business processes into four categories according to their main functions – operational, support, direction setting and managerial. Operational processes are the main processes that run across the organization to produce goods and services and are the core processes that create value for the customers. Support processes enable operational processes, whereas managerial and direction setting processes concern strategy and policy formulation and management. Business processes can also be classified into core, support and managerial processes and research highlights the importance of analysing and managing core business processes while making decisions regarding business process architecture and innovation management (Aparecida da Silva et al., 2012; Davenport,

1993; Harmon, 2007). Therefore, operational processes are usually the focus of BPM approaches to implement any process changes that eventually create more value to the customer.

What is Process Innovation?

Operational excellence depends on improving process performance on a continuum, reducing the cost of current operations while positioning the firm for future products and services. This is achieved through innovations in processes, adoption of technology, improved understanding of customer needs and other factors. Du Plessis (2007) defines process innovation as the creation of new knowledge and ideas that assist in improving a company's business processes and help to introduce new products and services. Business process orientation enables the company to focus its objectives through a cross-functional, outcome-oriented approach by prioritizing business processes, customer needs and requirements, while business process improvements are targeted at enhancing intra-organizational business processes (Nadarajah and Kadir, 2016; Trkman et al., 2015). This relationship between process orientation and process improvement is particularly evident in the service industry, where process innovation involves new developments in the organization's core processes in order to make core service products more attractive to the customer (Trkman et al., 2015). Hence, implementation of process innovation enables a company to better service customers' needs and expectations, and maintain a competitive advantage.

Types of Process Innovation

Process innovations by nature are complex since they may involve different combinations or variations of technologies, processes and approaches. Process innovation is broadly divided into two types, incremental and radical process innovation (Gloet and Terziovski, 2004; Megson and Hammer, 2004). Incremental innovations are modifications of existing products and services enhancing existing internal competencies and not requiring significant change to current business processes. Radical innovations, on the other hand, involve development and application of new technologies that eventually initiate different management practices, require new knowledge and skills in the organization or bring major enhancements to existing platforms and core business processes. Operational improvement or operational excellence aims to achieve high performance by using existing modes of operations without fundamentally changing current business processes, e.g. to reduce costs, delays and errors and to increase quality. Operational innovation initiates completely new ways of doing the company's core activities and brings major marketplace, strategic and operational benefits.

PROCESS INNOVATION USING A BUSINESS PROCESS MANAGEMENT FRAMEWORK

Introduction to BPM

BPM methodology for process innovation implementation has achieved significant adoption and success in many industries and firms. The discipline focuses on process-oriented knowledge creation within the organization and presents a variety of approaches to implement and manage process innovation to enhance the organization's core business processes. BPM has two objectives – improving business processes in the organization and at the same time evolving BPM capabilities (Rosemann and vom Brocke, 2015). Nadarajah and Kadir (2016) add the notion of connecting business process orientation and process improvement initiatives in the organization. Developing BPM capabilities or process orientation in the company is necessary in order to establish an infrastructure for more effective and efficient operational work and, hence, adjust to future improvements in the processes (Lehnert et al., 2017). Regarding business process improvement, it helps the company achieve higher process maturity levels and, eventually, change the centre of attraction of process from inward- to outward-looking – meaning that the focus is drawn more to customers' requirements and customer value creation (Nadarajah and Kadir, 2016).

The customer orientation is also crucial in defining BPM. Trkman et al. (2015) define BPM as the management discipline that takes into account customer requirements in order to redesign and improve internal business processes for the sake of higher customer satisfaction. In the service industry, when internal business processes are not in compliance with customers' awareness, a negative value gap arises and, therefore, the voice of the customer is taken into account when improving and redesigning business processes in order to minimize this gap and improve value for the customer (Pyon et al., 2011). Vom Brocke and Sinnl (2011) strengthen this insight and include customer orientation as one of the core values of BPM along with consistency, quality, process orientation, continuous improvements and responsiveness to any change. Jeston and Nelis (2006) state that in order to achieve organizational goals, BPM ought to be developed as a holistic practice by involving top management support, clearly defined roles within the company, a process-oriented culture, well-trained people and organizational management understanding. In other words, BPM should be seen as an integrated management approach or organizational capability of process-centric and customer-oriented organization that has its goals, people and technology integrated in both strategic and operational activities (Aparecida da Silva et al., 2012).

Core Elements of BPM

Rosemann and vom Brocke (2015) define six core elements of a BPM framework presenting the main principles and critical success factors behind managing, designing and changing business processes. These six elements are as follows:

1. *Strategic alignment:* BPM and its functions (e.g. design, execution, management and measurement) need to be closely aligned with the organization's strategic goals and specific strategic situations in order to ensure continuity and efficiency of business process improvement.
2. *Governance:* BPM governance establishes clear roles and responsibilities for project, programme, portfolio and operations management, as well as guiding process-related actions by creating decision-making and reward-system activities.
3. *Methods:* these are the set of tools and techniques used for enabling different activities along the process lifecycle and in the enterprise's BPM initiatives. For instance, these methods might constitute process modelling, business process improvement or analysis techniques.
4. *Information technology:* IT-based solutions that usually initiate significant business process redesigns and strengthen process awareness in the organization.
5. *People:* this element comprises people working in the organization who continuously develop their process management skills and knowledge in order to improve business processes and their performance.
6. *Culture:* it is the creation of the environment that emphasizes and enables various business process innovation initiatives. This includes specific values and methods that develop a BPM-supportive culture.

These six elements represent key factors that are necessary for successful BPM project implementation in the organization (Rosemann and vom Brocke, 2015). Over time these factors develop an organization's BPM capabilities and increase its maturity level which contributes to better business process performance over the long term.

Connection between BPM and Strategic Management

There is a tight link between BPM and strategic management. Islam and Daud Ahmed (2012) state that to implement process innovation, the top management should clearly communicate the essence of the change, create an appropriate environment for any transformations and provide a clear vision and benefits of the initiated change. Gębczyńska (2016) highlights the need to ensure consistency between process management activities and the strategy adopted within the organization. For this reason, strategic goals should be analysed at the beginning and based on the analysis the objectives of the core business process ought to be defined. Any activities or redesign initiatives undertaken in the core business process should be in alliance with the organization's strategic priorities.

Benefits of BPM

Numerous benefits of BPM are outlined in the academic literature. Hammer (2007) highlights significant improvements in cost, quality, time, and company profitability. Rosemann and vom Brocke (2015) note that a process focus development and continuous process innovations could lead to vast improvements in both a company's competitive performance and compliance of its whole system with process orientation, outcomes and customers. Sever (2007) adds some more benefits of BPM, from changing an organization's functional approach to implementing a process orientation, including:

1. Improvements in internal communication.
2. Better understanding of end-to-end processes.
3. Business processes have clearly defined inputs, outputs and work activities.
4. Taking a record of process performance enables better decision making.
5. A process performance driven culture also improves people management.
6. Reduction of rework done by different departments in the company.

In addition to improved operational performance measures BPM also supports organization functions and advances the enterprise's internal knowledge about business processes and customer value creation.

BPM Lifecycle

A lifecycle point of view is useful in understanding BPM adoption. Dumas et al. (2013) define the following stages for BPM adoption:

1. *Process identification:* this stage starts with identifying the operational problem to be addressed by the functional team and identifying the business process that is relevant to the proposed operational problem. The main output of this stage is process architecture that aims at collecting the related processes and measuring the value delivered by the specific process. In

other words, key process performance measures, i.e. cost, cycle time and quality, are identified to evaluate the state of the process.

2. *Process discovery:* once related processes and key process performance metrics are identified, the next step is to understand the current business process conducted in the organization. The typical outcome of this stage is an *As-is* business process model that presents the current sequence of the activities in the process and the way employees carry out their functions.

3. *Process analysis:* this stage consists of identifying and analysing the issue in the current business process. For instance, the possible impact of the issue is analysed, statistics of errors or amount of rework are gathered in order to provide process analysts with the information necessary to identify options for changing the process to improve key process performance measures. The stage is followed by the phase of identification and analysis of multiple potential opportunities to address the operational problem.

4. *Process redesign:* when understanding of operational issues in the current business process is gained and possible remedies are defined, the redesigned version of the process is proposed. In other words, the main outcome of this stage is a *To-be* business process model that includes solutions to the issues addressed in the *As-is* model. Process analysis and redesign stages are closely related as the best redesigned process is to be chosen after detailed analysis of the proposed options.

5. *Process implementation:* in this stage of the BPM lifecycle, the proposed *To-be* model is executed. The intended changes in the routines of working and/or IT systems in the organization are implemented to apply the redesigned business process in practice.

6. *Process monitoring and controlling:* the newly implemented process ought to be monitored in order to identify necessary adjustments for better business processes control. In this stage, relevant statistics are gathered and analysed in order to evaluate the key process performance indicators and the current state of the process. Hence, new operational problems could occur that require the repetition of the BPM lifecycle.

The BPM lifecycle ought to be seen as a circular activity as business processes should be continuously adapted and improved in accordance with changing customer needs and requirements, competition and new available technologies.

TOOLKIT FOR PROCESS INNOVATION

When choosing the appropriate BPM method for process innovation implementation, some criteria should be evaluated in addition to key process performance metrics. While implementing innovation, service companies should focus on the process of interaction with the customer as it is an integral part of the overall offering and creates service experience for the customer (Johne and Storey, 1998). According to Trkman et al. (2015), services mainly depend on interactions between service provider and the customer, and the behaviour of the customer has a major impact on the services. Hence, companies should also take into account customer business processes in order to respond to their changing needs and develop any improvements in internal business processes. Pyon et al. (2011) add that service improvement should be evaluated taking a process and customer point of view, especially in financial services companies, as value creation is closely linked with business processes in the back office of the company and process innovations co-created with the customers. Therefore, the specific BPM method is chosen by evaluating customers' needs and receiving continuous feedback from the customer.

There are a number of business process innovation implementation approaches that are applied in accordance with the organization's intended results of process change. Companies tend to implement process improvements by using different BPM methods and looking into process simplification, continuous improvements, process redesign, re-engineering to improve overall productivity, quality and overall operations management measures (Nadarajah and Kadir, 2016). The most commonly used approaches are CI and BPR methods (Gloet and Terziovski, 2004; Lehnert et al., 2017; Nadarajah and Kadir, 2016; Savolainen, 1999; Terziovski, 2012). Since these two approaches lead to different results – either minor process improvement or significant process improvements and redesign – these approaches are also described as incremental and radical process innovations, respectively. In the following sections the two most common BPM approaches, BPR and CI, are described in more detail.

Business Process Re-engineering

'Re-engineering' was first introduced in information technology but quite recently it has evolved into process change management methodology. The broader concept of 're-engineering' was firstly introduced by Hammer (1990) in his article 'Reengineering Work: Don't Automate, Obliterate'. BPR forces a firm to break away from the traditional way of organizing and conducting business and make radical changes in business process to achieve significant improvements in critical operational measurements – cost, quality, service and speed. BPR is often divided into IT-driven and quality-driven initiatives.

IT offers a number of ways to re-engineer the work as information technologies improve information access within the organization and inter-department coordination and have the potential to create new process design. IT capabilities enable the new concept of Case Management or Dynamic Case Management where powerful PC-based expert systems and automation of sub-processes support and allow case managers to handle individual cases throughout an end-to-end business process (Davis, 2013). Recent advances in robotics and machine learning have led to Robotics Process Automation (RPA), the automation of any repetitive routine process or series of activities that have consistent rules, and which is conducted wholly through interactions with IT applications. RPA in core business processes lowers process costs and lead-time, enables better control of errors and quality and improves accuracy.

Improved quality could be achieved through eliminating duplication of effort, non-value-creating transactional activities and delays in the process, and by defining clear roles and responsibilities within the process. Hammer (1990) stresses the importance of quality in BPR strategy by highlighting quality, innovation and service as the most important performance measures in the business. Tennant and Wu (2005) name quality improvement as one of the main BPR benefits together with productivity improvement, reduction in process cycle time, increased profitability and improved customer satisfaction. Hence, redesigning business processes based on quality improvement may lead to higher customer satisfaction and bring vast improvements in quality control.

Key steps in BPR implementation

BPR implementation involves the following key steps:

1. Developing a strategy for BPR implementation by defining targets, management approach and integrating leadership, re-engineering team, technology and methods.
2. Focusing redesign efforts on core business processes that have impact on competitive measures, such as customer service, quality, time and cost reduction.
3. Thinking big and initiating radical improvements by redesigning the entire business process.
4. Redesigning business process taking a cross-functional approach.
5. Enabling application of appropriate information technology.
6. Organizing work in the process by focusing on common outcomes instead of the task and functional goals.
7. Linking parallel activities and performing ongoing coordination instead of integrating its results.
8. Putting decision points in those activities where the work is done to empower employees to make decisions.

Challenges in BPR implementations

Firms often encounter challenges while re-engineering the business process. One of the barriers might be a high focus or concentration on technology, which may result in a redesigned process that becomes obsolete quickly. High prices of new technologies can also prevent enterprises from realizing quick improvements. Finally, an unhealthy organizational culture that does not support organizational change and leads to employee confrontation and fear can be a significant barrier in process redesign. Therefore, the top management of the company ought to evaluate and analyse these potential problems and prepare for them when initiating a BPR project.

Continuous Improvement Concept

Continuous improvement or incremental business process improvement is a collection of techniques that aim to incrementally improve and maintain existing business process performance and quality. CI is also a managerial approach that encourages ownership of responsibility for quality assurance by all levels in the organization and involvement of all employees in pursuing the organization's quality objectives. CI could be seen as a method to assure quality in every activity within the process by applying good practices derived from benchmarking in order to continuously improve customer satisfaction (Wilkinson et al., 1998, as cited in McAdam et al., 2000).

Lean methodology

Lean was a revolutionary managerial philosophy started by Toyota in the manufacturing industry and is based on application of statistical and quality control techniques to reduce waste in time, cost and defects. According to Browning and Sanders (2012), Lean methods assume a stable and routine process, a stable workforce and learning curves, high-volume production and taking out buffers from the process. Therefore, if these assumptions are met, the traditional Lean practices can be easily implemented in the service sector. In their research Heckl et al. (2010) found that the financial services sector is becoming more committed to efficient, standardized and automated processes, especially in the area of administrating customer-related outputs, such as payments/invoice transactions, processes that integrate self-devices, etc. Hence, Lean practices could be widely used in core customer-approaching business processes.

Types of Lean approaches

There are different ways organizations can use Lean to benefit from business process improvements. Browning and Sanders (2012) divide Lean into metaphorically named *liposuction* and *diet and exercise* approaches. The *liposuc-*

tion approach involves identifying non-value-added activities in the process and eliminating them. However, identification of activities that create no value is quite a tricky task as lack of value may not necessarily be associated with specific activities and may relate to incorrect input (Browning and Sanders, 2012). The *diet and exercise* method focuses on maximizing value of the business process by increasing its efficiency, adding some activities increasing total value of the process and developing knowledge about the overall process and its outputs through training and employee involvement. Both Lean approaches require system thinking and a holistic approach.

Harmon (2007) states that Lean principles concern process redesign and improvement and thus include both enterprise and process approaches – *Flow Kaizen* and *Process Kaizen*, respectively. *Flow Kaizen* focuses on identifying specific kinds of waste in high-level value-stream maps and eliminating or improving them, whereas *Process Kaizen* takes into account specific processes and elimination of wastes in them. The latter's main objective is to discard as many non-value-adding activities in the process as possible but to distinguish and keep those activities that support the company's functioning. In order to do so, seven types of wastes, referred to as the TIMWOOD framework, are defined in Lean: Transport time, Inventory, Motion of employees, Waiting time between process activities, Over-processing, Over-production and Defects (Schume, 2013). The generation of these wastes creates no value in the process and thus can be eliminated.

A variety of Lean approaches have been developed using specific industry or domain specific knowledge that focus on eliminating any waste in an organization's processes and flows and maximizing the value of the business process. Any Lean approach leads to incremental process innovations and key performance measure improvements. Therefore, a specific Lean approach ought to be chosen considering the operational problem raised and the organization's strategic priorities.

Lean Six Sigma

In recent years companies have started to use the Lean Six Sigma approach that blends methodologies and benefits of both Lean and Six Sigma. The latter approach focuses on the use of data and statistical analysis of business process in order to assess and improve the service-oriented process (Heckl et al., 2010). Taking a quality view, Six Sigma's goal is to reduce defects in the process to 3.4 per million opportunities in order to improve process quality and meet customer and stakeholders' requirements and expectations. Lean methodology focuses on process flow optimization by reducing or eliminating waste, while the Six Sigma approach emphasizes reduction of process variability based on statistical analysis so that the customers' experience is consistent with process outputs. Common Six Sigma implementations are based on the DMAIC cycle which includes the following stages (Magnusson et al., 2003):

1. *Define:* this stage focuses on generating and selecting improvement projects based on process performance, cost-saving potential, possible impact on customer satisfaction, technical and organizational complexity, and human resource availability. Thus, the variable to be improved is identified, the process is mapped, and performance is estimated.
2. *Measure:* in this stage the input factors that might have an influence on process performance are identified and ways to measure them are established.
3. *Analyse:* the key performance indicators are analysed by using statistical data and measurements in order to discover the root cause of the inadequate performance.
4. *Improve:* based on the knowledge gained in the analysis stage, the best solution to improve the process is defined and its implementations are operationalized.
5. *Control:* this stage involves verification that improvements are achieved and that the process is performing in an adequate manner. Also, the improved process is communicated within the organization.

As a result, Six Sigma implementation may result in a reduced number of non-value-added steps in the process, reduced cost due to poor quality, improved consistency of services due to reduction of variability in the process and increased employee morale (Heckl et al., 2010).

The integrated method of Lean Six Sigma is based on the knowledge, principles and tools of both methodologies and aims to increase both effectiveness and efficiency of the process. Thus, Lean Six Sigma brings double-sided benefit to the company in improved business performance and establishment of organizational climate supporting continuous, customer-driven innovations (Byrne et al., 2007). Due to its disciplined focus on customer and stakeholder requirements, detailed data and fact-based analysis this integrated methodology supports process-based transformations and creates a more innovative organizational culture (Lubowe and Blitz, 2008).

Integrated Strategy of CI and BPR

Even though the benefits gained from implementing continuous improvement and business process re-engineering approaches are obvious, many academics and practitioners claim that the gains from an integrated strategy are much more significant. Nadarajah and Kadir (2016) add that although BPR brings significant business process performance improvements, only integration with

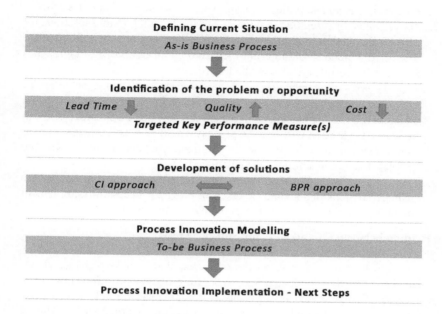

Figure 7.1   *Integrated model for process innovation*

a continuous improvement approach makes these gains sustainable and BPM practices effective. Business process improvement activities should first start with CI that builds a working base for process innovation (Harrington, 1995). Pilkauskaite (2018) developed a model that integrates BPM lifecycle, BPR and DMAIC cycle methodologies for process innovation projects (Figure 7.1). This model can be used by managers and team leaders for combining CI and BPR approaches to process improvement.

The research model involves the following stages:

1. *Defining current situation:* in this stage the current business process is described and mapped. As a result, the *As-is* business process is documented and process inputs, outputs and contributors are defined. This enables a better understanding of the end-to-end process and all activities involved.

2. *Identification of the problem or opportunity:* the key performance measurement is chosen to be improved based on the specific strategic goal and company's business model. One of the following key performance metrics is chosen – lead time reduction, quality improvement or cost reduction.

After the identification of targeted key performance measurement(s), process issues and activities for improvement are selected and described.

3. *Development of solutions:* in this stage of the model, possible solutions for process innovation to improve targeted key performance measurement are described. Potential solutions are focused on both CI and BPR approaches and possible results are also evaluated.

4. *Process innovation modelling:* as the sub-process or some activities of the process are chosen for process innovation implementation, the *To-be* business process is mapped. By having a documented *To-be* process, it can be seen what kind of redesign the process would have and process innovation implemented in the process. In addition, estimated results of possible process innovation solutions are calculated.

5. *Process innovation implementation:* this stage of the model presents all the managerial steps that should be taken in order to successfully implement the proposed process innovation implementation model.

Deciding between CI and BPR for Sub-processes

Based on a literature review, results of a case study and expert interviews, Pilkauskaite (2018) developed a framework for process innovation approaches which identifies common characteristics in order to evaluate a chosen business process or sub-process and decide which process innovation approach should be chosen in order to improve targeted key performance measures – CI or BPR (Figure 7.2).

1. *Value-addition:* if the process or sub-process is complex and its output brings high value to the end customer, it could be described as a high value-added process. This means that due to its complexity, if any error occurs, it might create many issues or cost a lot of time to fix any errors. Therefore, in order to minimize any risk of errors/defects, IT driven BPR solutions might be implemented. If the value addition in the process is lower, a CI approach may be taken to improve performance gradually over time.

2. *Dependency on external party:* this variable describes how much the process is dependent on an external party, such as client or end customer. The more the business process is dependent on external parties or the rules for handling specific cases are determined by the client, the more complexity and variability in volumes it may bring to the process. Hence, a BPR approach might be applied in the process to diminish the influence of the variability of the external party's input. Processes not dependent on external parties might be improved using a CI approach.

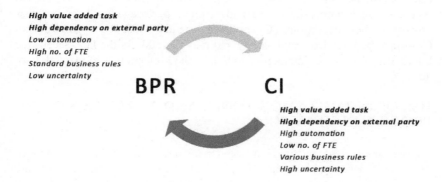

High value added task
High dependency on external party
Low automation
High no. of FTE
Standard business rules
Low uncertainty

BPR   CI

High value added task
High dependency on external party
High automation
Low no. of FTE
Various business rules
High uncertainty

Figure 7.2   Framework for choosing CI or BPR approach for process or sub-process

3. *Level of automation:* a low level of automation leads to a significant amount of manual work done by the responsible specialists. As a result, the lead time of the process is expanded due to the amount of manual work. Such process steps can benefit significantly from an IT driven BPR approach, while processes already having significant automation can benefit from CI.

4. *Number of full-time equivalents (FTE):* due to a low level of automation and a significant amount of manual work, some processes require a high number of FTE to handle both the process steps and the output of the process. Thus, the process cost is increased due to the high number of FTE, as well. The high number of FTE is evaluated taking into account the level of automation possible. As one of BPR's key aspects is application of IT solutions or revolutionary technology to simplify a process and improve key performance measures, the opportunities of IT implementation that would have an impact on the number of FTE should be evaluated at this stage.

5. *Standard business rules:* if a process involves little or no variability and there are standard business rules for handling any case and only few exceptions exist, IT software solutions could be implemented in a BPR approach.

6. *Degree of uncertainty:* this variable accounts for the understanding about the process that is gained among the process team. Greater understanding reduces uncertainty in the process and the process can be further improved using a BPR approach.

Thus, BPR should be used for process innovation implementation in specific areas in order to maintain a high value-added process, reduce the influence of external customers and increase the level of automation. Afterwards, the BPR effort should be followed by a CI approach since the business process should be continuously improved in order to maintain performance of the business process. In these conditions a CI approach instead of BPR is also possible, but CI brings the intended result slowly and may not address the key issue – the high level of customer interaction and, thus, the high amount of manual work needed.

USE OF OPTIMIZATION TOOLS AND ANALYTICS IN PROCESS INNOVATION

Rapid technological advances have seen many new solutions being introduced by vendors, which address specific problems faced by companies. Software tools that focus on optimizing Bill of Material management, or simplify and automate production planning and scheduling, or automate customer service and support or provide other optimization or automation have seen rapid adoption in industry, often using a BPR approach. While these tools are often domain specific, they all create significant change in the existing process and need to be implemented using a BPR framework.

In addition to complex technology tools, easy to use optimization methods, often implemented using common spreadsheet tools, can also enable significant process innovation. Gopal (2017) provides examples of significant improvements in supplier selection and the allocation process and in the inventory stratification process using a multi-criteria optimization approach, Analytical Hierarchy Process. These were implemented as part of a CI approach at client companies. Hence the use of algorithmic methods in a CI implementation can also yield significant benefits.

KEY SUCCESS FACTORS FOR PROCESS INNOVATION

Firm's Level of Innovation Maturity

Firms need to assess their maturity level before embarking on high-investment innovation efforts to increase the likelihood of successful outcomes. There are a number of process maturity models including the Capability Maturity Model (CMM) and the Process and Enterprise Maturity Model (Hammer, 2007). These models use a self-administered questionnaire that is answered by senior management to assess the maturity of the firm's process innovation capabilities. The Process and Enterprise Maturity Model (PEMM) uses two dimensions, process enablers and enterprise capabilities. Five process enablers – design, performers, owner, infrastructure and metrics – are needed to ensure high performance of the individual process. Four enterprise capabilities are also needed:

1. Strong leadership supporting creation of processes.
2. Culture valuing change, customer orientation, teamwork and personal accountability.
3. Expertise in process redesign and other change initiatives.
4. Governance of complex projects and improvement initiatives.

This integration of process enablers and enterprise capabilities is necessary for companies to maintain and transform a high-performance business process. In addition, the PEMM model also demands that all aspects of specific maturity level are to be completed before reaching the higher stage of BPM maturity. As a result, the company develops its BPM capabilities and gradually creates a process-oriented culture within the organization.

Gopal (2018) outlines an Operational Excellence Maturity Level (OEML) which categorizes companies based on existing operational practices, tenure of team members, leadership commitment to operational innovation, adherence

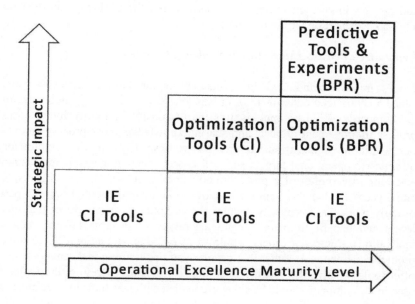

Figure 7.3   Maturity level and process innovation approaches

to standards like ISO, and other factors. Companies that are low on the OEML should first adopt CI approaches, especially Lean and Six Sigma methodologies, to gain control over process variation and motivate team members. As companies improve their OEML they can adopt higher-level process innovation tools and optimization methods successfully (Figure 7.3). If a poor performing, low OEML operation wants to adopt radically new methods or tools it needs to get the process expertise from industry experts, often through hiring experienced consultants. This effectively moves the firm to a higher maturity level and increases the likelihood of a successful BPR approach.

Senior Management Commitment and Communication

Senior management of the company ought to have a clear vision towards process innovation implementation and communicate an unambiguous message to the staff through specific operational targets. In addition, there should be a balance between strong governance of strategic priorities and giving flexibility to the employees to try new methods and creative solutions in order to improve core business processes. Top management should also act as a role model so that employees become willing followers of their ideas and process innovation initiatives. Consequently, the company can develop a process orientation within the company.

Centralized Process Innovation Knowledge Centre

Process improvement knowledge needs to be captured to drive innovation and hence a centralized department or at least one employee based on the size of the company should be appointed as the responsible authority for business process improvement projects and sharing knowledge about process innovation within the organization. For an effective reward system, the combination of concrete operational targets and soft aspects such as intrinsic motivation and supportive culture for process innovations should be used. As a result, employees' involvement in process innovation initiatives would become a part of daily work that eventually enables the company to reach higher maturity levels and benefit from an integrated strategy of incremental and radical innovations. Company leaders should focus on educating employees to solve problems and innovate rather than regularly giving training that cannot always offer tools to solve the specific operational problem. Therefore, the toolbox used in the company should be always amended with new tools that are created while solving specific business cases. Management and employees of the company should use both technological and human capital in order to initiate any kind of process innovation project since CI effort builds better process understanding and a base for greater process innovation projects. Otherwise, if companies become too dependent on IT and see process innovation opportunities based only on technology solutions, they sacrifice the gains resulting from CI initiatives. Thus, enterprises should work on small system improvements and incrementally achieve the stage of standardization that eventually would benefit from a new computer system.

Organizational Culture

A process-oriented culture should be supported by the top management and created through training about process improvement tools and specific strategic goals. In addition, both roles of process innovation ideas – suggesting and idea implementing and executing – should be defined as important for the company to benefit from continuity of process improvements. Also, the organizational culture should be accommodating and employees should feel motivated to participate in process innovation projects without fear of losing their jobs or being negatively affected by change. This could be done by openly communicating the results of each project and offering job opportunities for employees in those parts of the organization where workforce extension is needed. An organizational culture supportive of constant process improvement, providing opportunities to experiment and learn, and trusting employees are needed to have an effective process orientation in the company.

CONCLUSIONS

Organizations have tremendous opportunities to innovate their processes, provide new services and improve existing services while lowering costs. Using a combination of BPR and CI and adopting best practices, organizations, teams and individuals can all grow and provide better value to customers and to society.

REFERENCES

Aparecida da Silva, L., I. Pelogia Martins Damian and S. Inês Dallavalle de Pádua (2012), 'Process management tasks and barriers: functional to processes approach', *Business Process Management Journal*, 18(5), 762–776.

Armistead, C. and S. Machin (1997), 'Implications of business process management for operations management', *International Journal of Operations & Production Management*, 17(9), 886–898.

Browning, T.R. and N.R. Sanders (2012), 'Can innovation be lean?', *California Management Review*, 54(4), 5–19.

Byrne, G., D. Lubowe and A. Blitz (2007), 'Using a Lean Six Sigma approach to drive innovation', *Strategy & Leadership*, 35(2), 5–10.

Davenport, T.H. (1993), *Process Innovation: Reengineering Work through Information Technology*, Boston, MA: Harvard Business School Press.

Davis, D. (2013), 'Case closed? The difference between Dynamic Case Management (DMC) and Business Process Management (BPM)', accessed 15 December 2017 at https://www.processexcellencenetwork.com/business-process-management-bpm/articles/case-closed-the-difference-between-dynamic-case-ma.

Du Plessis, M. (2007), 'The role of knowledge management in innovation', *Journal of Knowledge Management*, 11(4), 20–29.

Dumas, M., M. La Rosa, J. Mendling and H. Reijers (2013), *Fundamentals of Business Process Management*, Heidelberg: Springer.

Gębczyńska, A. (2016), 'Strategy implementation efficiency on the process level', *Business Process Management Journal*, 22(6), 1079–1098.

Gloet, M. and M. Terziovski (2004), 'Exploring the relationship between knowledge management practices and innovation performance', *Journal of Manufacturing Technology Management*, 15(5), 402–409.

Gopal, G. (2017), 'Exciting developments in supply chain: from performance optimization analytics to blockchain experiments', paper presented at the Supply Chain Innovation Summit, 14–15 November.

Gopal, G. (2018), 'Operational excellence maturity level framework for process innovation success', Technical Report, Illinois Institute of Technology, Chicago.

Hammer, M. (1990), 'Re-engineering work: don't automate, obliterate', *Harvard Business Review*, 68(4), 104–112.

Hammer, M. (2007), 'The process audit', *Harvard Business Review*, 85(4), 111–123.

Hammer, M. and J. Champy (2006), *Re-engineering the Corporation: A Manifesto for Business*, New York: HarperCollins.

Harmon, P. (2007), *Business Process Change: A Guide for Business Managers and BPM and Six Sigma Professionals* (2nd ed.), Burlington, MA: Morgan Kaufmann Publishers.

Harrington, H.J. (1995), 'Continuous versus breakthrough improvement: finding the right answer', *Business Process Management Journal*, 1(3), 31–49.

Heckl, D., J. Moormann and M. Rosemann (2010), 'Uptake and success factors of Six Sigma in the financial services industry', *Business Process Management Journal*, 16(3), 436–472.

Islam, S. and M. Daud Ahmed (2012), 'Business process improvement of credit card department: case study of a multinational bank', *Business Process Management Journal*, 18(2), 284–303.

Jeston, J. and J. Nelis (2006), *Business Process Management: Practical Guidelines to Successful Implementations*, Oxford: Butterworth-Heinemann.

Johne, A. and C. Storey (1998), 'New service development: a review of the literature and annotated bibliography', *European Journal of Marketing*, 32(3/4), 184–251.

Kotler, P. (2000), *Marketing Management* (10th ed.), Englewood Cliffs, NJ: Prentice Hall International.

Lehnert, M., A. Linhart and M. Roeglinger (2017), 'Exploring the intersection of business process improvement and BPM capability development', *Business Process Management Journal*, 23(2), 275–292.

Lubowe, D. and A. Blitz (2008), 'Driving operational innovation using Lean Six Sigma', accessed 15 December 2017 at http://businessfinancemag.com/business-performance-management/driving-operational-innovation-using-lean-six-sigma.

Magnusson, K., B. Bergman and D. Kroslid (2003), *Six Sigma: The Pragmatic Approach* (2nd ed.), Lund: Studentlitteratur.

McAdam, R., P. Stevenson and G. Armstrong (2000), 'Innovative change management in SMEs: beyond continuous improvement', *Logistics Information Management*, 13(3), 138–149.

McKay, A. and Z. Radnor (1998), 'A characterization of a business process', *International Journal of Operations & Production Management*, 18(9/10), 924–936.

Megson, L. and M. Hammer (2004), 'Deep change: how operational innovation can transform your company', *Harvard Business Review*, 82(7/8), 182–183.

Nadarajah, D. and S.L. Kadir (2016), 'Measuring business process management using business process orientation and process improvement initiatives', *Business Process Management Journal*, 22(6), 1069–1078.

Neubauer, T. (2009), 'Um estudo empírico sobre o estado da gestão dos processos de negócio', *Business Process Management Journal*, 15(2), 166–183.

Pilkauskaite, E. (2018), 'Implementation of process innovation by integrating continuous improvement and business process re-engineering', Master's thesis, ISM University of Management and Economics, Lithuania.

Pyon, C.U., J.Y. Woo and S.C. Park (2011), 'Service improvement by business process management using customer complaints in financial service industry', *Expert Systems with Applications*, 38(4), 3267–3279.

Recker, J. (2014), 'Evidence-based business process management: using digital opportunities to drive organizational innovation', in J. vom Brocke and T. Schmiedel (eds.), *BPM – Driving Innovation in a Digital World: Management for Professionals*, Cham: Springer, 129–143.

Rosemann, M. and J. vom Brocke (2015), 'The six core elements of business process management', in J. vom Brocke and M. Rosemann (eds.), *Handbook on Business Process Management*, vol. 1: *Introduction, Methods, and Information Systems*, Heidelberg: Springer, 105–122.

Savolainen, T.I. (1999), 'Cycles of continuous improvement', *International Journal of Operations & Production Management*, 19(11), 1203–1222.

Schume, P. (2013), 'BPM Voices: BPM and Lean – a powerful combination for process', accessed 15 December 2017 at https://www.ibm.com/developerworks/bpm/bpmjournal/1308_col_schume/1308_schume.html.

Sever, K. (2007), 'The power of process orientation', *Quality Progress*, 40(1), 46–52.

Tennant, C. and Y. Wu (2005), 'The application of business process reengineering in the UK', *The TQM Magazine*, 17(6), 537–545.

Terziovski, M. (2002), 'Achieving performance excellence through an integrated strategy of radical innovation and continuous improvement', *Measuring Business Excellence*, 6(2), 5–14.

Terziovski, M. (2012), 'Exploring the effect of Six Sigma Quality (SSQ) on innovation and organisational ambidexterity', *Academy of Management Proceedings*, 2012(1), 13438.

Trkman, P., W. Mertens, S. Viaene and P. Gemmel (2015), 'From business process management to customer process management', *Business Process Management Journal*, 21(2), 250–266.

Vom Brocke, J. and T. Sinnl (2011), 'Culture in business process management: a literature review', *Business Process Management Journal*, 17(2), 357–378.

Wilkinson, A., T. Redman, E. Snape and M. Marchington (1998), *Managing with Total Quality Management: Theory and Practice*, Basingstoke: Macmillan.

8. New role of systems analysts in Agile requirements engineering

Alfredas Chmieliauskas, Kristina Grigorjevaite and Saulius Simkonis

INTRODUCTION

Financial and IT (Fintech) industries are among those who recently have become associated with a high degree of innovation. Innovations in new Fintech companies are easy to notice due to their product visibility. However, intensive process innovations that are not so visible for consumers often take place in old companies as they need to reinvent their ways of working in order to cope with new rivals while maintaining complex legacy infrastructure, meeting strict regulatory requirements and high customer demands for quality, security and availability.

The Agile development model is becoming more and more popular in big established companies. It promises faster time to market without compromising on quality. At the same time, it requires redesigning current processes, their interactions and changing competencies of people who currently work on those processes.

In this chapter we examine the changes being introduced to the role of a systems analyst while moving from the traditional, Waterfall, model to Agile in information systems development. Morrell et al.'s (2001) research indicates that the IT industry is typically characterized by two job titles – systems analysts and programmers. While systems analysts (SA) design requirements and functionalities of information systems (IS), programmers provide the working IS. In this research we focus on the following question: 'How do the changes in the process of requirements engineering (RE) when moving to the Agile development model impact the functions of SA and what are the core competencies required to fulfil these functions?'

CHANGES IN MODELS, PROCESSES AND ROLES IN IS DEVELOPMENT

Development of IS became one of the key drivers for the changing world and is widely named as an innovation in itself. While IS are available for every organization, the ability to use the IS to accomplish and foster business processes sets apart a successful organization from its competitors (He and Sheu, 2014). Taylan (2014) defines IS development as business re-engineering activity, as the development allows redefining business processes, their scope and work procedures. The attitude towards IS development shifted rapidly: from a simplistic, 'manufacturing-like' functional approach to complex, unique and difficult to automate strategic initiatives (Chan, 2000; Taylor, 2016). The shift in attitude might be a consequence of globalization and the understanding that IS development is directly related to business performance. The IS itself becomes an important driver in business innovation as its initiator, facilitator and enabler (Chan, 2000) is empowered to provide meaningful answers to the basic questions of the business: first of all – 'Why is there a need to add new functions to the current business?', then – 'Which operations and processes should be changed or developed for those functions?' and finally – 'How should the changes be implemented to reeengineer current business?'

IS development is often managed by projects. The traditional, linear (Waterfall) project management framework is no longer sufficient in the current ever-changing environment of rapid IS development. Agile is an approach to project management designed to meet the need for faster and more efficient introduction of changes in IS. It is important to mention that IS development is a process, which is intended to create a system to fulfil the needs of a client. The important part of IS development is Requirements Engineering (RE). This is a widely known term used to describe a process of gathering, specifying and managing client requirements for IS. The process has a direct effect both on the final product – the IS – and on its development process. Inappropriate or insufficient RE might lead to negative outcomes not just for the project, but also for the whole organization. RE is responsible for the definition of scope and activities to be performed. Hence, inappropriate work by a person who is responsible for RE, namely a systems analyst, might lead to project overrun, overspend, poor quality of final product, and financial and reputational losses for the company.

The chapter analyses the impact of changing project management models and RE activities on the new role of the systems analyst defined by the functions performed and the competencies required for fulfilling those functions.

Table 8.1   *Project success rate: Agile vs. Waterfall*

Model	Successful	Challenged	Failed
Agile	39%	52%	9%
Waterfall	11%	60%	29%

Changes in Models: From Waterfall to Agile

Project management has existed for centuries and is still growing as a desired profession (Schwalbe, 2010). Traditional definitions of project management mainly describe it as a way to organize and control activities, which are essential for achieving the project goal (Kapur, 2005), focusing on 'planning the work and working the plan' (Clements and Gido, 2006, p. 10). In the area of IT, project management is defined as 'the application of formal and informal knowledge, skills, tools and techniques to develop a system that provides a desired level of functionality on time and budget' (Martin et al., 2016, p. 52).

A successful project is supposed to finish on time, be within budget and cover all the originally specified requirements. Grech (2015) states that performance of IT projects increased as new project management models gained wider acceptance. This conclusion is also supported by other studies. Table 8.1 presents a summary of data from more than 10,000 projects relating success rate to the management model used (Hastle and Wojewoda, 2015).

With the Waterfall model losing the race for higher performance, a shift to the Agile model looks like a straightforward solution. But the main challenge in this regard is related to the fact that the change of underlying models requires not only redesigning the existing processes but also calls for new functions and competencies of the process participants. The nature of the required changes may be explained by comparing the basic concepts of the Waterfall and Agile approaches.

The Waterfall model is a sequential stage-based design approach used for decades in different areas of engineering, including software development. It assumes a largely one-directional flow of progress (thus the term 'waterfall') through certain stages, for example, analysis, design, implementation, testing, integration, and maintenance. The model allows for little flexibility with regard to scope changes both within each stage and – especially – between the stages.

In the context of IS development projects, for example, it means that after the elicitation of requirements, development starts and changes are not introduced until the end of the project. Nicholls et al. (2015) summarize the traditional project management model as one which highlights the importance of precisely defining the scope and avoiding any changes in it – i.e. follow the initial plan – otherwise the project is at risk of not being on time and on budget. The model usually defines analysis and coding as core activities in all IS development projects, regardless of size or complexity.

The analysis phase distributes the activities into elicitation, requirements gathering and analysis by itself. The initial step is to felicitate system requirements: the goal of the system and business case to solve. Requirements gathering is one of the core activities in the IS development, as the results of this process are high-level requirements for the software. These requirements state expectations for the system and functionalities to be developed. The third phase, analysis, starts only when requirements are gathered and confirmed. The analysis process defines preconditions that are more explicit, rules and description of the functionalities of the system. The output of analysis phase is documents, namely technical and functional specifications of IS. It is important to mention that the cornerstone of the Waterfall model is documentation, especially related to requirements, as it defines the scope and becomes an initial agreement between the IS development team and business representatives.

When the analysis phase is executed and approved, the program design phase starts. The result of system design is approved architecture of IS, which defines technical implementation of the system. The next phase, coding, is performed according to the written documentation, namely specification and architecture, defined in the previous phases. After the working code is in place, testing of the developed IS starts. The project manager delivers the final solution to the business representatives which approve the IS, starting the operations and maintenance phase, where the support team monitors the system and solves any issues, if they occur.

To sum up, the Waterfall model is still in wide use for IS development, especially for large and complex projects, but the ongoing trend to focus on adding value to the business as soon as possible pushes out the traditional model. And this is where the Agile model for IS development projects steps in.

Quick reaction to technological changes, re-planning, changes in scope and time are only some of the challenges that appear in the project lifecycle and need to be taken into account from the management perspective. There is a need for a model that is 'suitable for empirical, unpredictable and non-repeatable processes' (Cervone, 2011, p. 19). In 2001, a group of IT experts established the Agile Software Development Alliance (Nicholls et al., 2015). They started promoting an approach with a focus on flexibility to changes, customer requirements and deadlines. The key 12 principles were named the 'Agile Manifesto' (Beedle et al., 2001) underlining the working principles of the Agile model to satisfy the customer with changing requirements, transparency, regular deliveries and high quality final solutions. According to Schwaber (2004), Agile is supported by: visibility – the process must be visible for those who are in charge of the final solution; adaptation – quick response to the changes in requirements is part of the project; and inspection – responsible team members must regularly perform checks and detect issues that violate specifications. Agile is an umbrella term used for innovative project management practices, such as Scrum, Kanban, and Lean which 'enable offering [. . .] solutions through collaboration between self-organizing, cross-functional teams' (Denning, 2016, p. 11). Scrum is the most client-driven practice, therefore it is selected as a representative approach for this study. Agile was first applied in software development, but has extended its applicability to many fields (Nicholls et al., 2015; Sims and Johnson, 2012).

The significant feature of Agile project management is continuous acceptance of changing requirements that were considered 'frozen' in the Waterfall model (Misra et al., 2012). The changes in requirements allow for delivering the best solution for the business, with the key functionalities required. The core competencies for Agile project management are flexibility over predictability, value-driven versus plan-driven and incremental delivery as opposed to one-time delivery (Taylor, 2016). As the project manager's role has changed to that of facilitator rather than dictator, the role is still responsible for the results of the project, but is expected to delegate decision making to other team roles within the project (Taylor, 2016). Therefore, the self-organizing team is the basis for IS development in the Agile model. Among different Agile frameworks, Scrum is gaining more popularity recently. Scrum is based on roles, processes and artefacts. There are three major roles with different responsibilities within Scrum (Ozkan and Kucuk, 2016): the Product Owner (PO) which serves as an interface between stakeholders of the system and the development team; the Scrum Master responsible for enacting Scrum values by motivating the team to be as efficient and productive as possible; and the Scrum Development Team (SDT).

The framework of Scrum is like a project, repeated in small iterations (sprints). Each sprint has predefined activities, such as planning, development, testing, demo and retrospectives. Scrum starts with the definition of scope. Defined high-level requirements indicate the start of the development iterations. There are as many iterations as are required to cover the scope of the project. Each iteration starts with the predefined requirements, which can be introduced as user stories. At the second stage, the planning meeting defines the scope for iteration and priorities. During the planning meeting, the PO presents a backlog and SDT decides which functionalities must be included in the sprint to cover the required functionality for the particular iteration, sets the goal of iteration and breaks down those functionalities into the more technical tasks. After the planning, development starts. Execution of development is according to prioritization and when the first prioritized functionality is developed, the second one is started. Testing starts when the development team informs about the finished functionality. Development of planned functionalities closes when all user stories are finished and the goal of the iteration is met. The demo meeting is held on the last day of sprint for stakeholders of the project to show the progress and functionalities developed during an iteration, which will be passed for user acceptance testing. When all agreed functionalities for an interaction are developed, the business performs user acceptance testing. Retrospective meetings are held at the end of each interaction to discuss informally the iteration from the success and failure perspectives. The outcomes of the retrospective meeting are lessons learned and improvements for the process suggested for upcoming sprints. Although Agile is a widely used model in IS development, there are some drawbacks that should be taken into account. The major criticism is due to the changes in requirements. As the Agile team is flexible and adopts changes fast, there is a risk that the final solution ends up with an inappropriate application (Cervone, 2011).

To sum up, while drawbacks still exist in the model, organizations with the Agile mind-set are seen to adopt innovations more rapidly, have greater response to customer needs and higher satisfaction, demonstrate alignment with customer requirements, and have higher engagement from their employees. The aforementioned facts allow organizations to operate in line with the technological innovations, the globalized environment, and to be competitive in the market.

Change in Requirements Engineering Process: From Staged to Iterative

The final product (that is, the IS) depends on the requirements, listed by stakeholders, and the functionalities developed according to those requirements. Wysocki (2009) explains requirements as needs that define deliverables of the project before design and execution of the project. Requirements are the foundation for the project, because they state the problem the business intends to solve or new business opportunities that they are required to meet. Requirements engineering (RE) includes activities to identify the business need and the scope, analyse gathered information, and document and validate requirements for the system to be developed (Ramesh et al., 2010). Azanha et al. (2017) state that 35 per cent of the requirements change, while 65 per cent of specified requirements are never used. The volatility of requirements is considered a primary challenge to the IS development (Thakurta and Ahlemann, 2011). Salinas et al. (2008) point to five categories of activities in RE: requirements elicitation, requirements modelling, requirements specification, requirements validation and requirements management.

Requirements engineering differs in Waterfall and Agile IS development. Singh and Pandey (2017) define two major differences. Primarily, requirements gathering and analysis is performed prior to the start of the development in the Waterfall model, whereas in Agile, requirements engineering is performed simultaneously with other software development processes. Second, according to Agile, customer involvement is important during the whole development process, though in the Waterfall model, customer involvement is required only during the writing of requirements specifications. The changes to requirements and flexibility to those changes are essential to the Agile model; hence communication between the development team and the customer is inevitable. Rubin and Rubin (2011) state that explicit documentation in Waterfall, and only source code available as an artefact of documentation in Agile, define the core difference between RE practices.

To sum up, the requirements engineering process is critical for the success of IS development projects. Although it contributes only 7–10 per cent of the whole project effort, it can be the source for at least 15 per cent of the subsequent errors developed (Kulk and Verhoef, 2008). The findings of Paavola and Hallikainen (2016) identify the SA as the owner of the RE process. It is worth mentioning that close collaboration among managers, users and the SA is necessary to perform complete and effective RE processes. Researchers point to the growing importance of the role of the SA over the decades; it is the SA's job to gather the requirements, implement applications and perform problem solving (Lee, 2005). Thus, detailed analysis on the role of the systems analyst and changes in their role due to the changed project management and development approaches is presented below.

Change in the Role of the SA: From Static to Dynamic

Scholars investigate IS development from different perspectives. One of the areas of most interest is the roles and responsibilities in IT projects. Dennis et al. (2010) and Lerouge et al. (2005) emphasize the importance of the role of the SA in the software development lifecycle, mostly because the SA is familiar with the business situation and can identify opportunities for improvements in the business process and implement it in IS. In line with the importance of the SA, the research of Morrell et al. (2001) indicates that the IT industry may be characterized by two job titles only: SA and programmers.

The SA performs daily activities to give an organization the maximum benefit from the investment in technology and IS projects. The intention of the SA is to design a system that will increase business efficiency and decrease time spent on processes that can be automated. To do this, they can design an entirely new system or add functionalities for the existing one, in order to generate more value added to the business from the IS. The scope of SA activities increases from only gathering requirements for IS, to performing the same activity and supplementing it with communication with different stakeholders, and generating the best solution to satisfy the final customer. The first step in systems analysis is identification of the problem. The problem can be defined as a lack of functionalities in the existing system, or newly encountered features that are obstacles in reaching higher performance. The SA performs initial analysis by generating the statement of the problem as an output. Then, the SA gathers additional information to identify as many business problems and opportunities as possible. These activities continue until the SA is confident with the requirements. The key issues might be not noticed at first, but with repeated actions of information gathering, the importance of additional issues might be discovered.

The role of the SA in the Agile model differs from the one in the Waterfall model. Project management practices based on the Waterfall model use a command-and-control approach. Thus, the project manager's role is responsible for planning scope management, collecting requirements, defining scope, and creating the Work Breakdown Structure (Schwalbe, 2013). Requirements gathering is the first activity in the IS development project. In the Waterfall model, the project manager and the client define the requirements (Wysocki, 2009). The role of the SA starts only after the gathering of requirements and confirming them with the client. There is a high risk for scope creep when analysis starts. The SA starts framing the problem after defining the requirements, thus differences might appear from the initially defined problem to this, identified by the SA. The key role of the SA in the Waterfall model is performing analysis on the defined scope and writing the documentation. The output of SA activity is requirement specification, which is a guide for the development team as to what should appear in the final solution and how the system must behave.

The role of the SA in Agile is more difficult to define. The roles of Scrum Master, Product Owner and Development Team are defined in the Scrum Guide (Schwaber and Sutherland, 2017). The question under investigation is where the role of SA fits in the definition of roles and under what responsibilities. The nature of the work performed by the SA does not change: the SA is still a liaison between the team and the customer, problem-solver and requirements gatherer (Lee, 2005). But the first difference appears as the Agile model focuses on repeatable delivery in iterations. The SA performs analysis together with the business representatives and prioritizes requirements for the development team in response to changing requirements (Prasarnphanich et al., 2016). The SA is expected to perform analysis, define business problems and find solutions for the customer by developing the new IS or updating the existing one. Requirements elicitation happens during the development process. To be more precise, each iteration starts with analysis of requirements and functionalities and at the end the iteration is presented to the business representatives. It is one of the main differences between the Waterfall and Agile roles of the SA identified by Singh and Pandey (2017). This way, changes in requirements are rare or managed easily, because there is no need to change fully written documentation or almost developed IS. Second, extensive documentation is by nature not required from the SA in Agile, while in the Waterfall model the SA must prepare explicit documentation. Third, customer involvement in the IS development process is high, as there is continuous interaction between business representatives and the SA, which can lead to higher customer satisfaction (Dennis et al., 2010). Kelly (2010) describes the question of SA competencies and the role itself in Agile RE as still open and not fully covered by scholars.

To conclude, the role of the SA requires not just technical, but also functional and personal skills to be combined together, making the requirements transparent and comprehensible for other roles in the project. Lee (2005, p. 90) points out that the Fortune 500 companies 'expect their system analysts to become all-around athletes who play every corner of the field'. The SA role is difficult to define in Agile, as the emphasis is placed on the development team. Although the SA role does not itself involve development, it is perceived by the development team to be a managerial one (Kelly, 2010). The research described in the next section analyses expectations towards functions performed by the SA and the competencies required to perform those functions from the team's perspective.

RESEARCH FINDINGS

Research Framework

A qualitative research method (using semi-structured interviews as the data collection technique) was selected as most suitable for this study to analyse and understand the perception of SA functions and competencies while moving from the Waterfall model to Agile. The research design is based on a two-step approach: the first step focuses on the changes in SA functions, and in the second step the competencies required to perform the functions are identified.

The employees of the biggest Lithuanian IT organization were interviewed (17 extensive interviews were conducted). Interviewees were selected to fulfil the following conditions: work in different teams and projects, experience with Waterfall and Agile models, and direct working relationship with the SA. As the Agile model is a team-based approach, research conducted within the team is the most appropriate to define the competencies required for the role of SA as well as functions performed in Agile.

The theoretical research model is represented in Figure 8.1 where the consequences of moving from the Waterfall model to the Agile model in requirements engineering (transition A) are analysed in two consecutive steps:

- Step 1 includes analysis of the changes in SA functions (transition a11) implied by the requirements of the new Agile model (transition a12).
- Step 2 includes analysis of the changes in SA competencies (transition a21) implied by the new SA functions, identified in Step 1.

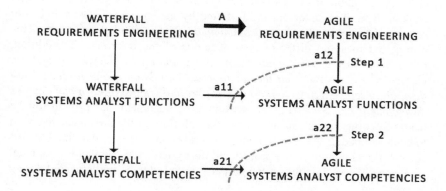

Figure 8.1   Two-step research model

The research in Step 2 consisted of identifying knowledge and skills and it also included ten competence elements defined as 'people competencies' in the IPMA Individual Competence Baseline framework ICB4 (International Project Management Association, 2015). ICB4 measures and improves individual competencies within the scope of project, programme or portfolio management. These competencies define 'personal and interpersonal competences required to successfully participate in or lead a project, programme or portfolio' (International Project Management Association, 2015, p. 26).

Changes in Functions of SA (Step 1)

The first insight from the interviews regarding the SA functions is that the SA role is the bridge between the business and development team. Typically, one respondent stated that the *'SA should understand how system implementation works and bring the requirements of business to the development team and technical implementation risks to the business'*. Another added that the *'SA needs to understand business language and explain to developers how to create the product as per those requirements. [The] Analyst is the main person who knows both sides and can translate everything to each side'*. To sum up, the SA is expected to be a translator from business language to technical language and vice versa.

The second insight is that the SA must be responsible for requirements gathering, elicitation and documentation. The written documentation must define all requirements from the business and be more business specific than technical document. There should be some technical details, but only key points for better understanding of business logic. When the requirements are clear, the function of the SA is to present those to the development team and explain them. The statement is illustrated by the statement *'The role clears requirements with business and communicates to the development team'*. This is required to avoid different interpretations of the document. In addition, respondents mentioned *'requirements are gathered by the system analyst. Unfortunately, we received the SA only at the middle of the project. Until then, all developers have to do analysis part and it slowed down our time for development by 75%'*. The SA must analyse, document and explain for the team all 'corner cases', scenarios and the full flow of the processes that need to be developed. It was mentioned by several team members that the SA must see the global picture of the project and the system, because the development team usually sees only the particular parts that need to be implemented during the iteration.

The third most commonly mentioned function for the role was support and micro-management. The team named support as the help required during the development process; when there are questions about the functionality, the SA must be the first contact person to eliminate obstacles and explain the business logic. If the SA cannot answer, the team expects the SA to contact business and clarify the possible scenarios. The micro-management mentioned by the team included planning the scope of the iterations, namely the sprint, monitoring the status of the iteration and encouraging the team to implement the plan. Additionally, respondents pointed out that the SA must know to whom to assign the task and who to push when work needs to be done.

The function of planning was the fourth SA function defined by the team. With regard to planning, as mentioned by the most of the team members, the SA is expected to plan the iterations and help the project manager to plan the scope of the whole project.

The fifth function is directly related to planning and support. The team defined decision making as one of the key functions. Although decision-making authority has some limitations for the role, it is perceived by the team that the SA makes decisions on what is going to be implemented in the system and during iterations. At the same time, the limitation of decision-making authority was highlighted. It was mentioned that this authority is required for the change management, where the SA must decide and agree with business regarding the change, in cases where the change is relatively small. If the change is big enough and affects the system in broader way, then the decision-making authority is handled by the project manager. Team members added that the *'SA must ensure that no breaking changes appear during the development and that this should be handled and negotiated by the SA with the business'*.

The last commonly mentioned function of the SA role was administrative work. The team pointed out that the SA should manage the backlog, bring items to the grooming meeting and manage releases to the production. The backlog management was explained as preparing the user stories for the development team and explaining them during the grooming meeting. In regards to the release management, it was mentioned that the SA must ensure that increments are actually delivered to the release.

The findings from Step 1 of the research identified several functions of the SA that are important from the team perspective: to be the bridge that links business and development team, perform requirements engineering, support the team and take care of micro-management and do administrative work.

Changes in Knowledge Required for SA (Step 2)

Interviewees were asked about their expectations towards the knowledge required for the SA. The answers were almost the same among all interviewees, although some contradictions appeared. The highest priority was given to knowledge in the business area. The team explained that the SA must have a broad understanding of the business area in which he or she is operating (*'The SA should have strong knowledge about portfolio and the project itself. By portfolio, I mean business area'*) along with knowledge about competitors and their business models. The second knowledge area required for the role was named as the fundamentals of IT or the development process. The knowledge was defined as crucial, because the SA must understand from the beginning until the end how development projects are executed. The following statements were made by almost all interviewees: *'Basics of IT fundamentals are mandatory when working with IT projects'*; *'When working in IT it is important to have at least basic knowledge of IT projects, how it is born and developed. This knowledge is crucial, as the SA should understand from the beginning until the end how the project is done'*. Although IT fundamentals were regarded as required for the role of SA, there were contradicting ideas as to whether that technical knowledge might encourage some limitations for the role: *'In addition, [the SA] should have some technical knowledge in order for better communication with developers. At least to think of solutions, propose them and discuss with technical team. On the other hand, if the person does not know technical details, she/he can propose more user-friendly solutions without thinking of technical limitations'*.

The third knowledge area was characterized by the team as 'psychology of individuals'. The core argument was that the SA works with many stakeholders and needs to know how to communicate efficiently and effectively. If the SA has specific questions or tasks, he or she must know which stakeholder to challenge to get the best result: *'Knowledge about your team you are working in. Psychology of people. If you have specific questions or tasks, you should know which person you should ask. Micro-management of the team. To know to whom to assign the task, whom to push, and track daily process'*.

The fourth knowledge area required by the SA was specifically underlined by the user experience designer and a software architect. They named knowledge of frameworks for project management and development as beneficial for the SA. The arguments were that the SA works a lot with business and needs to have knowledge on how projects are executed and how to deal with all stakeholders.

Changes in Skills Required for SA (Step 3)

The interviewees strongly highlighted communication skill as one of the core requirements for the SA: *'Communication is the most important skill because role should be able to talk with developers, managers, testers and many other people involved in the project'*. The SA must have the ability to approach stakeholders and extract information efficiently from them. The ability to think analytically is a supplementary skill that is needed for communication. In addition, *'analytical thinking is required as it helps the SA to communicate and gather requirements from business as well as lay down those requirements into the document in the way that all stakeholders understand'*. Analytical thinking allows the SA to connect all the information received into one general and broad picture of the software, with clarified processes and scope: *'it is difficult to communicate with business, as they are usually not so aware of the technical side, thus the SA must be able to communicate with them in their language while explaining technical details'*. Social or soft skills are also required for the role of SA: *'Of course, social skills are must have. The SA is probably the one who will have to deal with everyone a lot'*. The team expects the SA to deliver information ready before the development process and names the skill as organizational: to have the skill to plan the work, iterations and what should be delivered in order for the SA not to become a bottleneck.

The ability to negotiate was also mentioned by the team. According to the interviews, negotiation skill must be present when dealing with business. All interviewees mentioned that usually business asks for more functionalities to be implemented in the timeframe than it is possible to deliver. Interviewees expect the SA to handle this aspect and negotiate for them more time or less scope for iteration: *'Ability to openly discuss and negotiate with business'*. In addition, negotiation skill is required when business approach with new requirements. In this scenario, the SA must approach the team for technical details and negotiate with business for a better solution, as there can be technical obstacles to implementing the business need.

Changes in People Competencies for SA (Step 4)

This part of Step 2 was based on ten competence elements defined as 'people competencies' in the IPMA Individual Competence Baseline framework ICB4 (International Project Management Association, 2015).

The first competence in ICB4 is self-reflection and self-management. The team stated that *'it is one of the main parts of the work from what I see'*. The main argument was that if emotions are not handled well, it might affect negatively the work and result that the SA must achieve. *'Self-reflection is important because it is hard to be the bridge between people with different mind-sets so the person must be stable and have to understand that we are all different'*. The highest risk identified when the SA does not use self-reflection is that stakeholders might be offended by aggressive communication. This would definitely affect the information delivered and received to and by the systems analyst and pose a huge risk that the project would end in failure. The competence of self-management was perceived by interviewees as very important for the SA: *'it is part of SA work to be structured. Setting personal goals is important for SA because the SA should know the goal and push developers and business to achieve it'*. The SA must set personal goals and those tasks must be met prior to the deadline. In addition, *'developers and testers can be a huge mess and the SA is the person who must be structured and check the progress day after day'*.

The second competence is personal integrity and reliability. Interviewees mentioned that personal integrity is important for almost all roles, but the SA might require more in this respect because the role involves a great deal of communication and the SA needs to act according to ethical and moral values. This competence is without doubt one of the most important for the SA. Interviewees state that reliability of the SA must exist from several points of view. First of all, business must rely on the SA. If business does not regard the SA as reliable, there is a risk that they might not deliver all information needed for the project or start double-checking all decisions made by the SA. This might affect the whole project. This view of point was mentioned by interviewees: *'If business does not trust SA, they will start asking more and more details about implementation and management of the project'*; reliability is *'required because when business sets requirement it is crucial to rely on the SA that those requirements that are translated and communicated to developers are correct'*. Second, the team must rely on the SA. When the SA is regarded as reliable by the team, developers are not afraid to question the person and believe in the decisions made. Interviewees added that *'when the SA is not reliable, work takes more time to complete, as development team needs to communicate with business and within the team to figure out the requirements and logic behind the functionalities'*; *'I think SA is the person*

*whom everyone trusts a lot and if this person makes some mistake or some data
is incorrect, it creates some waterfall processes, which later on might evolve
into some bigger problem and the project might be corrupted'.*

The third competence is personal communication. The major arguments
mentioned during interviews were that this competence is self-explanatory
and if the SA communicates efficiently and effectively, analysis of business
needs is performed better, quicker and in a good quality manner: *'Definitely
required, because good communication with business and team members
makes project go faster. If the SA does not communicate in an effective and
efficient way, there is a high risk to project success'.* If this competence is
not strong enough, *'the SA cannot investigate all the business needs and later
when the product is presented to business it might appear that business needs
are not met. In this scenario the project can be treated as a failure'.*

The fourth competence is relationships and engagement. Interviewees
pointed out that building relationships helps to increase effectiveness of
communication and collaboration between stakeholders – *'knowing who to
ask opens the door'*, where 'who' stands for the already built relationships.
In addition, it makes information exchange smoother when people feel free
talking with the SA: *'People have to feel free when talking with the SA because
in other ways if they feel stressed or mad the information might be hidden from
the SA if people are afraid. When the relationship is absent, information can
be withheld from the start and appear in the middle of the project, affecting the
whole project and causing serious changes'.*

The fifth competence is leadership. *'It is required only if the SA wants to
become a project manager. This person is speaking to the whole team and
being able to round up and making proper decisions what to do next from
the current situation is important'.* Almost all answers indicated that project
manager mostly covers this competence.

The sixth competence defined is teamwork. Interviewees think that team
supporting varies from desirable to required for the role of SA: *'required,
because developers ask questions and the SA has to answer these questions
and explain business needs'*; *'support from the SA makes team members feel
better when they know that support of the SA is there'.* The team also stated
that SA work does not end when analysis is performed: *'There can be misun-
derstood parts by the team. So the SA should help during the process to explain
requirements and rules for implementation'.*

The seventh competence is conflict and crisis resolution. The answers vary
significantly regarding solving conflicts and crises. Interviewees mentioned
that the SA must be involved in the analysis of the crisis, as he or she is the
person who knows the system and business needs and can help to identify the
root cause of the problem. Besides, interviewees had the attitude that small

crises and issues should be handled by the SA, while organizational issues are the responsibility of a project manager.

The eighth competence is resourcefulness. *'Communication is the most needed competence and if it is present, frameworks for problem solving as well as techniques used do not matter at all'*. Although some conditions were added for problem solving: *'If the problem is technical, the SA can recommend something, but the decision is made by the team. If it is a business case and business logic problem, the SA has decision-making authority together with business'*.

The ninth competence is negotiation. Interviewees state that negotiation performed by SA is mainly with business: *'Required because not everything business is telling us or wants to be implemented can be doable or worth doing'*; *'the SA mainly negotiates about scope and features to implement, business requirements'*. This competence is needed to deal with business and negotiate regarding deadlines, scope, features and flow of the system. The team mentioned that the SA must have this competence for standing their ground and holding the position during the scope negotiation. In addition, it was mentioned that the SA must negotiate with the team as well: *'Everyone who has ever tried to communicate or negotiate with developers knows that it is required and very strong skills to negotiate [are needed]. There are usually negotiations about time frame to complete tasks. To do or not to do tasks'*.

The last, tenth competence is result orientation. Although there were some contradictions in the answers, the team suppose the SA to be result oriented. The main contradiction appears between *'Thus the SA must plan the scope and see the result. Must be oriented towards result but not the process'*, *'The SA has to have a broad view and should be oriented to the result'* and *'It is nature of work'* where interviewees said that the SA must be oriented to the final result, not to the process. Other interviewees mentioned that the SA is more important to orient activities to the process of development, rather than the final solution. The argument is that the final result might change slightly during the development, thus orientation towards process might bring more benefits.

DISCUSSION

The aim of this study is to identify the functions of the SA and their required competencies in the Agile model from a team perspective. Based on empirical results, here we discuss the theoretical and managerial implications of the findings.

The research was conducted to explore and analyse the functions that the SA should perform in the project or within the team and competencies required for these particular functions. In this respect, the literature clearly defines key functions of the SA in the traditional information systems development approach. The topic is analysed extensively with the core functions identified, such as gathering requirements (Cheney and Lyons, 1980), developing the system (Cheney and Lyons, 1980) and managing the implementation activities (Morrell et al., 2001). Our empirical research addressed the question about the changed role and functions of the SA in Agile RE. Here the findings exhibit differences from the existing theories. It can be stated that the differences in the functions appear depending on the selected IS development approach as well as the shifted mind-set in the sector.

It is important to mention that the rise of new IS development approaches, namely Agile, and the Scrum framework in particular, has had a profound effect on the role of the SA, not only in terms of the functions of the role, but also for the competencies required. Several new competencies supplement the initial functions, such as requirements gathering, development of the system and management of implementation activities.

The empirical research discovered that the team identifies five key functions of the role of the SA. The first item stated by the Scrum team aligns with that already defined in the Waterfall approach – to be a liaison between IT and the rest of the organization (Laudon and Laudon, 2004). This function requires the SA to gather information, explain requirements of the project to the development team, while still keeping in mind the risks of technical implementation and communicating them to business representatives so that they are aligned with it. In addition to the core function, empirical findings revealed that the SA must not only understand business problems, but also propose new solutions to solve them.

The second function of the SA also aligns with the existing literature, stating that the SA 'assists and guides the project team so that the team develops the right system in the effective way' (Dennis et al., 2010, p. 8). The interviewed team clearly positions support and micro-management to be one of the priority functions of the SA. Explaining to the team, support during the development process when uncertainties appear and need to be clarified, monitoring the status and even pushing the team for effective and efficient performance, were all mentioned during the research to support the second function. Although these functions have similarities with those in the Waterfall approach, it is obvious that the function of the SA has become wider in the sense that it is not only analysis and documentation that matters, but also it is important to perform managerial functions.

Further findings related to the functions of the SA have direct relations with Scrum, as they interrelate with Scrum roles and their functions. To be more precise, findings from the research highlight that the role of the SA is almost covered by the role of Product Owner in Scrum. New functions were emphasized such as decision making and planning. With the rise of the Agile approach, when the mind-set of IS development approaches changed, the new functions appear to be in high demand. The Product Owner, as defined in Scrum, has strong influence on the content of the iterations of the development team and has decision-making authority in regards to the functionalities of the system. Findings emphasize that the SA covers the role of Product Owner for these particular functions. The development team mentioned that the SA is responsible for the planning and scope of iterations. In addition, the SA is involved from the start when defining the whole scope of the project. This particular insight overcomes the divide between the responsibilities of the project manager in Waterfall and the systems analyst in Scrum, as the responsibility to define the scope of the project was initially only the project manager's responsibility. Although the last word still depends on the project manager, the SA assists the PM at the initial stage. This phenomenon can be explained through the changed attitude towards IS development approaches. Agile is based on the team and shared responsibilities within it. The SA is the person who has sufficient knowledge of how IS can solve the business problems and at the same time ensure that all IS standards are maintained. Bearing in mind this knowledge, the participation of the SA becomes crucial to avoid scope creep during the development. It can be one of the factors that influence decreased failure rates when comparing Agile and Waterfall approaches.

It is important to mention that the SA covers some functions of the Product Owner as well, which is a change from the traditional role of the SA. Not only is the planning and decision-making authority passed to the SA, but administrative functions as well. Managing the pool of tasks (or as described in Scrum, the backlog of user stories), describing and explaining those tasks, ensuring no break in changes and supporting the team – all these are functions in the new role of the SA.

The second question of our research and corresponding findings revealed the competencies required to perform newly identified and described functions in line with those initial ones from the Waterfall approach. The theoretical proposition of the research is to explore and analyse core competencies required from the systems analyst from the team's perspective. This particular approach was selected to fill a gap in the literature, where only insights from managerial positions have been discussed. As Agile is a team-oriented approach, the analysis focused on investigating the team's perspective towards the SA. The research about the competencies required began by asking the team to identify the skills they perceive to be important for the role of SA.

The findings of the research regarding skill sets and skills required by the SA differ slightly from those defined in Waterfall. The core finding is that skill sets and skills shifted more towards managerial competencies in Agile in comparison with Waterfall. While it is still beneficial for the SA to have some technical skills (e.g. the ability to use software or tools and visualize requirements), the higher priority by the Agile team is the SA's managerial skill set. The underlying idea of this finding is that in Agile, namely in Scrum, the technical skill set is covered by the SDT (Scrum Development Team) and the SA is intended to liaise between SDT and business, covering communication, planning and negotiation issues rather than bringing technical solutions to the team. The required competencies evaluated by the team are presented in Figure 8.2.

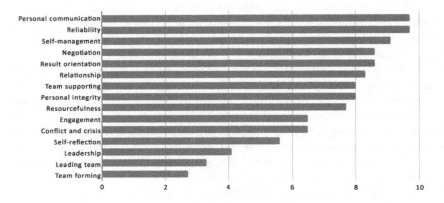

Figure 8.2   Competencies of SA

Figure 8.2 represents the most required competencies to be present at the top of the graph with the interviewees' percentage expression on the right. The results indicate that it is most important for the SA to be reliable, self-managed and communicate in an effective and efficient way. The three top competencies are highly interrelated. This is clearly visible in the interviewees' answers during the interviews. All of the team members highlighted that communication is the most important competence for the SA. Moreover, this competence aligns with the core function of SA – to be a bridge between business and the development team. Although communication is the core function, it cannot exist without reliability in the role. To be reliable means performing daily tasks dependably and according to expectations and agreed behaviour. This competence supplements communication, and vice versa. The combination of reliability and personal communication creates the skill set that if present in the role, boosts the results of analysis and the microclimate among stakeholders. When communication is effective and efficient and reliability exists in the relation between the stakeholders and the SA, requirements engineering goes smoother and with more value to the business and team. The process, by itself, cannot exist without these competencies, as if reliability is absent, the business or team will always have to check if the information provided is relevant and correct. In this situation, the bridge between business and the team, namely the SA, creates a bottleneck and more chaos than benefit. In addition, communication matters a lot, as it is one of the core functions identified in both Waterfall and Agile and supported by this research. Only effective and efficient communication allows requirements engineering to take place and ease the process of IS development. One of the supplements to communication is self-management, also identified in this research. Self-management includes dealing with continuously changing conditions and stressful situations, which allows improved communication in tough situations.

The next two competencies identified in the research as very important for the SA are to be skilled in negotiation and to be result oriented. The latter competence involves being focused on the goal of the project. This competence correlates with the functions defined to be mandatory for the SA. First, a result orientation helps the SA to focus on requirements gathering and the final product of the project – IS. In addition, the result oriented person foresees upcoming work and decisions that need to be made in the future for the success of the project. As stated by the team, planning and decision-making are functions of the SA, and therefore result orientation, as a competence, improves those functions also. The team gave the same level of importance to competence in negotiation. Negotiation competence entails the ability to balance between different expectations and interests of stakeholders, thus allowing agreement to be reached that satisfies all sides of interest. This competence is also important to support the functions of the SA, such as decision-making, support and micro-management.

In addition, research revealed that the competence of relationship helps to increase the performance of the systems analyst in terms of communicating, gathering requirements and even micro-management. The idea is that if the professional relationship with stakeholders is good, the SA can achieve greater and quicker results when performing daily tasks, such as requirements gathering and planning. In this way, stakeholders provide more information and decisions are made easier.

Team supporting and personal integrity were identified to be of the same importance for the team members. These competencies enable the SA to help and push the team to seek better results as well as to self-identify as part of the team. These competencies cover all the defined functions of the SA and show that the team is the most important unit in Agile IS development and every role in the project is there to support, help and increase the productivity of the team and to seek the best result. All the other analysed competencies were defined as of less importance for the role of systems analyst. The team expressed the view that competencies such as conflict and crisis management, engagement, leadership, etc. are more important for leaders or project managers than for systems analysts.

The research on the new role of SA in Agile requirements engineering reveals several managerial implications. First of all, the research clearly defines the core functions of the systems analyst in the Scrum team. This information can help project managers to define responsibilities within the team and set expectations for this particular role. In addition, when functions are clearly defined, it is easier for managers to evaluate the performance of the systems analyst by setting key performance indicators for the existing employees or when recruiting new ones.

Second, the competencies defined in the research can be used to improve the current performance of the SA in the team. The suggested approach is presented in Table 8.2, where the weight of each competency (W) is based on the research results presented in Figure 8.2. The gap (D − C) between desired level (D) and current level (C) should be assessed during interviews, and individual SA development priorities should be defined by multiplying the weight of the competency by the gap. This way, an individual learning path for the SA can be defined in order to track their progress.

There are several limitations to our research that should be considered and addressed in future academic studies. First, academic literature is currently available only from the viewpoint of managerial positions on the functions and

Table 8.2   *Suggested approach to evaluate SA competencies for improvements*

Competence	Weight	Current level	Desired level	Gap	Priority
	W	C	D	D − C	W × (D − C)
Reliability	9.7				
Personal communication	9.7				
Self-management	9.1				
Result orientation	8.6				
Negotiation	8.6				
Relationship	8.3				
Personal integrity	8.0				
Team supporting	8.0				
Resourcefulness	7.7				
Conflict and crisis	6.5				
Engagement	6.5				
Self-reflection	5.6				
Leadership	4.1				
Leading team	3.3				
Team forming	2.7				

competencies of the systems analyst. As Agile is a relatively new IS development approach compared to Waterfall, there is very limited information available about the functions of the systems analyst in Agile from the team's perspective. Thus, the findings of our research cannot be reliably compared to the existing literature at the moment.

Second, our research was conducted in only one company. Although the company is large, the perception of SA functions and competencies could be biased. The recommendation for future research would be to expand the sample of research and perform analysis in different companies.

CONCLUSIONS

The growing importance of the IT sector attracts scholars to pay attention not only to its technical side, but also to the innovation that arises in this sector, its impact in terms of globalization and the birth of new managerial solutions. As the numbers of IS development projects increase from year to year, it is important to investigate different approaches used in those projects to better understand their nature. This chapter has covered literature on changes in frameworks in use for IS development and the core differences between them. The traditional, Waterfall, project management approach is no longer adequate to deal with the realities of a fast-changing world and nowadays flexibility and quick reaction to changes are a must rather than a choice. It is here that Agile steps in with a different mind-set and approach. Our chapter has analysed the Waterfall and Agile approaches and the impact of the latter on one of the core activities in IS development – requirements engineering. The process has moved from static to dynamic and thus required changes to the owner of this process – the systems analyst. It is important to mention that our approach to the Agile mind-set regards the team as the most important unit which delivers value added in the project. Agile is keen on self-organized and self-managed teams, thus our study examines and elaborates on the functions of the systems analyst and the competencies required from the team's perspective, rather than from the managerial one. With this perspective, our research conceptualized frameworks for IS development and the changes that have an impact on requirements engineering. We have highlighted the importance of the role of the owner for the requirements engineering process and raised the question about the SA's role in Agile RE.

The literature review laid the ground for our theoretical model. We identified that two-layered research was needed to pursue our analysis. First of all, we carried out a review of changes in frameworks of IS development and requirements engineering and identified the functions of SA in Agile requirements engineering. The research revealed that the functions became broader in Agile requirements engineering compared to the Waterfall approach. Although requirements engineering remains one of the core functions, namely requirements gathering, elicitation and documentation, the significance of the role lies more in the managerial and communication part. Research results claim that being a liaison between business and development team is the function that makes the role unique. Moreover, the role is considered to have responsibilities and functions that are predefined ones for the role of Product Owner in Scrum, in line with functions of support to the team and micro-management. This change in the framework of project management methodology brought a new mind-set to the role of the systems analyst and broadened our perception of it.

The second part of the research intended to define the competencies required for the identified functions. As the functions have broadened in Agile, different competencies are required to fulfil these functions. The competencies were analysed using the IPMA Individual Competence Baseline framework (International Project Management Association, 2015). In line with the Eye of Competence, 15 competencies were analysed and the most important competencies were defined by the Scrum Development Team to be required for the role of systems analyst. Two of the core competencies are reliability and personal communication. The reason for these competencies to be at the top of the priority list is that they directly align with the function of being a liaison between team and business. The SA must ensure information transfer from the business needs to the development team in order to develop the IS in such a way that business can use it and it fully aligns with their expectations. Errors in this function and competencies can cause serious problems and even the failure of the project. The reliability of the SA is also important so that stakeholders do not withhold information or need to double check if the SA is working as expected. The competencies of self-management, result orientation and negotiation were also identified to be in the top five of the priority list. All these competencies help the SA to perform the core functions and create value added to the project and company.

The results of our research were discussed within the company and admitted to be important and significant for fostering the role of the SA. Moreover, managerial implications were provided for human resource specialists and the manager of the project. First of all, the identified functions of the SA in Agile can be used to improve the SA's position description in the company and outline the responsibilities that must be covered by this role. In addition, our model will allow the current situation to be evaluated in order to create a plan as to what actions should be taken to increase the most important competencies. The results of the study will enable the right employees to be selected for the role of SA and help to develop the most important competencies for the existing employees in the company.

REFERENCES

Azanha, A., A. Argoud, B. Camargo Jr. and P. Antoniolli (2017), 'Agile project management with Scrum', *International Journal of Managing Projects in Business*, 10(1), 121–142.

Beedle, M., A. Bennekum, A. Cockburn, W. Cunningham, M. Fowler, J. Highsmith, R. Hunt, R. Jeffries, J. Kern, B. Marick, R. Martin, K. Schwaber, J. Sutherland and D. A. Thomas (2001), *Manifesto for Agile Software Development*. Retrieved from http://agilemanifesto.org.

Cervone, H.F. (2011), 'Understanding agile project management methods using Scrum', *OCLC Systems and Services: International Digital Library Perspectives*, 27(1), 18–22.

Chan, S. (2000), 'Information technology in business processes', *Business Process Management Journal*, 6(3), 224–237.

Cheney, P.H. and N.R. Lyons (1980), 'Information systems skill requirements: a survey', *MIS Quarterly*, 4(1), 35–43.

Clements, J.P. and J. Gido (2006), *Effective Project Management*, Mason, OH: Thomson/South-Western.

Denning, S. (2016), 'How to make the whole organization Agile', *Strategy & Leadership*, 44(4), 10–17.

Dennis, A., B.H. Wixom and R.M. Roth (2010), *Systems Analysis and Design*, Hoboken, NJ: John Wiley.

Grech, T. (2015), 'The intersection of agile and waterfall', *Industrial Engineering*, August, 47–49.

Hastle, S. and S. Wojewoda (2015), *Standish Group 2015 Chaos Report – Q&A with Jennifer Lynch*, 4 October. Retrieved from https://www.infoq.com/articles/standish-chaos-2015.

He, X.J. and M. Sheu (2014), 'Efficacy of functional user impact on information system development', *Management Research Review*, 37(10), 902–911.

International Project Management Association (2015), *Individual Competence Baseline for Project, Programme and Portfolio Management* (4th ed.), Nijkerk, Netherlands.

Kapur, G.K. (2005), *Project Management for Information, Technology, Business, and Certification*, Upper Saddle River, NJ: Pearson/Prentice Hall.

Kelly, A. (2010), 'I'm a business analyst. Get me out of here', *Overload*, 98, 4–8.

Kulk, G. and C. Verhoef (2008), 'Quantifying requirements volatility effects', *Science of Computer Programming*, 72, 136–175.

Laudon, K.C. and J.P. Laudon (2004), *Management Information Systems: Managing the Digital Firm* (8th ed.), Hoboken, NJ: Pearson.

Lee, C.K. (2005), 'Analysis of skill requirements for system analysts in Fortune 500 organizations', *Journal of Computer Information Systems*, 45(4), 84–92.

Lerouge, C., S. Newton and E. Blanton (2005), 'Exploring the systems analyst skill set: perceptions, preferences, age and gender', *Journal of Computer Information Systems*, 45(3), 12–23.

Martin, N., J. Pearson and K. Furumo (2016), 'IS project management: size, practices and the project management office', *Journal of Computer Information Systems*, 47(2), 52–60.

Misra, S., V. Kumar, U. Kumar, K. Fantazy and M. Akhter (2012), 'Agile software development practices: evolution, principles, and criticism', *International Journal of Quality & Reliability Management*, 29(9), 972–980.

Morrell, J., C. Mawhinney, G. Morris, W. Haga and A. Smolkina (2001), 'The systems analyst: a post mortem?' Retrieved from https://www.researchgate.net/publication/242248394_the_systems_analyst_a_post_morte.

Nicholls, G.M., N.A. Lewis and T. Eschenbach (2015), 'Determining when simplified Agile project management is right for small teams', *Engineering Management Journal*, 27(1), 3–10.

Ozkan, N. and C. Kucuk (2016), 'A systematic approach to project related concepts of Scrum', *Review of International Comparative Management*, 17(4), 320–334.

Paavola, R. and P. Hallikainen (2016), 'Antecedents for successful collaboration in requirements engineering', *VINE Journal of Information and Knowledge Management Systems*, 46(3), 353–370.

Prasarnphanich, P., B. Janz and J. Patel (2016), 'Towards a better understanding of system analysts' tacit knowledge', *Information Technology & People*, 29(1), 69–98.

Ramesh, B., L. Cao and R. Baskerville (2010), 'Agile requirements engineering practices and challenges: an empirical study', *Information Systems Journal*, 20(5), 449–480.

Rubin, E. and H. Rubin (2011), 'Supporting agile software development through active documentation', *Requirements Engineering*, 16, 117–132.

Salinas, M., G. Prudhomme and D. Brissaud (2008), 'Requirement-oriented activities in an engineering design process', *International Journal of Computer Integrated Manufacturing*, 21(2), 127–138.

Schwaber, K. (2004), *Agile Project Management with Scrum*, Redmond, WA: Microsoft Press.

Schwaber, K. and J. Sutherland (2017), 'The scrum guide', 18 November. Retrieved from http://www.scrumguides.org/docs/scrumguide/v2017/2017-Scrum-Guide-US.pdf#zoom=100.

Schwalbe, K. (2010), *Managing Information Technology Projects*. London: Cengage Learning.

Schwalbe, K. (2013), *An Introduction to Project Management*, Minneapolis, MN: Kathy Schwalbe LLC.

Sims, C. and H.L. Johnson (2012), *Scrum: A Breathtakingly Brief and Agile Introduction*. Dymaxicon.

Singh, A. and D. Pandey (2017), 'Implementation of requirement engineering in Extreme Programing and Scrum', *International Journal of Advanced Research in Computer Science*, 8(5), 621–624.

Taylan, O. (2014), 'IT project risk assessment of learning organizations by fuzzy set and systems', *International Journal of Organizational Analysis*, 22(2), 161–180.

Taylor, K.J. (2016), 'Adopting Agile software development: the project manager experience', *Information Technology & People*, 29(4), 670–687.

Thakurta, R. and F. Ahlemann (2011), 'Understanding requirement volatility in software projects', *Engineering Management Journal*, 23(3), 3–7.

Wysocki, R.K. (2009), *Effective Project Management: Traditional, Agile, Extreme*, Hoboken, NJ: Wiley Technology.

PART V

Human resource innovation management

9. Transforming human resource management: innovative e-HRM value creation for multinational companies

Vida Škudienė, Gintare Vezeliene and Olga Stangej

INTRODUCTION

Technology has become a key wheel of today's organizations. The rapid development of advanced information technology (IT) solutions has impelled businesses to adopt innovative IT tools to be able to successfully compete in the global market. Technology advancement in human resource management (HRM) is considered to be one of the critical driving forces for the overall strength, efficiency and productivity of an organization (Kohansal et al., 2016). Through technology-fostered HRM practices, including recruitment, selection, training and retention, organizations have greater access to talents, which in turn promotes organizational competitiveness.

A rather new phenomenon, known as electronic human resource management (e-HRM) has evolved to support the human actors in the delivery of HRM functions, tasks and performance through planning, provision, implementation, operation and application of information technology (Strohmeier, 2007). At its core, e-HRM employs web-based and data archiving technologies that enhance existing human resource practices to make them more meaningful, systematic and result-oriented as well as cost-effective for organizations (Islam, 2016). Consequently, managing a large number of employees in multinational organizations has become more efficient through the implementation of technological solutions. Extant studies already confirm that companies that adopt sophisticated HR technologies, known as 'e-HRM', outperform their counterparts (Johnson and Gueutal, 2011). As a result, HRM is becoming a more technology-based function.

However, although extant studies relate e-HRM to increased efficiency of HRM processes, service delivery, greater strategic contribution (Ruël and Bondarouk, 2013) and value creation (Parry, 2011; Parry and Tyson, 2010), the findings on how value is created for an organization through the adoption of e-HRM remain fragmented. This chapter is based on an empirical study conducted with an aim to investigate how multinational companies create value through e-HRM practices. As it has been proven that cultural practices can moderate the relationship between e-HRM and organizational outcomes (Peretz and Parry, 2016), the study has been based on multinational companies that embrace a culturally diverse context. From a practitioner's standpoint, this subject is specifically critical to multinational companies, since while the adoption of latest technology tools for HRM transformation may lead to benefits, if not properly employed they may cause problems, such as depersonalization of HRM (Parry and Tyson, 2010).

TRANSFORMATION OF HRM FUNCTIONS

Human resource management has long been associated with administrative tasks. Back in the 1960s, HR practitioners mainly dealt with administrative functions and roles, including management of employee and payroll data. When financial recession occurred in the 1970s, however, HRM practitioners were expected to develop solutions for optimization of employee-associated costs. The computer boom that began in the 1980s eventually resulted in HRM providing the data for organization management. Finally, at the end of the 1990s, IT was already integrated into almost all HRM domains, and a contemporary approach to managing human resources became inevitable (Analoui, 2007). As a result, a gradual transition from traditional HRM practices to e-HRM emerged. The last few decades have highlighted the need to reframe the HRM function as more strategic (Marler and Fisher, 2013). However, the alignment of HRM goals with organizational goals has been challenging due to its twofold contribution. On the one side, HRM is expected to enact the role of a strategic business partner for a company, oriented towards maximization of human capital, the pursuit of business interests and increased profitability. At the same time, HRM entities serve as the employees' advocates. This dual mission calls for effective management of both soft and hard sides of HRM.

As businesses expect HRM to be strategic and yield greater value-adding capabilities, HRM practitioners have started to consider how to incorporate this new transformation and tailor High-Performance Work Systems to achieve optimum impact (Schuler and Jackson, 2000). Overall, effective HRM may lead to cost reduction and improved service quality that altogether may result in increased business performance (Strohmeier, 2009). However, the literature on HRM highlights the importance of HR practitioners becoming more strategic (Ruël et al., 2007). As Conaton (2014) notes, perceptions of the strategic effectiveness of HRM can be enhanced through electronic human resource management. Indeed, e-HRM is based on a broader conception of HRM data and functions. Not only does it serve as a tool for storing all HRM-related data, but it also aids in forecasting the future of HRM and the effect of changes in HRM policies and programs (Rothwell and Kazanas, 1988). By investing in e-HRM, organizations can store, manipulate and retrieve HR-related data that, in turn, opens doors for strategic HRM through web-based technologies. In line with these calls, in order to stay competitive in the global arena and achieve operational, relational and strategic advantages, companies invest in innovative HRM solutions (Bondarouk et al., 2017; Marler and Parry, 2016; Strohmeier, 2009). Based on the traditional AMO (ability, motivation and opportunity) model for HRM (Applebaum et al., 2000), organizations focus not only on the administrative or operational sides of HRM, but also invest in practices related to employee empowerment, ability, and motivation. In sum, the literature on e-HRM (Buckley et al., 2004; Gardner et al., 2003; Ruël et al., 2007) outlines three main goals of e-HRM across three domains that all create value for the organization:

- Increase efficiency and be more cost-effective within the HRM department (operational domain).
- Improve HRM service quality to both employees and management (relational domain).
- Become a strategic partner in achieving organizational goals (strategic-transformational domain).

These domains serve as the framework for the research presented in this chapter.

Operational e-HRM Domain

Traditionally, human resources are assumed to perform tasks related to transactional activities (Bussler and Davis, 2001). Scholars (for example Huselid et al., 1997) agree that organizational competitive advantage on operational activities is very limited unless performed efficiently. Hence, the majority of companies aim at maximum efficiency and minimum costs and resources. In this vein, they identify that most routine tasks can be conducted through the enablement of a manager, employee self-service or automated transactions. E-core HRM practices provide organizations with instant access to employee data and typically involve an employee self-service portal for editing their personal information or requesting changes from HR managers. Access to personal HR-related data promotes employee trust and has a positive impact on organizational culture (Rietsema, 2017). Additionally, e-core HRM provides a comprehensive database solution, where management and employees can monitor organizational structure, employee involvement, awards, competencies, job information, and public profiles of colleagues (Deshwal, 2015). With a role-based permission access tool, different management groups can view and edit their subordinates' personal or employment information, manage time-off requests, and use more functions, depending on the maturity of e-HRM implementation. Altogether, e-core HRM stores HR-related data and assists HR managers in fulfilling the majority of HRM administrative tasks.

Relational e-HRM Domain

Alongside delivering multiple transactional procedures, relational e-HRM refers to people management and includes HR planning, acquisition, development, and compensation, and is often linked to organizational culture (Foster, 2009). The relational process is considered to create high value for the business, as, for example, sound recruitment fosters access to skilled labour (Foster, 2009; Huselid et al., 2005). In this vein, e-recruitment and selection, e-training and development, e-compensation and e-performance management contribute to the e-HRM relational dimension.

E-recruitment and selection
In general, the ultimate goal of recruitment is to attract a workforce whose skills correspond to organizational goals, objectives and values (Oswal and Narayanappa, 2014). With the first arrival of information and communication technology applications designed for recruitment, companies turned to computers as a recruiting tool by announcing vacant positions online, thus attracting candidates both from the local region and globally (Deshwal, 2015). While additionally employing internal databases of current staff profiles, e-recruitment and selection have been widely used by companies due to shorter recruitment cycles, sharper targeting of applicants, reduced costs through the elimination of 'middlemen', and global coverage (Analoui, 2007).

E-training and development
While training practices help employees to enrich their knowledge and skills required for business and customer service (Oswal and Narayanappa, 2014), companies increasingly select e-training and development systems. Such an approach provides always-accessible learning material and reduces direct training costs through limited needs for lecturers, printed materials or learning facilities (Deshwal, 2015) and indirect costs such as travel or equipment expenses. As it also enables the employees to familiarize themselves with the latest information and technological advancement relative to the firm, organizations develop and upload their own material to the intranet.

E-performance management

E-performance management is a web-based appraisal e-HRM practice that permits effective assessment of employee skills, knowledge and job performance and automated linkage of performance level with employee compensation (Oswal and Narayanappa, 2014). It further provides employees with tools to add, edit and track their performance as well as monitor their competencies within the organization, thereby paving the way for transparent and efficient performance monitoring.

E-compensation

Regardless of its size, every organization is engaged in compensation planning of its employees (Deshwal, 2015), while compensation itself has become a critical factor in the competition for talents over the recent years. Hence, the ultimate purpose of e-compensation is to aid managers in designing employee compensation, benefit and incentive systems, schemes and packages aligned with budget guidelines. It also helps to track the compensation distribution among employees and ensure justice (Oswal and Narayanappa, 2014).

Strategic-Transformational e-HRM Domain

This category includes non-transactional HR activities, including HR strategy, workforce planning, and business development. E-HRM proposes complex human capital analytics tools for the management to produce data-driven insights about HRM processes and workforce, such as gaps that impede organizational results (SAP SuccessFactors, 2017), and align them with strategic decisions. By tracking trends in recruiting, retirement, retention, headcount and HR strategy, the management can mitigate risks, improve workforce planning and scenarios and successfully model HR composition and expenses. E-HRM enables HR professionals to access all the data that is compiled in one place and derive decisions from the analysis. Thus, it serves as a powerful strategic tool and makes a great base for HRM to enact its new role as a strategic partner in the organization. All three above-mentioned domains and respective practices, discussed further in the next section, were integrated into the research methodology.

METHODOLOGY

Stemming from traditional HRM literature, a corresponding shift from traditional practices to e-HRM practices has been observed as a positive influence on value-creating outcomes. For the purpose of the empirical study discussed in this chapter, the value was considered as (1) operational cost reduction, (2) improved HR service quality, and (3) enhanced strategic capabilities. The primary purpose of HRM is to fulfil administrative activities – keep records of employees, manage payroll tasks, monitor time and attendance, and store HRM-related data. 'Operational costs' are decreased by implementing core e-HRM practices, where all essential HRM information is unified, and administrative workload is reduced once automated processes are implemented. 'Improved HR service quality' is the result of 'relational e-HRM practices' that have been adopted from the traditional AMO model (Applebaum et al., 2000), including employee ability, motivation and opportunity enhancement practices. Lastly, a new transformational role of HRM is enacted through e-workforce analytics practice, which provides significant insights into the workforce and assists HR managers in increasing 'strategic capabilities' within the organization. Hence, three major e-HRM practices – core, relational and strategic – are shaped to serve different goals of e-HRM and create value for multinational organizations.

Research Context and Sample

Complex e-HRM systems are primarily designed for large organizations that involve ample resources and capital. The study presented in this chapter focuses on multinational corporations based in Lithuania, where growth tendencies are observed. A multinational company in this study is defined as a multinational corporation (MNC) that owns and controls the production of goods and services in at least one country other than its home country. It typically has business units in different countries and a centralized global head office where global management – including HRM – is coordinated. As reported by the Lithuanian Department of Statistics, in the year 2015, 3,938 organizations in Lithuania were controlled by foreign entities, and this number continues to grow (Statistics Lithuania, 2017). Driven by the aim to analyse multinational profit-oriented companies, a purposive sampling technique was used, when participants are selected based on predefined criteria relevant to a particular research question (Mack et al., 2005). A multinational company in this study was required to meet one specific criterion – to have adopted at least one e-HRM practice in its organization. For result validity purposes, companies in different sectors were selected. In order to embrace the most significant aspect of an in-depth interview – the qualifications of the interviewee (Neelankavil, 2007; Rowley, 2012) – interviewees from each organization were selected based on their position, knowledge and experience in adoption and integration of e-HRM in their organizations. The sample size was increased until saturation point was reached and collected information became repetitive. In sum, interviews with 13 HRM managers, each representing a different company, were conducted in 2017.

Three firms (Alpha, Beta, Gamma) operated in the IT sector, delivering advertising technology, computer technology and IT consulting, software and hardware solutions for transport telematics. One firm (Delta) operated in the energy sector with a focus on oil and gas products. Four multinational companies (Epsilon, Zeta, Eta, Theta) were from the financial sector, representing banks and credit management companies. One MNC (Sigma) operated in the professional services sector, delivering insurance, tax, consulting and advisory services. Two firms (Iota and Kappa) operated in the consumer staples sector – food processing, food and beverage retail. One company (Upsilon) was based in the transportation sector, distributing commercial vehicles and trucks as well as providing repair and maintenance services. Finally, one multinational company (Omega) operated in the consumer discretionary field, offering translation services worldwide and other business solutions (see Appendix Table 9.A.1).

Research Instrument

The structured interviews were composed of three parts. First, an interview would begin with two introductory questions about the particular systems that organizations used for different e-HRM practices. To derive a pattern about the trends of the systems, it was inquired what systems the companies used specifically and how long e-HRM had been implemented. The second part of the interview focused on how each process (operational, relational, strategic-transformational) created value for the multinational organization. The third part comprised questions intended to measure whether e-HRM practices contributed to e-HRM value outcome and if it did, how. In order to compare traditional versus e-HRM practices, interviewees were asked to measure how HRM practices improved or were weakened after installing e-HRM based on a Stapel scale. The interviewees indicated how valuable each of the practices was on a scale from -3 to $+3$ (0 indicating traditional HRM), pointing at the direction and weight of change after e-HRM practice was implemented, as well as the advantages and disadvantages in value creation through e-HRM.

FINDINGS

The collected data revealed that different systems for different practices of e-HRM are being used by multinational companies, including, for example, Workday, Oracle Platform, Kenexa, My Work-Life, and People Soft, while companies that have been using e-HRM practices for many years have migrated from older to more advanced systems. A high number of system alternatives available for e-HRM practices indicate intense competition in the market. Interestingly, most HRM specialists could not specify or recall the duration of e-HRM application in their companies. As they indicated, companies have been using electronic HRM for many years, moving from older to newer, more advanced solutions. This finding may denote that the usage of electronic HRM for large, profit-oriented multinational corporations, having many employees worldwide, is a routine practice.

An investigation into potential operational cost reduction for multinational companies due to the usage of e-core HRM confirmed that the majority of interviewees (10 out of 13) agree that e-core HRM contributes to operational cost reduction within their organizations. Time and resource efficiency were outlined as the main advantages/benefits. Managers noticed that less time and human resources were required due to process automation, such as the delivery of automatic approvals, or electronic documentation. Another highlighted advantage was the key HRM data being stored in one place enabling companies to monitor, plan, conveniently edit HRM-related data and report accurately. Two organizations (Kappa and Omega) specifically found the possible integration with other Enterprise Resource Planning (ERP) systems to be valuable. All of these factors contribute to operational cost reduction and HRM specialists agreed that in future, a new, more advanced, innovative Workday system, which would likely reduce operational costs, would be employed. Interestingly, all interviewees highlighted some challenges while using e-core HRM despite not questioning the value added to operational cost reduction. Companies agreed that e-core HRM adoption required large primary investments. It also took significant time resources for learning to use the e-HRM tools and exploit their functions to the full. Nevertheless, all interviewees stressed that advantages outweighed the challenges.

Based on the research results, 12 out of 13 companies have shifted to e-recruitment and selection. The interviewees pointed out that these solutions improve the quality of HRM. Among the most noticeable benefits of e-recruitment and selection, the managers emphasize that, primarily, e-recruitment and selection offer easy and convenient tracking, monitoring, and streaming of the entire process. HR recruiters can filter and rank candidates according to organizational needs and communicate the open positions. Also, e-recruitment and selection solutions enable them to track if individual HR recruitment task execution is in line with the predefined timeline and stay notified about upcoming deadlines. Another great advantage seen by the interviewees is a large database of potential candidates. This e-HRM practice provides historical information and options for reviewing candidate profiles in the future when a similar position is vacant. Sigma and Epsilon managers additionally highlight that e-recruitment and selection help to reduce the amount of manual work since automatic letters of notification and candidate pools are created by default. As a result, e-recruitment and selection can speed up communication with potential candidates. Finally, Alpha, Gamma and Omega companies appreciated that multiple stakeholders can be engaged in the process. For example, managers also have access to the electronic forms and can track and monitor if the new member has already been added to the team, as well as leave feedback. These benefits can ensure fast and effective coordination of the recruitment and selection process.

However, companies pointed to some challenges as well. Alpha outlined that this particular electronic practice is lacking analytical tools for the applicant. Hence, it is hard to conduct proper reporting. Sigma stressed out that the human factor cannot be eliminated from the process, as assessment results might be affected by external factors, and only one HR team member could observe the potential of the candidate. Iota, Kappa and Theta have recorded numerous IT issues, which sometimes can interrupt the process. Given the above, companies are still satisfied with the electronic recruitment and selection, as it secures the safety of candidates' personal data and increases transparency throughout the process. The average score given for the value created while using this e-HRM practice was 2.5 out of 3.

According to the research results, companies agree that e-training and development improve HR service quality (Alpha is not using this practice). Multinational corporations mostly value flexibility, ease and convenience of e-training and development platforms. Employee potential can be developed individually since they can enrol in specific training according to their needs and choose from a wide range of courses, webinars and other types of learning. As confirmed by Sigma, Iota, and Omega, it significantly reduces costs in comparison to face-to-face training. What is more, Sigma, Beta, Zeta and Eta signified the convenience of learning since learning materials were accessible anytime and anywhere. Interestingly, Theta mentioned that electronic practice was valuable for industry learning activities that were mandatory in their organization, including training based on the company values and navigating the employees in the industry and the field. From an HRM perspective, electronic learning and development allowed easy and convenient tracking of employee progress, as indicated by Zeta and Sigma, which was also one of the milestones discussed during the further performance stages. In sum, flexible, adaptable and convenient opportunities for employee development seem to be the company top priority nowadays.

On the other hand, Kappa only noted the value of e-training at the beginning of employment, whereas it is not claimed to be effective in further stages. Likewise, other interviewees noted that online classrooms, webinars and online conferences would never replace the value gained from face-to-face training. Sigma mentioned that, in particular, e-learning could not be effective for particular topics, such as soft skills, and sales training. The reason behind this was that such training required personal coaching, knowledge sharing and face-to-face feedback and it was challenging for the companies to find the balance in budget between electronic and face-to-face training. Nevertheless, the average score for these practices was 2.2 out of 3, indicating that organizations were satisfied with the e-learning opportunities.

The findings revealed that 10 out of 13 multinational companies used electronic performance management practice at work, and they increased HRM quality. Companies admitted that the progress of their workforce could be evaluated and monitored in the system. As Delta, Beta and Iota noted, user access, granted for employees and managers, enabled them to edit goals, mark their progress and complete status, once achieved. Sigma emphasized the fact that it is a more accurate and faster way to gather data for career growth. Iota also valued the transparency of this e-HRM practice that permits historical records, tracking and analysis of workforce performance. Likewise, Sigma mentioned that with the help of electronic performance management, the business could compare the results with other target groups. Gamma also reported tracking key performance management indicators during the year. Furthermore, as mentioned by Beta, feedback about job performance could be gathered from different stakeholders, which also added more validity to performance evaluation. Given these points, companies could gain adequate insights into employee growth.

However, some uncertainties about electronic performance management were still present. For example, Iota questioned the quality of performance evaluation as employees lacked discipline and commitment to the e-performance management process. They often forgot to update the status of their goals and make them accurate in the first place. Similarly, Beta noted that achievement of goals could be hardly measurable, such as in innovations. Another concern, expressed by Sigma, related to the feedback collection, which still needs to be face-to-face in order to promote personal growth. Hence, electronic performance management could sometimes lack validity. In the Alpha case, the company did not see any value from e-performance management as they still relied on traditional practice and most of the work had to be done in Excel, not in the separate e-compensation system. Given the above-mentioned challenges and taking into account the benefits, the average score for e-performance management was 2 (slightly below the average compared to other e-HRM practices).

As for e-compensation, 77 per cent of the interviewees indicated that it improved HRM quality. The majority of the companies noted that due to e-compensation practice, human errors were avoided and data accuracy increased substantially. Also, Delta, Sigma, Beta, Zeta, Omega and Theta benefited from automated processes, including automatic estimations of compensation, salaries, overtime and bonuses, while the manual workload was reduced. Finally, the e-compensation was valuable since it helped the management to plan and track compensation budget (for Sigma, Beta, Upsilon and Omega) and inform the employees about the compensation decisions being made (for Delta and Omega).

Among other benefits, automatic workflows were triggered and sent to HR for approvals, when compensation-related data was being changed. Then, notifications were made about the upcoming need to edit employment contracts. As Sigma, Eta and Omega indicated, due to the e-compensation solution, the process was much faster and daily routines of compensation planning were better operationalized. What is more, the HR representative from Delta mentioned that great value was added since electronic compensation could be integrated with different ERP systems, for example finance and material management.

However, some challenges were being faced by Alpha. Even though automated workflows were helpful, this company could not use an e-compensation practice since it did not take into consideration differences in the national laws regarding payroll. Hence, the company was forced to hire external consultants to work on estimation and payroll creation for different branches located globally. As for Epsilon, they did not see any value added for HRM quality, naming their electronic compensation practice as 'standard' and not customized to their business needs. Meanwhile, for the rest of the analysed companies, e-compensation was a time-saving IT solution for HRM team members (with an average score of 2.2 out of 3).

Based on the data, it is important to notice that only two companies of the research sample used electronic workforce analytics (Zeta and Theta). Zeta had introduced this e-HRM practice but had not started to use it yet, so could not comment on the actual value being added. They did believe that in the future this would allow gathering meaningful insights for the workforce. Iota, based in Lithuania, did not have access to workforce analytics due to being in a small market, but such e-HRM practice is used on a global scale. As for companies Zeta and Theta, this tool allowed gathering insights faster and more efficiently. As a result, much time was saved due to less manual work, also facilitating decision making, when data-based strategic decisions need to be taken. Interestingly, two firms – Alpha and Delta – had especially emphasized the need for such e-HRM practice. They noticed that major analysis was carried out manually and was time-consuming. As Delta suggested, it would be very helpful to have such an e-practice full of analytical tools that promote data-driven decisions.

Interestingly, Zeta noticed some challenges as well. Firstly, some analytical tools were too advanced and required time to learn. Therefore, some employees preferred traditional and much simpler methods of deriving some data. Secondly, the insights derived from the e-workforce analytics were still hardly trusted by managers related to some data inconsistency occurring from time to time and evoked by multiple reasons varying from lack of knowledge to technology-related problems. Hence, e-workforce analytics was still making its way to broad recognition, as it involved learning and high initial investment. In the long term, companies, however, tend to acknowledge the advantages and used workforce data strategically to drive business impact (the average score for this type of electronic HRM solution is 1.3).

Finally, all interviewees were asked if they agreed that electronic human resource management created value for multinational companies, and if yes, how that value was created. Key insights from each interview are outlined below.

Alpha. The interviewee agreed with the statement, stating that time efficiency, communication efficiency, optimization of data and its accuracy achieved through e-HRM solutions were highly valuable to the company. According to Alpha, e-HRM also helped to make valid decisions based on actual data analysis. As the representative noted, even though HRM was about people, today's business was focusing on numbers. In order to have these numbers, data must have been presented in the most convenient way that was offered by e-HRM.

Delta. The interviewee agreed with the statement. The key message heard from its HRM representative was that HRM was getting more digitalized every day and she believed that big data-driven solutions and artificial intelligence were the future of e-HRM.

Beta. The interviewee agreed with the statement. For the company, e-HRM was a great solution due to time and cost-efficiency. Less technical work was required from the HRM team, more accurate data and analysis were available, and historical information was also stored in one place. That helped them a lot in budgeting and organizational strategic planning.

Epsilon. The interviewee agreed with the statement as e-HRM brought additional value in the light of large numbers of employees and complex organizational structures in different countries. E-HRM aided in coordination of every process, from recruitment and selection activities to performance management. Employee-friendly interface, easy usage, availability of data and fast access to it were the most valuable features of e-HRM.

Iota. The interviewee partially agreed with the statement. On a global scale, process management, efficient measurement and cost-effectiveness were highly valuable. According to the interviewee, e-HRM was the right way to transmit a consistent message, common benchmarks, knowledge transfer, and analysis. For small markets like Lithuania, HRM required a lot of work outside the e-HRM practices that ultimately raised questions about benefits and value added to the local business unit.

Kappa concluded that a key benefit for the company was the ability to update all information about candidates and current employees in one place.

Automation of processes, a smaller number of employees needed, and integration with other ERP solutions, such as supply chain management, were also considered to be highly valuable for this company.

Gamma. According to the interviewee, e-HRM undoubtedly created value. It saved time, resources and costs. Also, the practices were especially valuable for the HR department as the majority of the work involved sensitive employee information. Hence, Gamma highly valued the option to limit access to specific information for particular users.

Zeta. The interviewee agreed with the statement. According to the company, the more processes were standardized and automated, the more time the HRM team had to focus on other areas like analysis, insights, and strategic planning that were more beneficial rather than recording information manually. As the HRM representative from Zeta noted, each improvement of the e-HRM practice reduced manual work, and saved much time as there are many workflows triggered in HRM processes. In other words, the less the company was involved in daily manual operations execution, the more it could focus on strategic planning and analysis.

Upsilon. The interviewee partially supported the statement. The HR consultant from Upsilon noted that single e-HRM by itself did not add additional value for them. However, if all e-HRM practices were integrated, then the value would obviously have been created.

Omega. The interviewee strongly agreed with the statement that e-HRM created value for multinational organizations. In the interviewee's opinion, some of the e-HRM benefits for international organizations were that the HR function could be more efficient, improve service delivery and facilitate its transformation into a more strategic role. Also, e-HRM allowed HR staff to spend more time on research about how to support the organization in achieving its business strategy.

Eta. The interviewee agreed with the statement: e-HRM created value for the organization through improving service quality to employees by increasing the speed of HRM operations. E-HRM improved accuracy and reduced errors in data and it was safer for keeping records. Finally, it substantially helped in generating reports and conducting analysis based on any type of information about the workforce. As a result, the HR department benefits from more time available to focus on strategic HR issues.

Theta. The company agreed with the statement: e-HRM enabled the company to avoid manual mistakes, saved time, costs and resources, made processes more transparent and created an opportunity for employees and clients to develop, as they were all engaged in e-HRM ongoing development.

The summary of the final results suggests that interviewees agreed with the statement that e-HRM practices and solutions have created value for them (2.1 out of 3). The most valuable e-HRM practice was electronic recruitment and selection. Except for Upsilon, which did not use this solution, all companies had given scores of 2 or 3. The least valuable practice with the average score of 1.3 was workforce analytics – only three companies used it. The highest scores for electronic HRM solutions were given by Omega and Eta, which had evaluated the e-HRM practices they used as very valuable (average score is 3). The lowest score was given by Iota (average score is 1) possibly related to the fact that Lithuania was considered a small market and that the access to e-HRM practices was very restricted. However, the HRM representative from Iota did see the value of these solutions on a global scale.

DISCUSSION

Even though the HRM role has dramatically changed over the past decades, the HRM priority is to administer employee information. As Thomas et al. (2001) suggest, the key role for HR managers is to administer information regarding time-off, and monitor employee size, number of external workers, consultants, temporary and part-time employees. Also, HR practitioners need to keep a record of operational data concerning the employees – their personal data, employment-related data, track assignment history, work location, career plans and availability for job redeployment or reassignment. Such key HRM activities place a high administrative burden on HR management, which, according to estimates by Snell et al. (2001), constitutes approximately 75 per cent of HRM workload. To decrease operational costs and gain an edge over its competitors, organizations are forced to invest in new technologies and solutions. In this way, traditional human resource management regarding administrative and transactional functions of HRM has gradually shifted to electronic human resource management for HRM administration activities, called e-core HRM.

Introduction of e-core HRM decreases the administrative burden on HR management to a great extent. As noted by Olivas-Lujan et al. (2007, p. 418), 'automation of HRM tasks and practices is replacing traditional paper-and-pencil, labour-intensive HRM tasks, into efficient, fast-response activities'. The findings of this study allude to the reduction in HRM administrative functions also outlined by a number of authors (Imperatori, 2014). The managers acknowledged the value being created through process automation, reduced number of employees needed, accessibility of employee data using one large database, reduced time and workload on administrative tasks and materials required for managing core HR activities. Nevertheless, while a relatively low status of the HRM field is sometimes recognized (Imperatori, 2014), the decrease in the administrative part should not be associated with a decreasing capacity, but rather with the newly opening perspectives for advancing the HRM potential as a key player in organizational strategy. As Panos and Bellou

(2016) noted, e-HRM can play a facilitating role in achieving transformational outcomes in the context of strategic change.

However, some challenges regarding e-core HRM are still noticeable in the findings of both previous and the presented studies. Chapman and Webster (2003) and Martin and Reddington (2010) notice that electronic HRM demands high initial investments, both in terms of employee training and the implementation itself. In Beta's case, the company did not see any value of e-core HRM at the moment, since they only started using this e-HRM practice a few months ago and it was currently raising more questions than adding benefits for operational activities. Therefore, HRM representatives from Beta noticed that extensive training was required for both employees and HRM staff. However, in the future, the company was expecting to reduce administrative burdens and save operational costs.

As for other challenges, Olivas-Lujan et al. (2007) argue that e-HRM is a growing tendency and one day it might become universalized under the dual impact of globalization and technology for firms willing to compete worldwide. It is beneficial that e-HRM is standardized to support process automation. However, country-specific attributes should also be considered. Taking these challenges into account, cost savings due to e-core HRM stem from automation and reducing the administrative burden on HRM, and, as previous research shows (Hawking et al., 2004; Ruël et al., 2007; Strohmeier, 2007), in the long run, e-core HRM can reduce operation costs to multinational organizations. These observations also correspond to empirical research results showing that 77 per cent of multinational firms acknowledged the fact that e-core HRM reduced operational costs for them.

E-Recruitment and Selection

Based on the traditional AMO model, ability-enhancing practices like recruitment and selection should be designed in a way to develop and attain the best employees for a position. Likewise, Oswal and Narayanappa (2014) argue that to attract the best possible candidate with a required set of skills and competencies for the position, traditional recruitment based on local paper advertisements, local employment office postings, and word-of-mouth has been replaced by web-based technologies. Nowadays, candidates are mainly hired through specialized internet-based job posting boards or company web pages. Likewise, the power of social media should not be forgotten, as shown by Olivas-Lujan et al. (2007). As Analoui (2007) notes, such modern electronic recruitment methods provide global coverage and ensure that the best possible candidate can be reached regardless of his or her current location as web-based technologies have no international boundaries.

With the introduction of e-recruitment and selection, the expectations have been set high. Analoui (2007) argues that electronic HRM practice for recruitment and selection should centralize and standardize record-keeping of potential candidates. Indeed, based on the research findings from 13 companies that use this e-HRM solution, 10 of them agree that high value is created due to the ease of tracking, storing and monitoring applicant data. Among other key advantages, firms notice that HR recruiters can shortlist candidates based on scoring, ranking and feedback gathered from many stakeholders, quickly start advertising the newly vacant position and schedule global video interviews. This corresponds to Analoui's (2007) observation that e-recruitment and selection allow better targeting, making identification of applicants more accurate. What is more, managers agree that e-recruitment and selection help to reduce the amount of manual work since automatic letters of notification and candidate pools are created by default. As a result, this electronic practice fosters communication among potential candidates. As Analoui (2007) points out, such efficiency in cost and time due to the automation of the staff requisition creation and approval process reduces the opportunity costs of not filling a position. All in all, HRM representatives noticed value being added as such functionalities and capabilities empowered HRM service quality.

Interestingly, one of the main observations from empirical research is that e-recruitment and selection might be inefficient in terms of volume and quality (Analoui, 2007). According to Analoui (2007), it is believed that for recruitment specialists, it takes time to sort out targeted applicants. Also, high storage capacity is required to keep all applicants' information. What is more, it is expected that the increased reach of potential candidates might lower the overall quality of candidates. However, as mentioned by managers, this electronic practice had highly effective scanning tools and reduced the workload for HR. Also, as noticed by Gamma, the high number of applicants allowed having a rich database of candidates that would be valuable in the future when future positions need to be filled. Therefore, managers confirmed that electronic practices for recruitment and selection were valuable as HRM service quality was increased due to the factors mentioned above.

E-Training and Development

As the traditional AMO model states, extensive training is needed to ensure that an employee has the required skills and competencies to do his or her job (Fu et al., 2013). The impetus to shift towards electronic training and development has increased due to issues associated with traditional training. As Pfeffer (1994) notes, traditional face-to-face training has been criticized for being too costly, inconvenient, and not customizable. Indeed, the majority of companies mentioned that key value was added by electronic training since it is an economical and fast way of learning which can be accessible all the time and everywhere. Beta managers valued a wide scope of thoughtfully designed courses available that allowed each employee to choose learning material according to their diverse learning styles. In fact, as noticed by Andriotis (2016), one of the main goals of e-learning is to offer an individualized learning experience that claims lower costs and ensures a self-paced learning environment.

Another great advantage of web-based training is that it can measure employee progress more effectively (Analoui, 2007). However, Beta challenged this theoretical proposition by saying that some globally set measurement indicators were very hard to implement and measure on a local scale, like, for example, innovation. This also suggests that electronic learning requires a great deal of self-direction and discipline in order to be successful (Andriotis, 2016). However, traditional methods may not be always less effective in comparison to electronic solutions. As mentioned by managers, the value gained from face-to-face training was much higher for some particular types of training, including those dedicated to empowering employee soft skills, or sales training. Foster (2009), for example, claims that such training is based on real-time responsiveness, peer-to-peer live learning, coaching, and on-the-spot feedback provided by instructors. It is considered as a direct, dynamic and social activity. Meanwhile, online training is effective on a bigger scale, as a large employee base across multiple locations can join and attend the same training. To sum up, even though empirical findings signify that online training cannot replace all forms of traditional e-learning, yet, it is still providing flexibility, consistency and assessment that are greatly valued by multinational companies.

E-Compensation

Stemming from the traditional AMO model, employee motivation can be increased in a variety of ways. As Munteanu (2014) notes, a motivating compensation system can escalate workforce performance and contribute to better overall organizational results. Traditional ways of managing compensation, as argued by Wright (2003), have been varying, static and arduous in nature. Separate spreadsheets used for each employee only focused on employee tasks and duties and provided information only on a 'need-to-know' basis. Hence, companies began developing compensation practice based on a business strategy that would enable the identification of key characteristics of jobs through job analysis (Munteanu, 2014). As a result, a gradual shift from traditional to electronic practice has taken place. The companies involved in the presented study also have followed this trend.

As noted in the existing literature, the compensation process can be facilitated in several ways due to e-compensation. Among major benefits, first of all, an electronic e-HRM solution helps to collect job analysis data and determine the relative worth associated with jobs (Dulebohn and Marler, 2005; Stone et al., 2006). Correspondingly, Beta managers value to a great extent the opportunity to plan and track compensation budget. As Munteanu (2014) observes, in later stages, data gathered on compensation can be turned into evaluation points and integrated with a labour market and this process, in turn, creates a framework for pay grades and establishes pay levels at the organizational level. As a result, e-compensation creates the impetus for HR practitioners to develop budgets, monitor the determinants of incentives, and foster the fairness of salary allocation decisions.

What is more, electronic HRM for compensation allows communicating information regarding employee benefits and payroll more effectively. Research by Gueutal and Falbe (2005) shows that people are not always familiar with the benefits that they are eligible for. What is valuable in such e-HRM practice is that employees can choose benefit plans online and track their compensation-related data, ensuring transparency within the organization with regards to compensation-related information. Such academic findings correspond to the research findings to a great extent: the managers mentioned that e-compensation ensured the accuracy of data, speeded up communication and kept employees updated regarding financial and non-financial compensation. Hence, a greater level of transparency could be ensured that, in turn, increased procedural, distributive, informational and interpersonal justice within the organization.

However, Alpha managers recognized some e-compensation issues. They noticed that such e-HRM practice lacked the ability to be customized and found it hard to calculate benefits and pay for different branches of the company located globally. Hence, in Alpha's case, the company was forced to hire an external consultant and did not use e-HRM internally. As a response to the customizability issue, academic literature notices some challenges for e-HRM. The key idea of e-HRM practices is to centralize and globalize HRM processes. However, differences and inconsistencies in countries' laws regarding compensation make it very complex to standardize. A high level of customizability is required, which essentially increases overall costs of e-compensation development and maintenance for the firm. As a result, some companies opt to outsource this practice of e-HRM.

All in all, the studied companies agreed that e-compensation outweighs these challenges and increases HR service quality, indicating that multinational organizations were collectively moving towards modernized compensation solutions. From emerging literature, it becomes more evident that by clarifying expectations towards benefits and salary, using compensation structures to support changing business needs, and aligning them to business strategies, HR can achieve more with compensation planning than ever before.

E-Performance Management

Derived from the AMO model, the traditional paper-based appraisal process is becoming obsolete. As study findings showed, 10 out of 13 firms were using this e-HRM solution and nine of them firmly agreed that e-performance management helped to increase HRM service quality.

According to Cardy and Miller (2005), such a web-based HRM solution enables HR and line managers to evaluate employee performance, write reviews and collect feedback about their subordinates. Likewise, among most answers gathered from HR representatives, the main benefit was the opportunity to monitor and edit employee goals and track their performance. Also, employees could be empowered as they engage in their performance tracking; they could set up their own goals and make suggestions on how their performance and career path could be elevated within the organization. Another interesting finding corresponding to academic literature is that e-performance management allows collecting feedback from different stakeholders that is especially perceived as valuable by Beta. In the same way, Gueutal and Falbe (2005) find that 360° feedback is empowered through IT-enabled performance management, as emails asking to assess the employee are sent to multiple raters. Later, the data can be merged and results analysed in order to collect in-depth recommendations for future career growth.

However, literature, as well as our empirical research findings, observes one of the key challenges in terms of e-performance management. As Stone et al. (2006) argue, such e-HRM practice is still not able to measure all aspects of employee behaviours that are required for an organization to be successful. What is more, electronic performance management has little or no capacity to evaluate organizational citizenship and collaboration. Academic literature and empirical findings show the same concerns. In particular, Beta mentioned that some achievements of goals were hardly measurable, like team innovation, and could not depict the real progress of an employee. Also, managers emphasized face-to-face feedback, as it was, according to the company, vital for personal growth, and could not be replaced by technologies. At the same time, firms seemed to value the control given by e-performance management towards employee behaviour that allowed ensuring its alignment with organizational goals.

Strategic-Transformational Domain

From a strategic human resource management point of view, HRM activities should be planned to enable a company to achieve its business goals and objectives (Analoui, 2007). This perspective suggests that the workforce is nowadays treated as a core element for achieving a competitive advantage over competitors. The strategic response to unprecedented external and internal factors that affect business is needed. Indeed, all HRM specialists in our empirical research have indicated that nowadays management is expecting HRM to be more engaged in the formulation of corporate strategy and act as a business partner towards achieving organizational goals. Hence, to empower decision making, HRM is pressured to base its propositions on real data analysis using various forms of analytical tools, in line with the finding that the strategic orientation of the HR function can be considered a prerequisite for e-HRM embracement by the organization (Lazazzara and Galanaki, 2018).

In light of the emerging business need for powerful analytical tools to gather in-depth insights, e-workforce analytics is being developed. As scholars observe, the implications of such electronic practice are significant in terms of acquiring and retaining a valuable talent pool, identifying requisite skills and knowledge, developing strategies for workforce reductions, retraining or succession (Olivas-Lujan et al., 2007; Sutcliffe, 2017; Torres-Coronas and Arias-Oliva, 2011). Referring to our empirical research results, there was a strong consensus among interviewees with respect to the importance of electronic HR analytics. However, there was a notable gap between the importance placed on e-HRM analytics and the actual results within organizations: Beta had only recently deployed this practice. Given the advantages of a faster and more efficient way of gathering insights and the reduced amount of manual work required, companies still found it challenging to use e-workforce analytics. Based on expert opinions, electronic workforce analytical tools were too advanced and required considerable time investments in learning. Therefore, some managers preferred traditional methods over the modern approach to derive data. Another problem was that the insights gathered by the electronic tools were still hardly trusted by managers. This was due to some data inconsistencies occurring from time to time. Nevertheless, companies, as well as scholars, are confident about how well-informed decisions play an essential role in implementing successful business response to competition, and for that, a consistent analytical point of reference is inevitable.

MANAGERIAL IMPLICATIONS

Deployment of e-core HRM requires large primary investments and a steep learning curve. Hence, extensive training for HRM personnel and employees is required in order to be able to exploit the opportunities of this e-HRM practice to the full.

Some aspects should be taken into account by the management regarding e-recruitment and selection. First of all, based on HRM experts' opinion, the human factor cannot be eliminated from the process, because sometimes the results of evaluations might be affected by external factors, and only the HRM team member could observe the potential of the candidate. Hence, e-recruitment and selection should allow capturing valuable feedback from HR and should not eliminate face-to-face interaction. Secondly, companies are still facing IT issues. Hence, 24/7 IT support should be ensured for HRM practitioners.

For some topics, e-learning is not effective (soft skills training, sales training), as personal coaching, knowledge sharing, and face-to-face feedback are very important. Hence, HR managers should request more functionalities from e-learning and development that would allow using video conferencing infrastructure and ensuring instant connectivity to subject matter experts to be able to gather valuable, on-the-spot feedback and coaching.

Some companies still find it challenging to integrate differences in countries' laws regarding payroll. Adding more capabilities to customize e-compensation would be valuable to multinational companies. Hence, additional investments should be considered by the management.

HR managers noticed that achievement of goals could be hard to measure. Hence, it is recommended for organizations to decide on SMART goals that would be specific, measurable, achievable, relevant, and time-bound. This would allow e-performance management to be more accurate and precise.

A data-driven mind-set is essential in the successful integration of e-workforce analytics. Hence, it is important to organize meetings and put emphasis on a common organizational approach towards acceptance of data-driven decision making that is empowered by insightful e-workforce analytics. Meanwhile, this e-HRM practice itself could be more user-friendly and less complex to use.

All in all, management of organizations should continue improving HRM processes and upgrade systems for e-HRM practices accordingly, train employees on how to use the systems, and provide instant technical help for them.

CONCLUSIONS

With the fast-changing environment of the business world and intense competition, managers are constantly pressured with innovation adoption decisions. To stay competitive, e-HRM has emerged as an innovation in managing people, as it reduces the administrative burden on HRM personnel, increases

HRM quality and enhances strategic capabilities of HRM (Analoui, 2007; Foster, 2009; Ruël et al., 2007; Strohmeier, 2007). However, emerging academic literature on e-HRM lacks an integrative multi-level theory on e-HRM (Marler and Fisher, 2013; Ruël and Van der Kaap, 2012). Literature highlights the recent shift from traditional human resource management to e-HRM. Electronic core HRM has replaced traditional operational activities of HRM regarding information request handling, workforce administration, and time management. Relational activities of HRM such as recruitment and selection, training and development, compensation and performance management have shifted to electronic practices like e-recruitment and selection, e-training and development, e-compensation and e-performance management. From the emerging literature, it is noticeable that HRM business partners become more engaged in the formulation of corporate strategy, and for them, a consistent analytical point of reference is needed to ground their decisions influencing overall business performance. For this, e-workforce analytics has been developed. All these e-HRM practices have formulated a conceptual research model, aiming to test how valuable each of them is with regard to operational cost reduction, improved HRM quality and increased strategic capability.

The research conducted with HRM professionals from multinational companies operating in Lithuania showed the strong and positive value of using e-HRM. The managers firmly agree with the statement that e-HRM creates value for them, with e-recruitment and selection being the most valuable and e-performance management being the weakest e-HRM practice. However, companies also see some challenges including less social interaction and a steep learning curve in using such electronic practices for managing people. In sum, e-core HRM is considered valuable, primarily, through the decreased administrative burden on HRM, increased reporting capabilities, a large database of employees' records, process automation and a reduced amount of paperwork, materials and equipment needed. As for e-recruitment and selection, it provides ease of tracking, monitoring, and streaming the entire process, reduces manual workload, fosters communication, safely stores information about job candidates and ensures accurate evaluation by many stakeholders. Furthermore, e-training and development is greatly valued by the companies due to the wide scope of training available to employees at all times and everywhere, the ability to monitor and track progress, and reduced costs for employee training. E-compensation provides more accurate data and process automation and helps managers to plan and track compensation budget. Meanwhile, e-performance management is valuable for its functionalities to monitor and edit employee goals, evaluate employee progress, accurately gather data regarding career growth within the organization and collect performance evaluations from different stakeholders.

Finally, e-workforce analytics empowers HRM professionals to gather insights about the workforce and make more accurate decisions based on real-time data. To sum up, these main advantages help multinational organizations to decrease operational costs, improve HR service quality and enhance the strategic capabilities of HRM. Research findings also indicate perceived difficulties of using e-HRM. The main challenges are that multinational organizations lack a data-driven mind-set towards workforce analytics. Also, even though it is beneficial that e-HRM is standardized and fosters process automation, country-specific attributes should also be considered. In addition, e-HRM requires instant technical IT support for all users so that HRM process flow does not stop.

In sum, there is emerging evidence that, nowadays, firms operating in highly competitive markets perceive the development of HRM strategy in alliance with corporate goals as essential. To be as cost-effective as possible, HRM business partners agree to dedicate as many HRM functions to e-HRM as possible and reduce human interaction. However, it seems that HRM can be overly focused on policy development, placing corporate objectives at the forefront. Ideally, individual values and goals should match with organizational objectives. Yet, assuring such consistency in practice is a daunting task that may result in conflicts between employees and HRM and have a detrimental effect on business performance. This problem ultimately raises a question as to what extent e-HRM can enable companies to manage people effectively. Nevertheless, innovative e-HRM seems to be vital for multinational companies to leverage competitive advantage in the global market and manage global HRM processes. For more than four decades, the increased number of multinational companies that have adopted e-HRM signifies that e-HRM technology is becoming more valuable and addresses the emerging trends of the digital workforce, providing an engaging and cohesive employee experience. With the growing e-HRM practices, HRM can finally pursue the role it has long been assigned – to foster organizational competitiveness as a strategic partner while effectively nurturing immediate relationships with employees through actual and virtual space simultaneously.

REFERENCES

Analoui, F. (2007), *Strategic Human Resource Management*, London: Thomson.
Andriotis, N. (2016), 'Online learning vs traditional formats: the big 4 benefits of elearning', accessed 20 October 2017 at http://www.efrontlearning.com.
Appelbaum, E., T. Bailey, P. Berg and A.L. Kalleberg (2000), *Manufacturing Advantage: Why High-Performance Work Systems Pay Off*, London: ILR Press.
Bondarouk, T., E. Parry and E. Furtmueller (2017), 'Electronic HRM: four decades of research on adoption and consequences', *International Journal of Human Resource Management*, 28(1), 98–131.

Buckley P., K. Minnette, D. Joy and J. Michaelis (2004), 'The use of an automated employment recruiting and screening system for temporary professional employees: a case study', *Human Resource Management*, 43(2/3), 233–241.

Bussler, L. and E. Davis (2001), 'Information systems: the quiet revolution in human resource management', *Journal of Computer Information Systems*, 42(2), 17–20.

Cardy, R.L. and J.S. Miller (2005), 'eHR and performance management: a consideration of positive potential and the dark side', in H.G. Gueutal and D.L. Stone (eds.), *The Brave New World of EHR: Human Resources Management in the Digital Age*, San Francisco: Jossey-Bass, 138–165.

Chapman, D.S. and J. Webster (2003), 'The use of technologies in the recruiting, screening, and selection processes for job candidates', *International Journal of Selection and Assessment*, 11, 113–120.

Conaton, S. (2014), 'Realizing the potential of strategic human resource management: employee self-advocacy in the information age', *Cornell HR Review*, accessed 25 October 2017 at http://digitalcommons.ilr.cornell.edu/chrr/68.

Deshwal, P. (2015), 'Role of e-HRM in organizational effectiveness and sustainability', *International Journal of Applied Research*, 1(12), 605–609.

Dulebohn, J.H. and J.H. Marler (2005), 'E-compensation: the potential to transform practice?', in H.G. Gueutal and D.L. Stone (eds.), *The Brave New World of EHR: Human Resources Management in the Digital Age*, San Francisco: Jossey-Bass, 166–189.

Foster, S. (2009), 'Making sense of e-HRM: technological frames, value creation and competitive advantage', Doctoral Dissertation, University of Hertfordshire.

Fu, N., P.C. Flood, J. Bosak, T. Morris and P. O'Regan (2013), 'Exploring the performance effect of HPWS on professional service supply chain management', *Supply Chain Management – An International Journal*, 18(3), 292–307.

Gardner, S., D. Lepak and K. Bartel (2003), 'Virtual HR: the impact of information technology on the human resource professional', *Journal of Vocational Behavior*, 63(2), 159–179.

Gueutal, H.G. and C.M. Falbe (2005), 'eHR: trends in delivery methods', in H.G. Gueutal and D.L. Stone (eds.), *The Brave New World of EHR: Human Resources Management in the Digital Age*, San Francisco: Jossey-Bass, 190–225.

Hawking P., A. Stein and S. Foster (2004), 'E-HR and employee self-service: a case study of a Victorian public sector organization', *Journal of Issues in Informing Science and Information Technology*, 1, 1019–1026.

Huselid, M.A., B.E. Becker and R.W. Beatty (2005), *The Workforce Scorecard: Managing Human Capital to Execute Strategy*, Boston, MA: Harvard Business School Press.

Huselid, M. A., S. Jackson and R.S. Schuler (1997), 'Technical and strategic human resource management effectiveness as determinants of HRM performance', *Academy of Management Journal*, 40(1), 171–188.

Imperatori, B. (2014), 'The unexpected side of relational e-HRM: developing trust in the HR department', *Employee Relations*, 36(4), 376–397.

Islam, M.S. (2016), 'Evaluating the practices of electronic human resources management (E-HRM) as a key tool of technology driven human resources management function in organizations: a comparative study in public sector and private sector enterprises of Bangladesh', *Journal of Business and Management*, 18(11), 1–8.

Johnson, R.D. and H.G. Gueutal (2011), 'Transforming HR through technology: the use of E-HR and HRIS in organizations', in *Society for Human Resource Management Effective Practice*, Guidelines Series, Alexandria, VA.

Kohansal, M.A., T. Sadegh and M. Haghsenas (2016), 'E-HRM: from acceptance to value creation', *Journal of Information Technology Management*, 27(1), 18–27.

Lazazzara, A. and E. Galanaki (2018), 'E-HRM adoption and usage: a cross-national analysis of enabling factors', in C. Rossignoli, F. Virili and S. Za (eds.), *Digital Technology and Organizational Change*, Cham: Springer, 125–140.

Mack, N., C. Woodsong, K.M. Macqueen, G. Guest and E. Namey (2005), 'Qualitative research methods overview', in Family Health International, *Qualitative Research Methods: A Data Collector's Field Guide*, North Carolina: Family Health International, 1–12.

Marler, J.H. and S.L. Fisher (2013), 'An evidence-based review of e-HRM and strategic human resource management', *Human Resource Management Review*, 23(1), 18–36.

Marler, J.H. and E. Parry (2016), 'Human resource management, strategic involvement and e-HRM technology', *International Journal of Human Resource Management*, 27(9), 2233–2253.

Martin, G. and M. Reddington (2010), 'Theorizing the links between e-HR and strategic HRM: a model, case illustration and reflections', *International Journal of Human Resource Management*, 21(10), 1553–1574.

Munteanu, A. (2014), 'What means high performance work practices for human resources in an organization?', *Annals of the University of Petrosani, Economics*, 14(1), 243–250.

Neelankavil, J. (2007), *International Business Research*, Armonk, NY: M.E. Sharpe.

Olivas-Lujan, M.R., J. Ramirez and L. Zapata-Cantu (2007), 'E-HRM in Mexico: adapting innovations for global competitiveness', *International Journal of Manpower*, 28(5), 418–434.

Oswal, N. and G.L. Narayanappa (2014), 'Evolution of HRM to E-HRM to achieve organizational effectiveness and sustainability', *International Journal of Recent Development in Engineering and Technology*, 2(4), 7–14.

Panos, S. and V. Bellou (2016), 'Maximizing e-HRM outcomes: a moderated mediation path', *Management Decision*, 54(5), 1088–1109.

Parry, E. (2011), 'An examination of e-HRM as means to increase the value of the HR function', *International Journal of Human Resource Management*, 22(5), 1146–1162.

Parry, E. and S. Tyson (2010), 'Desired goals and actual outcomes of e-HRM', *Human Resource Management Journal*, 21(3), 335–354.

Peretz, H. and E. Parry (2016), 'Impact of national culture on the use and outcomes of E-HRM', *Academy of Management Annual Proceedings*, article 10891.

Pfeffer, J. (1994). *Competitive Advantage Through People*, Boston, MA: Harvard Business School Press.

Rietsema, D. (2017), 'What is core HR? – HR payroll systems', accessed 25 October 2017 at https://www.hrpayrollsystems.net/core-hr/.

Rothwell, W.J. and H.C. Kazanas (1988), 'The workforce analyst', in *Strategic Human Resources Planning and Management*, Englewood Cliffs, NJ: Prentice Hall.

Rowley, J. (2012), 'Conducting research interviews', *Management Research Review*, 35(3/4), 260–271.

Ruël, H. and T. Bondarouk (2013), 'Introduction: Thematic issue on e-HRM in an international context: an emerging topic for research', *European Journal of International Management*, 7(4), 369–372.

Ruël, H., T. Bondarouk and M. Van der Vald (2007), 'The contribution of e-HRM to HRM effectiveness', *Employee Relations*, 29(3), 280–291.

Ruël, H. and H. Van der Kaap (2012), 'E-HRM usage and value creation: does a facilitating context matter?', *German Journal of Human Resource Management: Zeitschrift für Personalforschung*, 26(3), 260–281.

SAP SuccessFactors (2017), 'Increase the effectiveness and visibility of HR with human capital analytics', accessed 11 October 2017 at http://www.successfactors.com.

Schuler, R.S. and S.E. Jackson (2000), 'HR as a source of shareholder value', in R.S. Schuler and S.E. Jackson (eds.), *Strategic Human Resource Management*, Oxford: Blackwell.

Snell, S.A., D. Stueber and D.P. Lepak (2001), 'Virtual HR departments: getting out of the middle', paper presented at the School of Industrial and Labor Relations, Center for Advanced Human Resource Studies (CAHRS Working Paper #01-08), Ithaca, NY: Cornell University.

Statistics Lithuania (2017), 'Number of foreign-controlled enterprises', accessed 11 October 2017 at https://osp.stat.gov.lt/statistiniu-rodikliu-analize#/.

Stone, D.L., E.F. Stone-Romero and K. Lukaszewski (2006), 'Factors affecting the acceptance and effectiveness of electronic human resource systems', *Human Resource Management Review*, 16(2), 229–244.

Strohmeier, S. (2007), 'Research in e-HRM: review and implications', *Human Resource Management Review*, 17(1), 19–37.

Strohmeier, S. (2009), 'Concepts of e-HRM consequences: a categorisation, review and suggestion', *International Journal of Human Resource Management*, 20, 528–543.

Sutcliffe, S. (2017), 'Must-read HR analytics articles', accessed 5 January 2017 at https://www.visier.com/clarity/must-read-hr-analytics-articles-successful-2017/.

Thomas, S., M.R. Skitmore and T. Sharma (2001), 'Towards a human resource information system for Australian construction companies', *Engineering, Construction and Architectural Management*, 8(4), 238–249.

Torres-Coronas, T. and M. Arias-Oliva (2011), 'E-HRM challenges and opportunities', in *Encyclopedia of Human Resources Information Systems: Challenges in e-HRM*, Hershey, PA: Information Science Reference.

Wright, A. (2003), 'Tools for automating complex compensation programs', *Compensation & Benefits Review*, 35(6), 53–61.

APPENDIX

Table 9.A.1   *List of the respondents*

No.	Company Name	Sector
1.	Alpha	Information Technology
2.	Delta	Energy
3.	Sigma	Professional Services
4.	Beta	Information Technology
5.	Epsilon	Financials
6.	Iota	Consumer Staples
7.	Kappa	Consumer Staples
8.	Gamma	Information Technology
9.	Zeta	Financials
10.	Upsilon	Transportation
11.	Omega	Consumer Discretionary
12.	Eta	Financials
13.	Theta	Financials

10. Human resource management perspective on innovation

Daniel Paulino Teixeira Lopes

INTRODUCTION

As other chapters have pointed out, innovation is a complex phenomenon and requires multiple perspectives for its better understanding. Strategic and technological views on the development of new or significantly improved products and business processes (OECD, 2018) have provided essential viewpoints to analyze innovation. Furthermore, one can argue that combining technological and non-technological innovations is required to achieve sustainable competitive advantages and improve organizational performance (Cerne et al., 2016; Le Bas et al., 2015).

Advancing the 'classic literature' on technological innovation (Fagerberg et al., 2012), several works (e.g. Birkinshaw et al., 2008; Damanpour, 2014; Lam, 2005; Volberda et al., 2013) have sought to understand management innovation – a term that will be used here as a synonym for organizational innovation. Notably, the adoption of management activities and practices, management processes, and organizational structures that are new to the adopting organization should be seen as a management innovation, which differs concerning complexity and determinants from technological innovations.

Human resources-related factors can be regarded as an essential determinant either to technological innovation (Liu et al., 2017; Seeck and Diehl, 2017) or to management innovation (Birkinshaw et al., 2008; Crossan and Apaydin, 2010; Volberda et al., 2013). However, according to Laursen and Foss (2014), researchers should explore the relationship between human resources management (HRM) and different innovation types.

It is reasonable to recognize that there is a 'boom' in publications on this relationship (Ruël et al., 2014, p. 468). Indeed, researchers' interest in a more in-depth examination of the relationship between HRM practices and innovation is a recent phenomenon (Jackson et al., 2014; Laursen and Foss, 2014).

This chapter aims to explore innovation as both an inherent and an adjoining phenomenon to contemporary HRM. The guiding questions are (1) what innovation-focused HRM practices lead to what type of innovation (technological *versus* managerial), and (2) what are the characteristics of HRM innovations compared to other management innovations?

Thus, this chapter briefly discusses HRM practices that lead to innovative products and processes, as well as to new managerial activities and practices, management processes, and organizational structures. Then, management innovations – such as those in HRM – are conceptualized according to different realms and complexity levels. Empirically, the shreds of evidence on these issues are brought from a PhD thesis that examined whether HRM practices toward product and process innovation were also related to the adoption of management innovation (Lopes, 2017).

This chapter is organized into five further sections, including this introduction. The next two sections discuss the relationship between HRM and innovation, and the main categories for analyzing management innovation. The following section outlines the methodological procedures based on a survey of Brazilian organizations. In the fourth section, the results are provided and discussed based on a descriptive analysis of the survey data. In the last section, the final considerations are formulated, including limitations and recommendations for future studies.

INNOVATION AND HR CONFIGURATIONS

Human resources management can be regarded as a strategic capability (Kim and Lee, 2012) that may be difficult for other organizations to imitate. Each organization's HRM is path dependent, that is, it tends to evolve in its own way and follows unique historical conditions. Wright et al. (2008) claim that some capabilities are hard to imitate because of their causal ambiguity. Also, these authors note that inimitability arises from socially intricate resources or due to the long time it takes to imitate them.

In this theoretical perspective, the ability to manage human resources becomes strategic provided that it fosters unique sources of sustainable competitive advantage, for example, by nurturing innovation. Organizations should create, develop, combine and effectively exploit HRM capabilities in a singular way (Colbert, 2008). Ultimately, innovation in HRM (or "HRM innovation" as posed here) may bring heterogeneity to organizations to the point of leading them to different behaviors and performances.

Becker and Huselid (2006) argue that HRM models should support strategic business processes and ensure effective strategy implementation. More than one HR architecture – with practices that are universal, contingent or consistent vertically and horizontally (Delery and Doty, 1996) – may coexist in organizations (Becker and Huselid, 2006).

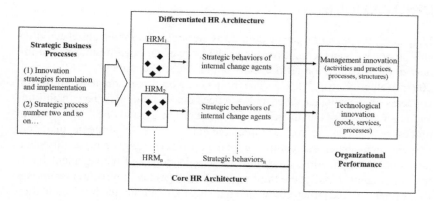

Figure 10.1   Relating HRM to different types of innovation

Figure 10.1 illustrates how HRM architecture can assimilate innovation. The three large blocks of this figure represent, from left to right, the organization's strategic business processes, the differentiated and core HR architectures, and organizational performance. The formulation and implementation of management innovation – and technological innovation-related strategies – are taken as strategic business processes. According to Becker and Huselid (2006), such processes are supported by specific practices underlying the common core of HR architecture. However, for each of those strategic business processes, different practices are required to prompt specific strategic behaviors. Such behaviors will lead to specific management innovation and technological innovation outcomes that are expected to contribute to organizational performance. Previous research has analyzed recruitment and retention, delegation of responsibility, employee training, internal communication, and incentives as HRM practices that mostly contribute to innovation and organizational performance (Laursen and Foss, 2014; Oke et al., 2012; Shipton et al., 2006; Wang and Zang, 2005). Positive effects can be strengthened when these practices are complementary – that is, consistent with each other (Laursen and Foss, 2003, 2014) – and systemic (Jiang et al., 2012; Jørgensen et al., 2011).

Indeed, the practices mentioned above may contribute to technological innovation as well as to management innovation. However, attention should also be paid to how innovative is human resources management. A broader perspective on innovation not only as an end but also as a means is required from scholars and practitioners. This concern is part of a rationale in which organizations seek competitive advantages based on the ability to improve or even reinvent their management.

REALMS AND COMPLEXITY OF MANAGEMENT INNOVATIONS

Management innovation can be defined as the adoption of managerial activities and practices, management processes, and organizational structures that are new to the organization (Birkinshaw et al., 2008; Damanpour, 2014; Hamel, 2007; Volberda et al., 2013). The first realm of a management innovation concerns changes in activities and practices due to new roles, responsibilities and other aspects of a manager's daily routine. The second one – management processes – refers to, for example, the introduction of strategic planning, knowledge management, capital budgeting, project management, quality management, re-engineering, recruitment and selection, and management information systems. Finally, the third realm of management innovation comprises new organizational structures, which may be, for example, the implementation of a matrix or projected structure, business units, departments, decentralization efforts and self-managed teams.

Therefore, management innovations differ not only from technological innovations but also from each other. On the one hand, it is important here to find connections between HRM and organizational structures, HRM and management processes, and among HRM and managerial activities and practices. In other words, it would not be feasible to make a generic connection between HRM and management innovation, since the latter is not a homogeneous phenomenon (Damanpour, 2014). By understanding the multiple realms of management innovations, HRM has the opportunity to expand its role within organizations – not only as an administration expert but also as a strategic business partner and change agent (Ulrich, 1998).

On the other hand, differently from supporting management innovations in diverse areas, it is crucial to recognize innovation in human resources management. Some researchers have analyzed HRM innovations, as can be seen in Agarwala (2003), Cristallini (2011), Kossek (1987), Lin (2011), Wolfe (1995) and Wolfe et al. (2006). From a historical perspective, Mol and Birkinshaw (2008) have identified the emergence, during the nineteenth century, of corporate well-being practices, professional managers, and corporate education systems as the main HRM innovations. The twentieth century saw the creation of pay-for-performance systems, assessment centers, T-groups, quality of life initiatives at work, mentoring and executive coaching, and 360-degree feedback. Virtually, these HRM innovations were all created by one or a few organizations and diffused over time (Mol and Birkinshaw, 2008).

As seen through these examples, it is clear that they vary regarding complexity, and the literature on management innovation has explored this issue (Volberda et al., 2013). The attributes that confer complexity to a management innovation are: adaptability (flexibility and variability), operational complexity (difficulty to use and implement), degree of novelty (radical or incremental, depending on the level of abandonment of what was previously done and past competencies), uncertain outcomes (lack of clarity between innovation and its results), tacit character, rarity (in the case of creation), and difficulty in replicating, protecting, testing, observing and identifying its limits (Damanpour, 2014; Mol and Birkinshaw, 2014; Rogers, 2003).

This brief discussion of the realms and complexity of management innovations is necessary to properly analyze their interface with human resources management, as can be seen in the next section, which shows the study methodology.

METHODOLOGY

This chapter is based on a survey conducted for doctoral research (Lopes, 2017). A new questionnaire (see Appendix Table 10.A.1) was developed because existing ones, mainly based on the *Oslo Manual* (OECD, 2005), do not cover the set of constructs and variables of interest. The self-administered questionnaire consisted mainly of five-point Likert-type questions: from '1 – Completely disagree' to '5 – Completely agree'. Scale validation was carried out in four stages: generation and selection of an initial pool of 442 items; content and writing improvement; cognitive interviews; and pre-test (Netemeyer et al., 2003). Scales were successfully evaluated through measures of reliability, convergent validity, residuals, and discriminant validity.

The questionnaire was structured with 32 items: two items for measuring technological innovation in products and processes, based on OECD (2005) and Foss et al. (2011); three items for management innovation realms, based on OECD (2005), Birkinshaw et al. (2008), Hamel (2007) and Walker et al. (2010); seven items for management innovation complexity, built on Rogers (2003), Damanpour (2014) and Ansari et al. (2014); and twenty items for innovation-focused HRM practices, taken from Chen and Huang (2009), Foss et al. (2011), Laursen and Foss (2014) and Delery and Doty (1996). As for technological and management innovation measurement, respondents were asked about those innovations adopted between 2014 and 2016.

Also, an open-ended question was included to ensure that respondents understood questions about management innovation's realms and complexity on which they were responding. This questionnaire design allowed the identification of names for each management innovation, which in turn also enabled the identification of each HRM innovation (Table 10.1). Therefore, the study instrument captured both existing innovation-focused HRM practices and management innovations, including those in HRM – to be precise, HRM innovations. As for other management innovations, HRM ones were characterized concerning realms and complexity.

The initial sample included 1,111 Brazilian organizations (non-probabilistic), with no restrictions on sector or size, and questionnaires were answered by directors, functional managers, project managers, or respondents who performed related activities. Data were collected in 2016, between June 8 and July 15. Managers from different Brazilian states returned a total of 416 valid questionnaires. About 60 percent of sample respondents were from medium and large organizations (100 or more employees). The distribution of organizations among sectors was as follows: 68 percent in services (mostly knowledge-intensive service firms), 20.7 percent in manufacturing and 11.3 percent in other sectors, such as public administration and civil construction.

FINDINGS

A higher proportion of innovative organizations characterized the sample of this study. The percentage of organizations that implemented at least one innovation in a product (goods or services) or process between 2014 and 2016 was above 90 percent. Product improvement was observed in 26 percent of organizations, whereas 27.2 percent implemented new-to-firm product (good or service), and 37.3 percent implemented new-to-market product innovation. As for process innovation, 33.9 percent of organizations improved existing processes, 31.7 percent implemented new-to-firm processes, and 26 percent implemented new-to-industry process innovation. On the other hand, 267 organizations (64 percent) had implemented at least one management innovation between 2014 and 2016.

Innovation-Focused HRM Practices in Innovative and Non-Innovative Organizations

In general, there was a more significant presence of innovation-focused human resource management practices in organizations with product/process or management innovations than in organizations without it. The differences between means for each HRM practice according to innovation type are reported as follows.

In organizations with product or process innovation, each of the five innovation-focused HRM practices had the following means: 3.5 for recruitment and retention; 3.4 for training; 3.7 for delegation; 2.9 for incentives; and 3.1 for communication. In organizations without product or process innovation, the following means were found: 3.3 for recruitment and retention; 3.2 for training; 3.6 for delegation; 2.6 for incentives; and 2.6 for communication.

These means show that organizations that did not innovate in products or processes obtained lower means for innovation-focused HRM practices. The most significant gaps between organizations that innovated and those that did not innovate in products or processes were found for communication and incentives. As the mean for delegation was higher than for other practices and similar both for organizations with and without product or process innovation, such practices seem to have become common to the sample's organizations independently on their technological innovativeness.

In the case of organizations that implemented management innovation, means for all five practices were higher when compared to means of organizations without management innovation. The most significant difference between means was found for training variables (3.6 versus 3.1), and the narrowest differences were found for recruitment and retention (3.6 versus 3.3) and communication variables (3.2 versus 2.9). Means were 3.1 for incentives and 3.8 for delegation in organizations with management innovation, whereas in organizations without management innovation they were, respectively, 2.7 and 3.4.

Results for each of the variables of innovation-focused HRM practices reveal that the highest mean (4.3) concerned a delegation variable that referred to the degree to which employees were allowed to suggest work improvements. The lower means (below 3, the scale's neutral point) concerned variables of incentives, communication, and recruitment and retention. Regarding incentives, lower means were obtained for the following variables: "There is a clear link between performance and reward" (2.9), "Salary is determined by the willingness to improve skills and upgrade knowledge" (2.4) and "Salary is associated with the ability and willingness to share knowledge" (2.8). Among communication practices, the surveyed organizations had lower means for job rotation (2.7) and formal mechanisms for information and knowledge sharing (2.9), such as knowledge management, complaints resolution system and suggestion program. The practice of recruitment and retention with the lowest mean was "Individuals have clear career paths within the organization" (2.9).

Human Resources Management Innovations

Of the 267 organizations with management innovation implemented between 2014 and 2016, 48 implemented HRM innovation (18 percent). Table 10.1 shows denominations for each of them, that is, the names respondents gave to what his/her organization introduced between 2014 and 2016. For ease of understanding, these denominations were grouped by HRM practice. HRM innovations introduced between 2014 and 2016 ranged from specific novelties in performance management, leadership training programs, job rotation and

Table 10.1 Denominations of HRM innovations

HRM Practices	HRM Innovations	
Recruitment and retention	–Jobs and salary plan –Restructuring of recruitment and selection process	–Creating an administrative-accounting job role
Training	–Competence center –Competence management –Deep learning –Introduction of a new model of values and behaviors for professionals –Leadership development and restructuring –Learning tracks	–Mentoring program –New business unit, management training, internal MBA –Professional certification –Professional development program –Profile mapping program –Training improvement –Development tracks
Delegation	–Automated workday control management –Home office –HR autonomy	–Group management implementation –Personal and group quality management
Communication	–Collaborative management –Full flexibility policy for working time and place of work –HR news	–Job rotation –Pro-win knowledge management –Specialty committee –Storytelling
Incentives	–High performance program –Incentive program –Objectives and key results management –Performance and competence appraisal –Performance appraisal –Performance management –Variable compensation	–Performance management/restructuring/ Leadership appraisal program –Recognition of knowledge and competence –Results-based management –Performance appraisal based on revenue –Productivity management
Other	–HR restructuring –Organizational culture –Organizational transformation, management model, technology in human capital management	–Process management; change management –Strength-based people management –Values-based management –HR structuring –HR redefinition

competence management, to broader programs concerning HR restructuring, organizational culture and change management.

Although denominations help us in illustrating research data, they do not provide an in-depth explanation of the specific HRM innovations. Therefore, it is useful to take the distinctive realms of a management innovation to characterize this set of 48 HRM innovations, as well as to understand the differences between them and other management innovations (Table 10.2).

Table 10.2   *Means of management innovation realms for innovation*

Management Innovation Realms	Human Resources Management Innovation (means)	Other Management Innovations (means)
Significant changes to management activities and practices	4.0	3.8
Introduction of new management processes, techniques and tools	3.9	4.1
Introduction of new organizational structures	4.0	4.1

Table 10.2 shows that, in comparison to innovations in areas such as strategy, finance, operations, marketing and IT management, the surveyed HRM innovations also brought novelties to managerial activities and practices, management processes and organizational structures. Table 10.2 indicates that HRM innovations affected these realms in substantial ways, changing slightly more managerial daily routines and organizational structures than management innovation in other areas.

In addition, results reveal HRM innovations' complexities in comparison to other management innovations. At first sight, means were the same (3.0) for the difficulty to understand, use and/or implement them. However, respondents suggest that HRM innovations are more complex as they involve more management areas than other management innovations (mean of 4.2 versus 4.0). HRM innovations also encompassed organizations in a systemic way (4.3) in comparison to other management innovations (4.0). Contrasted to the latter, HRM innovations are less complex in terms of making significant adaptations from the original practice (2.6 versus 3.0), as well as in terms of difficulty to align the novelties with values or organizations' past experiences (2.7 versus 2.9). In the same vein, the degree of novelty was lower for HRM innovations (3.5), that is, they were less radical than management innovation in other areas (3.7). Still, respondents mostly disagreed with the uncertainty of impact from surveyed management innovations, including those on HRM (2.4) and on other areas (2.1).

There is an apparent contradiction here, since innovation involves taking risks. Despite the systemic and radical nature of management innovations, respondents suggest their results or impact are mostly predictable. Reinforcing this contradiction is the neutrality of respondents concerning difficulties of understanding, using and implementing management innovations, as well as their compatibility with the organizations' values and past experiences or the degree of adaptation from the original practice. Therefore, at least for this sample, HRM innovations are not as sophisticated in this respect as they do not require as much adaptation, in comparison to innovations in other areas of management.

CONCLUSIONS

By analyzing innovation from the perspective of human resource management, this chapter explores the interplay between them as complex phenomena. Specific practices, preferably complementary, are required to foster innovation in organizations. The configuration of recruitment and retention, delegation of responsibility, employee training, internal communication and incentive practices influences innovation types in various ways. Thus, differentiated HRM architectures are implemented to foster distinct types of innovations, as was seen for technological innovation in products and processes and management innovation. Worth highlighting was the fact that the surveyed HRM practices are more likely to be established in innovative organizations than in those without innovation.

The findings also reinforce a complicated relationship between management innovation and human resources. HRM innovations, that is, innovation in the management of human resources, are as complex as innovation in other management areas. The HRM innovations studied substantially affected management activities and practices and represented the introduction of new management processes and organizational structures. Also, those innovations involved other management areas and were radical and systemic to a certain extent. However, they did not require as much adaptation, in comparison to innovations in other areas of management.

This chapter has shown that innovation, including in HRM, is not a homogeneous event. This brings new challenges to the HRM function: it should continually evaluate its role and continually adapt or even reinvent itself. One possible way is by definitively incorporating different types of innovation to the HRM agenda or, alternatively, even recapturing innovation-focused managerial practices hosted by other organizational functions (for example, by quality management or knowledge management functions).

From the practitioners' viewpoints, organizations should explore practices that are better suited to their internal contexts. A consistent fit is required between the HRM architecture and innovation strategies, as well as among HRM practices. Configurations should vary according to both the intended technological and non-technological innovations and the extent of their change and complexity. In this perspective, HRM innovation may be a means to obtain a better fit and to minimize the natural uncertainties of innovation processes.

Finally, management innovations should be analyzed in more detail, reflecting their distinctive realms and complexity, particularly in the case of HRM innovations. Therefore, researchers should consider multiple levels of analysis, ranging from those closest to the action of individuals who implement or use innovations to higher ones, such as an organizational level of analysis. As for future studies, the same survey data should be explored through other techniques, for example, searching for the effects from the selected HR practices on technological innovation and management innovation. Also, it may be necessary to survey other HRM practices – possibly more traditional ones, not necessarily focused on product and process innovation – to analyze their relationship with management innovation.

REFERENCES

Agarwala, T. (2003), 'Innovative human resource practices and organizational commitment: an empirical investigation', *International Journal of Human Resource Management*, 14(2), 175–197.

Ansari, S., J. Reinecke and A. Spaan (2014), 'How are practices made to vary? Managing practice adaptation in a multinational corporation', *Organization Studies*, 35(9), 1313–1341.

Becker, B.E. and M.A. Huselid (2006), 'Strategic human resources management: where do we go from here?', *Journal of Management*, 32(6), 898–925.

Birkinshaw, J., G. Hamel and M.J. Mol (2008), 'Management innovation', *Academy of Management Review*, 33(4), 825–845.

Cerne, M., R. Kase and M. Skerlavaj (2016), 'Non-technological innovation research: evaluating the intellectual structure and prospects of an emerging field', *Scandinavian Journal of Management*, 32(2), 69–85.

Chen, C.-J. and J.-W. Huang (2009), 'Strategic human resource practices and innovation performance: the mediating role of knowledge management capacity', *Journal of Business Research*, 62(1), 104–114.

Colbert, B.A. (2008), 'The complex resource-based view: implications for theory and practice in strategic human resource management', in R.S. Schuler and S.E. Jackson (eds.), *Strategic Human Resource Management*, Malden, MA: Blackwell Publishing, 98–123.

Cristallini, V. (2011), 'L'amélioration du management des personnes comme innovation majeure et responsable en matière de GRH', *Revue Sciences de Gestion*, 83, 109–132.

Crossan, M.M. and M. Apaydin (2010), 'A multi-dimensional framework of organizational innovation: a systematic review of the literature', *Journal of Management Studies*, 47(6), 1154–1191.

Damanpour, F. (2014), 'Footnotes to research on management innovation', *Organization Studies*, 35(9), 1265–1285.

Delery, J.E. and D.H. Doty (1996), 'Modes of theorizing in strategic human resource management: tests of universalistic, contingency, and configurational performance predictions', *Academy of Management Journal*, 39(4), 802–835.

Fagerberg, J., M. Fosaas and K. Sapprasert (2012), 'Innovation: exploring the knowledge base', *Research Policy*, 41(7), 1132–1153.

Foss, N.J., K. Laursen and T. Pedersen (2011), 'Linking customer interaction and innovation: the mediating role of new organizational practices', *Organization Science*, 22(4), 980–999.

Hamel, G. (2007), *The Future of Management*, Boston, MA: Harvard Business School Publishing.

Jackson, S.E., R.S. Schuler and K. Jiang (2014), 'An aspirational framework for strategic human resource management', *The Academy of Management Annals*, 8(1), 1–56.

Jiang, K., D.P. Lepak, K. Han, Y. Hong, A. Kim and A.-L. Winkler (2012), 'Clarifying the construct of human resource systems: relating human resource management to employee performance', *Human Resource Management Review*, 22(2), 73–85.

Jørgensen, F., K. Becker and J. Matthews (2011), 'The HRM practices of innovative knowledge-intensive firms', *International Journal of Technology Management*, 56(2–4), 123–137.

Kim, A. and C. Lee (2012), 'How does HRM enhance strategic capabilities? Evidence from the Korean management consulting industry', *International Journal of Human Resource Management*, 23(1), 126–146.

Kossek, E.E. (1987), 'Human resources management innovations', *Human Resource Management*, 26(1), 71–92.

Lam, A. (2005), 'Organizational innovation', in J. Fagerberg, D. Mowery and R. Nelson (eds.), *The Oxford Handbook of Innovation*, Oxford: Oxford University Press, 115–147.

Laursen, K. and N.J. Foss (2003), 'New human resource management practices, complementarities and the impact on innovation performance', *Cambridge Journal of Economics*, 27(2), 243–263.

Laursen, K. and N.J. Foss (2014), 'Human resource management practices and innovation', in M. Dodgson, D.M. Gann and N. Phillips (eds.), *The Oxford Handbook of Innovation Management*, Oxford: Oxford University Press, 505–529.

Le Bas, C., C. Mothe and T.U. Nguyen-Thi (2015), 'The differentiated impacts of organizational innovation practices on technological innovation persistence', *European Journal of Innovation Management*, 18(1), 110–127.

Lin, L.-H. (2011), 'Electronic human resource management and organizational innovation: the roles of information technology and virtual organizational structure', *International Journal of Human Resource Management*, 22(2), 235–257.

Liu, D., Y. Gong, J. Zhou and J.-C. Huang (2017), 'Human resource systems, employee creativity, and firm innovation: the moderating role of firm ownership', *Academy of Management Journal*, 60(3), 1164–1188.

Lopes, D.P.T. (2017), 'Inovação gerencial na perspectiva da gestão de recursos humanos', Tese de Doutorado, UFMG, Belo Horizonte.

Mol, M.J. and J. Birkinshaw (2008), *Giant Steps in Management*, Harlow: Prentice Hall.

Mol, M.J. and J. Birkinshaw (2014), 'The role of external involvement in the creation of management innovations', *Organization Studies*, 35(9), 1287–1312.

Netemeyer, R.G., W.O. Bearden and S. Sharma (2003), *Scaling Procedures: Issues and Applications*, Thousand Oaks, CA: Sage Publications.

OECD (2005), *Oslo Manual* (3rd ed.), Paris: OECD Publishing.

OECD (2018), *Oslo Manual* (4th ed.), Paris: OECD Publishing.

Oke, A., F.O. Walumbwa and A. Myers (2012), 'Innovation strategy, human resource policy, and firms' revenue growth: the roles of environmental uncertainty and innovation performance', *Decision Sciences*, 43(2), 273–302.

Rogers, E.M. (2003), *Diffusion of Innovations* (5th ed.), New York: Free Press.

Ruël, H., T. Bondarouk, H. Florén and J. Rundquist (2014), 'Human resource management and firm innovativeness in a European context: advancing our understanding of the relationship (Introduction to the thematic issue)', *European Journal of International Management*, 8(5), 465–471.

Seeck, H. and M.-R. Diehl (2017), 'A literature review on HRM and innovation: taking stock and future directions', *International Journal of Human Resource Management*, 28(6), 913–944.

Shipton, H., M.A. West, J. Dawson, K. Birdi and M. Patterson (2006), 'HRM as a predictor of innovation', *Human Resource Management Journal*, 16(1), 3–27.

Ulrich, D. (1998), *Os campeões de recursos humanos*, São Paulo: Futura.

Volberda, H.W., F.A.J. Van Den Bosch and C.V. Heij (2013), 'Management innovation: management as fertile ground for innovation', *European Management Review*, 10(1), 1–15.

Walker, R.M., F. Damanpour and C.A. Deve ce (2010), 'Management innovation and organizational performance: the mediating effect of performance management', *Journal of Public Administration Research and Theory*, 21(2), 367–386.

Wang, Z. and Z. Zang (2005), 'Strategic human resources, innovation and entrepreneurship fit: a cross-regional comparative model', *International Journal of Manpower*, 26(6), 544–559.

Wolfe, R. (1995), 'Human resource management innovations: determinants of their adoption and implementation', *Human Resource Management*, 34(2), 313–327.

Wolfe, R., P.M. Wright and D.L. Smart (2006), 'Radical HRM innovation and competitive advantage: the Moneyball story', *Human Resource Management*, 45(1), 111–145.

Wright, P.M., B.B. Dunford and S.A. Snell (2008), 'Human resources and the resource-based view of the firm', in R.S. Schuler and S.E. Jackson (eds.), *Strategic Human Resource Management*, Malden, MA: Blackwell Publishing, 76–97.

APPENDIX

Table 10.A.1   Questionnaire structure

Questionnaire sections and variables	
A. Product and process innovation	
	Implementation of product (good or service) innovation
	Implementation of process innovation
B. Management innovation [this set of questions was answered only by respondents that identified management innovation implementation between 2014 and 2016. In such cases, they first answered an open-ended question requesting the management innovation name, which was used for subsequent statements in this category]	
Realms	This innovation significantly changed our management activities and practices
	This innovation introduced new management processes, techniques and tools
	This innovation introduced new organizational structures
Complexity	This innovation involved multiple management areas
	This was a radical innovation, with a significant departure from previous practices
	This innovation was difficult to understand, use and/or implement
	It was difficult to align this innovation with our values and/or past experiences
	We had to make significant adaptations from the original practice
	This innovation encompassed our organization in a systemic way (not just a part of it)
	There was great uncertainty about the impact of this innovation
C. Innovation-focused HRM practices	
Delegation	In my organization, employees are allowed to make decisions
	Employees are allowed to suggest improvements to work
	Employees' voices are valued by the organization
	Employees are engaged in teams with high degree of autonomy
Incentives	There is a clear link between performance and reward
	There is a formal employee performance appraisal with feedback
	Salary is determined by the willingness to improve skills and upgrade knowledge
	Salary is associated with the ability and willingness to share knowledge
Communication	There is an exchange of information between employees across departments
	Communication flows between supervisors and subordinates
	Employees are allowed to participate in job rotation
	There are formal mechanisms for information and knowledge sharing
Training	Formal training programs are offered to employees
	Training policies and programs are comprehensive
	There is training for new hires
	There is training for problem-solving ability

Questionnaire sections and variables	
	There is selectivity in hiring
Recruitment and retention	Employees are selected for expertise and skills
	Individuals have clear career paths within the organization
	The organization prioritizes the internal promotion of its employees

11. On the emotions that spark innovative and entrepreneurial behaviors in employees

Fabian Bernhard

INTRODUCTION

During the past years academic scholars and practitioners have become increasingly attracted by the role of emotions in innovation and entrepreneurship. This interest is warranted as several studies underpin the role affect can play in our creative thinking and the implementation of new ideas. Accordingly, people in business have started asking which emotions may be particularly beneficial in initiating new entrepreneurial endeavors in employees. By understanding which feelings foster and which ones prevent innovative entrepreneurship, one could pursue strategies towards a favorable emotional climate that enhances innovative thinking and behaving. What organizational climate should managers and owners of businesses foster to make their workforce more inventive? And are only positive emotions beneficial to creative behavior, or can negative emotions also elicit innovativeness? This chapter aims at offering a first response to these pressing questions by providing a brief overview on the current state of research on how different emotional affect relates to employees' innovative and entrepreneurial behaviors. Accordingly, innovation managers can gain by understanding how to train their emotional awareness and to set the appropriate emotional triggers for an innovative organizational climate.

Research on continuous entrepreneurship and innovation is in demand. Startup founders are constantly on the lookout for new business ideas, established family businesses seek ways to break through the ties of tradition that prevent the next generation being entrepreneurial (Filser et al., 2018; Kellermanns et al., 2008; Vuori and Huy, 2016; Zahra, 2005), and other kinds of organizations try to overcome organizational inertia but motivate their members to behave in innovative and entrepreneurial ways (Jong et al., 2015). Finding answers as to why some people are better at spotting and acting upon new business opportunities touches many fields of study. But especially the fields of entrepreneurship and applied psychology have been looking into factors within the individual that make us more innovative. And lately, the emotional states under which entrepreneurial intentions and actions emerge have gained much attention (Bernoster et al., 2018; Cardon et al., 2012; Delgado García et al., 2015). Important but unanswered questions are: Which emotions make us innovative and entrepreneurial? Can certain emotional states and moods be triggered to make organizational members more creative? And if so, which organizational climate should managers and owners of businesses foster to make their workforce more innovative? Are only positive emotions beneficial, or can negative emotions also elicit innovativeness? Following this stream, researchers have started looking for answers to the question of which feelings make us more innovative in our business behavior. The goal of the present chapter is to offer insight on this question in the light of current knowledge found in the academic literature.

RESEARCH INTO INNOVATIVE ENTREPRENEURSHIP AND EMOTIONS, MOODS AND FEELINGS

The growing interest in the relationship between psychological affect and entrepreneurial and innovative behaviors is rooted in three arguments (Bernoster et al., 2018; Delgado García et al., 2015). First, starting a new business is more than a rationally planned behavior. Understanding entrepreneurship as a pure act of rationality does not take into account the interrelatedness between cognition and affect (e.g. Bower, 1983). Many acts of entrepreneurship find their origin in emotions; be it that certain emotions trigger creative thinking; be it that negative emotions make us yearn for implementing change and trying out new things; or be it that some positive emotions make us more susceptible to spotting business opportunities. Having a clear understanding on this connection can enable opportunities to steer the power of certain emotions into advantageous directions. Second, it has been argued that the startup process of new ventures is characterized by many ups and downs (Cook, 1986). As a result, trying to implement one's own business ideas under chaotic and complex situations can be similar to an emotional rollercoaster. Entrepreneurs are frequently exposed to emotions that test their resilience. Under such conditions emotion and affect may play an elevated role in cognition. Third, not only the frequency of occurrence but also the intensity of emotions is stronger in an entrepreneurial context. Entrepreneurs may be intensely affected by the current condition of their venture as they often strongly identify with it. After all, they put significant investment in terms of time and personal energy into the implementation of their ideas. Furthermore, entrepreneurial success is closely linked with their self-esteem and own financial situation. Given this close connection between the founder and his or her venture, the strong influence of affect on cognition may be especially prominent among entrepreneurial people.

In the literature several terms are used to describe the influence of affect on entrepreneurs' cognition and behaviors. Given the multifaceted terminology it can easily lead to confusion. Some authors refer to more general terms such as "affect" (Baron, 2008), "emotion" (Foo, 2011) and "mood" (Perry-Smith and Coff, 2011), while others research discrete basic emotions such as "anger," "fear," and "joy" (Welpe et al., 2012), but also discrete cognitive emotions such as "shame" or "guilt" (Bernhard, 2018). From a psychological perspective and in line with Frijda (1986), the concepts related to affect differ in several dimensions. Moods on the one side remain stable over some time, create only lower levels of arousal, and are not consciously connected to a specific event, person or object. Emotions, on the other side, can quickly come to existence, remain only for a limited period of time, create high levels of arousal, and are regularly tied to a specific event, person or object. Both forms of affect can vary in their valence and intensity. Moreover, emotions have been described as contagious, changing the level of analysis from individual to group level (Mackie et al., 2000; Smith et al., 2007). Given these multilayered aspects of affect, complexity rises, which has led to a fragmented and theoretically inconsistent body of literature on how affect relates to entrepreneurship (Delgado García et al., 2015). To make things worse, entrepreneurship is a process consisting of different stages, and authors have usually focused only on one part of it, creating even more fragmented answers. As affect might have different influence on the various stages along this process, the inconsistency in studies makes a complete understanding even more difficult. In the following, the main findings of prominent studies will be summarized.

THE BENEFITS OF POSITIVE AFFECT

The majority of studies highlight the benefits of positive affect. For example, conceptual work by Baron et al. (2012) point towards the beneficial effects positive affect can have on new venture development and growth. People with a disposition towards positive emotions and moods generally perform well in opportunity recognition and evaluation and effective decision making. However, the authors also mention that this relationship is of a curvilinear nature. Overly strong tendencies for positive affect can lead to increased impulsiveness, distraction from self-monitoring and proneness for more cognitive errors.

Empirical evidence backs the proposed beneficial aspects of positive emotions. A study by Baron and Tang (2011) indicates that positive affect among founding entrepreneurs is significantly related to their creativity and that creativity, in turn, is positively related to firm-level innovation. In another study Foo and colleagues (2009) asked 46 entrepreneurs twice per day on their levels of affect over a period of over three weeks. They found that positive affect can predict venture effort beyond what is immediately required and that positive emotions prolonged the temporal perspectives. In another article Foo and colleagues (2015) argue that particularly positive affect and its activation work together to impact opportunity identification. Williamson and colleagues (2019) found that high-activation positive moods were precursors of innovative behaviors of entrepreneurs on a given day. Other studies support the view on the beneficial outcomes of positive affect from a different perspective. For example, research by Naudé et al. (2014) links a nation's level of happiness with the entrepreneurial activities of its citizens. Countries where people tend towards positive emotions seem to provide better soil for entrepreneurship. Finally, empirical studies in Eastern parts of the world, e.g. China, also show relationships between positive affect and innovative work behavior (Li et al., 2017).

THE BENEFITS OF NEGATIVE AFFECT

The connection between negative affects and entrepreneurial behaviors might be less apparent. After all, the image of an entrepreneur is shaped by a positive-thinking, upbeat-mood personality and just does not seem to fit with negativity (Patzelt and Shepherd, 2011). Indeed, De Dreu et al. (2008) highlight that deactivating moods such as feeling sad or depressed lead to less creative fluency and originality. With decreased creativity it seems that entrepreneurial endeavors become less likely. In the same vein, Doern and Goss (2014) show that negative emotions in the social processes of entrepreneurship can destroy entrepreneurial motivation and direct attention and energy away from business growth and development. In fact, those who remain self-employed have been argued to simply better cope with negative emotions (Patzelt and Shepherd, 2011).

Latest findings, however, have called into question the pessimistic view on negative affect in the prevalent literature. For example in two studies by Foo (2011) results indicate that anger, which qualifies as an emotion with negative valence, can lead to more positive opportunity evaluations. This in turn may support entrepreneurial endeavors. Similarly, Welpe et al. (2012) show that joy, but also the negative feeling of anger, can increase entrepreneurial exploitation. Participants were also more likely to positively connect opportunity evaluation and exploitation under the emotions of joy and anger. Fear on the other side reduced the same connection. Similar findings are reported by Vuori and Huy (2016) who show that the experience of fear was one of the reasons why Nokia became less innovative. Lastly, empirical research by Bernhard (2018) reported that study participants with tendencies for the negative cognitive emotion of guilt were more prone to behave in entrepreneurial and innovative ways, and were more likely to start their own business.

CONCLUSIONS

The question of which emotions drive entrepreneurship has been called a "hot topic" (Cardon et al., 2012). Research and practice alike have found great interest in the influence of affect on entrepreneurial thinking and acting. In spite of the attention given to the topic, its complexity and the fast development of the field, academic results on the question of which feelings make us entrepreneurial are still inconclusive and fragmented. The present chapter has offered a glimpse into the latest findings. Most research lays out the beneficial effects of positive emotions. Yet also some of the negative feelings have been connected to entrepreneurial behaviors. New theorizing in the field of creativity research, however, has suggested that the change of emotions, the so-called affective shift (Bledow et al., 2011, 2013), interacts with and triggers motivational forces related to engagement and thus potentially entrepreneurial behaviors. Future research will show the way and produce new insights. Academia is thus encouraged to create new understanding by providing overarching theories across levels of analysis and along the stages of the entrepreneurial process.

For practitioners these findings are worthwhile as they promise benefits on several levels. For example, studies have shown that managers who create suitable emotional climates can expect increased company performance, revenue growth and outcome growth (Ozcelik et al., 2008). Similarly, recent findings suggest that innovation managers who understand emotions are able to influence employees' creativity via organizational culture (Jafri et al., 2016). Lastly, also the link between people's emotional competencies and innovation performance has been successfully tested (Zhang et al., 2015). As such, research has offered managers important tools. Understanding the role of emotions and strengthening one's emotional intelligence promises to be an essential management tool in the innovation management process.

REFERENCES

Baron, R.A. (2008), 'The role of affect in the entrepreneurial process', *Academy of Management Review*, 33(2), 328–340.

Baron, R.A., K.M. Hmieleski and R.A. Henry (2012), 'Entrepreneurs' dispositional positive affect: the potential benefits – and potential costs – of being "up"', *Journal of Business Venturing*, 27(3), 310–324.

Baron, R.A. and J. Tang (2011), 'The role of entrepreneurs in firm-level innovation: joint effects of positive affect, creativity, and environmental dynamism', *Journal of Business Venturing*, 26(1), 49–60.

Bernhard, F. (2018), 'Self-conscious emotions and entrepreneurial behavior, intent, and execution', paper presented at the Annual Meeting of the Academy of Management, Chicago, IL.

Bernoster, I., J. Mukerjee and R. Thurik (2018), 'The role of affect in entrepreneurial orientation', *Small Business Economics*, http://hdl.handle.net/1765/112098.

Bledow, R., K. Rosing and M. Frese (2013), 'A dynamic perspective on affect and creativity', *Academy of Management Journal*, 56(2), 432–450.

Bledow, R., A. Schmitt, M. Frese and J. Kühnel (2011), 'The affective shift model of work engagement', *Journal of Applied Psychology*, 96(6), 1246–1257.

Bower, G.H. (1983), 'Affect and cognition', *Philosophical Transactions of the Royal Society of London B: Biolgical Sciences*, 302(1110), 387–402.

Cardon, M.S., M.D. Foo, D. Shepherd and J. Wiklund (2012), 'Exploring the heart: entrepreneurial emotion is a hot topic', *Entrepreneurship Theory and Practice*, 36(1), 1–10.

Cook, J.R. (1986), *The Start-Up Entrepreneur: How You Can Succeed in Building Your Own Company into a Major Enterprise Starting from Scratch*, New York: Dutton.

De Dreu, C.K., M. Baas and B.A. Nijstad (2008), 'Hedonic tone and activation level in the mood-creativity link: toward a dual pathway to creativity model', *Journal of Personality and Social Psychology*, 94(5), 739–756.

Delgado García, J.B., E. Quevedo Puente and V. Blanco Mazagatos (2015), 'How affect relates to entrepreneurship: a systematic review of the literature and research agenda', *International Journal of Management Reviews*, 17(2), 191–211.

Doern, R. and D. Goss (2014), 'The role of negative emotions in the social processes of entrepreneurship: power rituals and shame-related appeasement behaviors', *Entrepreneurship Theory and Practice*, 38(4), 863–890.

Filser, M., A. De Massis, J. Gast, S. Kraus and T. Niemand (2018), 'Tracing the roots of innovativeness in family SMEs: the effect of family functionality and socioemotional wealth', *Journal of Product Innovation Management*, 35(4), 609–628.

Foo, M.D. (2011), 'Emotions and entrepreneurial opportunity evaluation', *Entrepreneurship Theory and Practice*, 35(2), 375–393.

Foo, M.D., M.A. Uy and R.A. Baron (2009), 'How do feelings influence effort? An empirical study of entrepreneurs' affect and venture effort', *Journal of Applied Psychology*, 94(4), 1086–1094.

Foo, M.D., M.A. Uy and C. Murnieks (2015), 'Beyond affective valence: untangling valence and activation influences on opportunity identification', *Entrepreneurship Theory and Practice*, 39(2), 407–431.

Frijda, N.H. (1986), *The Emotions*, Cambridge: Cambridge University Press.

Jafri, M.H., C. Dem and S. Choden (2016), 'Emotional intelligence and employee creativity: moderating role of proactive personality and organizational climate', *Business Perspectives and Research*, 4(1), 54–66.

Jong, J.P., S.K. Parker, S. Wennekers and C.H. Wu. (2015), 'Entrepreneurial behavior in organizations: does job design matter?', *Entrepreneurship Theory and Practice*, 39(4), 981–995.

Kellermanns, F.W., K.A. Eddleston, T. Barnett and A. Pearson (2008), 'An exploratory study of family member characteristics and involvement: effects on entrepreneurial behavior in the family firm', *Family Business Review*, 21(1), 1–14.

Li, M., Y. Liu, L. Liu and Z. Wang (2017), 'Proactive personality and innovative work behavior: the mediating effects of affective states and creative self-efficacy in teachers', *Current Psychology*, 36(4), 697–706.

Mackie, D.M., T. Devos and E.R. Smith (2000), 'Intergroup emotions: explaining offensive action tendencies in an intergroup context', *Journal of Personality and Social Psychology*, 79(4), 602–616.

Naudé, W., J.E. Amorós and O. Cristi (2014), '"Surfeiting, the appetite may sicken": entrepreneurship and happiness', *Small Business Economics*, 42(3), 523–540.

Ozcelik, H., N. Langton and H. Aldrich (2008), 'Doing well and doing good: the relationship between leadership practices that facilitate a positive emotional climate and organizational performance', *Journal of Managerial Psychology*, 23(2), 186–203.

Patzelt, H. and D.A. Shepherd (2011), 'Negative emotions of an entrepreneurial career: self-employment and regulatory coping behaviors', *Journal of Business Venturing*, 26(2), 226–238.

Perry-Smith, J.E. and R.W. Coff (2011), 'In the mood for entrepreneurial creativity? How optimal group affect differs for generating and selecting ideas for new ventures', *Strategic Entrepreneurship Journal*, 5(3), 247–268.

Smith, E.R., C.R. Seger and D.M. Mackie (2007), 'Can emotions be truly group level? Evidence regarding four conceptual criteria', *Journal of Personality and Social Psychology*, 93(3), 431–446.

Vuori, T.O. and Q.N. Huy (2016), 'Distributed attention and shared emotions in the innovation process: how Nokia lost the smartphone battle', *Administrative Science Quarterly*, 61(1), 9–51.

Welpe, I.M., M. Spörrle, D. Grichnik, T. Michl and D.B. Audretsch (2012), 'Emotions and opportunities: the interplay of opportunity evaluation, fear, joy, and anger as antecedent of entrepreneurial exploitation', *Entrepreneurship Theory and Practice*, 36(1), 69–96.

Williamson, A.J., M. Battisti, M. Leatherbee and J.J. Gish (2019), 'Rest, zest, and my innovative best: sleep and mood as drivers of entrepreneurs' innovative behavior', *Entrepreneurship Theory and Practice*, 43(3), 582–610.

Zahra, S.A. (2005), 'Entrepreneurial risk taking in family firms', *Family Business Review*, 18(1), 23–40.

Zhang, S.J., Y.Q. Chen and H. Sun (2015), 'Emotional intelligence, conflict management styles, and innovation performance: an empirical study of Chinese employees', *International Journal of Conflict Management*, 26(4), 450–478.

PART VI

Case study

12. UPS Lithuania – choose your own salary

Vida Škudienė and Ilona Buciuniene

BACKGROUND

UPS Lithuania was established by a person with revolutionary ideas and brave vision for a company in independent Lithuania. CEO Vladas Lasas believed that employees could do the job as well as he or even better. His status did not mean a lot to him. He used to delegate the work to others and his head was always full of ideas that very often were ahead of their time. As early as 2007, he introduced the idea of using electric motor-bicycles. In order to minimize impact on the environment, the company bought three electric motor-bicycles. It was a great opportunity to save costs and environment. Thus, UPS Lithuania became the first company in Lithuania to use such modern and ecological transportation.

The company did not have formal written values, although the core value in the company had always been fairness: *'Fairness for colleagues, oneself and job you do. The employees with different values and consciousness usually leave the company'*, claimed Vladas Lasas. The company and its employees held the values of responsibility and fairness, even when it was not financially beneficial. The company employees always informed the authorities if they suspected any unfair delivery or use of a stolen credit card.

Vladas Lasas was proud of his colleagues and family. He had two children of his own and had adopted two. Therefore, nobody was surprised when a support programme for a foster home for children was started. It became a tradition to visit the foster home at least twice a year and provide as much support for the children as possible. The employees initiated the fund 'Child Support'. The fund established a private foster home for children called 'Home Fireplace' and found sponsors for it. With the sponsors' help they bought a house with a large garden. The home fostered eight children. The founders' aim was to create an environment close to a real family for the children. The company employees could receive tax-free loans if needed.

Once Vladas Lasas read *Maverick: The Success Story Behind the World's Most Unusual Workplace* by Ricardo Semler he was mesmerized by the idea presented in the book: to allow employees to define their salary by themselves. He wanted to implement the idea in his company but realized that it was too early and the company was not mature enough for such change; however, he was sure that some day he would introduce this idea to his company.

CONTEXT OF THE INNOVATION

In 2004 Lithuania joined the EU and many qualified people emigrated to Western European countries and the USA seeking better salaries and quality of life. Consequently, many companies started to feel the lack of qualified employees. Due to emigration and the decreasing birth rate in Lithuania, the number of potential employees had been shrinking and the mobility of employees from company to company increased. The increase in demand in the labour market caused a tendency among employees to change jobs. Companies were fighting for skilled employees and were raising their salaries. However, the salary increase did not enhance employee motivation and commitment to an organization. Companies invested a lot in human resources: training, organizational culture and the formation of an attractive employer image.

UPS Lithuania, as an authorized Service Contractor of a big international company, had to follow the international service delivery standards very strictly, but they could create and implement the HRM policies and decisions locally. Vladas Lasas reacted to the labour market situation similarly: he started reviewing salaries twice a year. Still, the company employees were not satisfied with the salary levels and the way the salaries were defined. Annual employee turnover was 12.8 per cent. Luckily the company received EU funding to implement an HRM development program. The main aim of this program was orientated towards customer service improvement by developing general employee skills. The project lasted two years and 66 employees out of 76 participated in the training. The training was very successful: consultancy companies gave a high assessment of the culture of the company and the maturity of their employees. The employees highlighted the company's values, discussed why they appreciated the company, were proud of it and enjoyed working for it. Vladas Lasas knew – now it was the time to start the change.

IMPLEMENTATION

Having analysed the company's income and costs, and the increase in the company profit, the shareholders increased the employee salary budget by 19 per cent. Only the project team – the CEO, the Head of the HR department and the senior accountant – were aware of this decision. The supervisors of the departments were asked to determine their department employees' salaries, taking into consideration their accomplishments: work quality, participation in company activities, teamwork and proposed innovative ideas. After that, the suggested salary increase was presented and discussed with the vice president. The senior accountant presented the data about employee salaries to the Head of the HR department.

The company CEO wrote a letter to all the employees. A corporate envelope was sent to every employee with the letter (see example in the Appendix), including a questionnaire, an extract from the book *Maverick*, the company's structure, and the individual employee's salary data. The latter document gave information on how much money from the employee's gross salary the company paid for social insurance (33.8 per cent), citizenship income taxes (27 per cent) and the final net salary, which the employee received. This information allowed employees to better understand the full costs of their salary and how much every employee paid to the government. It was not usual practice at that time in Lithuania for companies to inform their employees about payment costs. The project group wanted employees to evaluate not only the salary that they received but also the taxes that were paid by an employee and the company to the government.

The Head of the HR department arranged meetings in every department and presented the new project 'Choose Your Own Salary' idea. After the meeting, every employee received a personal envelope, was asked to fill in the questionnaire and return it to their supervisor within 24 hours. Then the supervisors sent the questionnaires to the Head of the HR department.

RESULTS

The Head of HR department conducted the questionnaire analysis and presented the results to the project team. The results were as follows: 39 per cent of employees' salary expectations matched the company's plan or were even lower than was planned by their supervisors, 40 per cent of employees requested a slightly higher salary whilst 21 per cent of employees' expectations differed by 15 per cent from the planned.

The Head of HR department arranged personal meetings with every employee to discuss the results: the employee's salary, responsibility, commitment and career. Many employees confessed that they had asked for a higher salary just to receive the amount they wanted. After the meetings, 74 per cent of employees were very happy because they received the salary they requested and it matched the company's appointed sum, 13 per cent of employees were satisfied because they received salaries which differed only slightly from the requested salary and it was discussed what they had to do in order to receive the higher salary, and 13 per cent of employees were unsatisfied because their expectations were not met.

The unsatisfied employees participated in a second meeting to analyse the situation more thoroughly. After the second meeting, the salary was increased for one employee because he was able to prove that he deserved that salary, one employee left the company, one employee agreed with the decision to compensate her salary increase by other measures, and two employees were still not satisfied. An action plan for these employees on how it would be possible to increase their salary was prepared. The project results were presented to all the employees.

After a year, the second part of the project was carried out in the same way as the first. This time, the CEO wrote another letter with a questionnaire. The findings of the questionnaire indicated that 85.5 per cent of employees were very satisfied. The remainder, 14.5 per cent of employees, were unsatisfied. Even after the personal meetings, the results were the same. The feedback from the employees was very good.

The project 'Choose Your Own Salary' was very successful: the effort was reflected in the results. Employee voice mailboxes were provided in every department as employees requested. Personal interviews with employees were arranged according to the employees' request, as they wanted more personal attention from the managers. Employees could talk to their supervisors and CEO once in three months, a new mid-year bonus scheme was introduced and a facility room for carriers was constructed. Employee turnover dropped to 4.4 per cent.

DISCUSSION QUESTIONS

1. What are the aspects that enabled UPS Lithuania to innovate? Support your answer with reference to Chapters 9, 10 and 11.
2. Is the learning of this organization transferable to other organizations? Yes/No. Why? Support your answer with reference to Chapter 2.
3. Compare Japanese and UPS Lithuania organizational culture patterns supporting innovations. Refer to Chapter 3.
4. What are the main success factors allowing the introduction of such an innovative compensation system in the company? Refer to Chapter 6.
5. Describe how the four innovation perspectives (strategic, product/service, process, and people) are being manifested in UPS Lithuania. Support your answer with reference to the relevant book chapters.

APPENDIX

Dear Rimantas,

You and all your colleagues created this company. This process did not last just one year and we all should be proud of our company: our company is the most famous in Lithuania. UAB 'Skubios Siuntos' company is part of everyone's life story. If you are with us, it means this story is important to you, as every child is important for a parent, although your child may also have drawbacks.

Why do you work in our company? How would you like to improve it? How could it become a better place for you to work? How would it be able to help you accomplish your aims and be more beneficial to you? What should the company be aiming for? These are difficult questions to answer. You should be sure that your voice is important and that a lot depends on you.

Today, when we discuss salary issues, it depends on you what salary you will allocate to yourself. We are asking you to 'choose your own salary'. You will see it is not that easy. You will find in the envelope an extract from R. Semler's book *Maverick: The Success Story Behind the World's Most Unusual Workplace* to assist you in making the decision. Think about what salary you expect, what salary you think your work would be valued at in another company in Lithuania, what salary you would be satisfied with and what your salary should be in a year or two. Fifteen years ago, an average salary in our company was 50 USA dollars. Calculate how much your salary has increased now.

What else is important for you in our company? What matters should more time and attention be devoted to and what matters should be avoided? You will find in the attachment more information for your consideration and a short questionnaire that we ask you to fill in and return to your supervisor within 24 hours in an envelope. We want to make changes as soon as possible, in October, don't we?

Do not hesitate and ask if you need explanation or any misunderstanding occurs. Mistakes are possible every time when you do something new. We want to say thank you to our managers for their initiative, work and responsibility while organizing this discussion.

Good ideas and good luck!

Sincerely, CEO Vladas Lasas

We would like to remind you these facts: (1) the salary fund since last year was increased by 19 per cent; (2) the information about the money you earned is provided in Table 12.A.1.

Table 12.A.1   Information about the earned money and taxes

Month	Company allocated money for your salary	Social insurance tax 33.8 per cent	Citizenship insurance tax 27 per cent	Salary after taxes
Jan	4471	1159	827	2485
Feb	4471	1160	827	2484
March	5768	1496	1094	3178
April	5603	1453	1060	3090
May	4715	1223	877	2615
June	5949	1543	1131	3275
July	6433	1669	1231	3533
Aug	5704	1480	1081	3143
Total	**43115**	**11186**	**8127**	**23803**

Index

Abbeglen, J.C. 28, 30
affect
   affective shift 186
   benefits of negative 185–6
   benefits of positive 184–5
   relationship with entrepreneurial and
      innovative behaviors 183–4
   role in creative thinking 182
Agile development model
   change from Waterfall model
      116–19
   change in RE process 119–20
   definition 115
   growth in popularity 114
   project success rate 116
   research findings 130–135
   research framework 122–3
   role of SA in 120–122, 130, 134,
      135–6
   study conclusions 135–6
Amabile, T. 31, 32
AMO model 142, 145, 154, 155, 156,
   158
'Andon' 34–5
Apple 3, 27
As-is business process 99, 105
aspiration, high 38, 42
automation level 107
automotive industry 7–8
   see also Toyota Motor Corporation

benchmarking 50
best practices in NPD *see* new product
   development (NPD)
BPM *see* business process management
   (BPM)
brainstorming 53
Brazilian organizations
   HRM innovations 173–6
   innovation-focused HRM practices
      in 172–3

methodology 171–2
questionnaire sent to 180–181
study conclusions and future
   research avenues 176–7
'Bushi-do' outlook 29
business competencies *see* competencies
business process
   To-be business process 106
   defining 94–5
   high-performance 109
   HRM for supporting strategic 168
   improvement
      activities 105
      continuous 108
      implementing 100
      incremental 102
      recommendations 110
   As-is 105
   Lean approaches for 102–3
   overview 94–6
   value creation linked with 100
business process management (BPM)
   benefits 98
   commonest approaches
      BPR 100–102
      CI 102–4
      deciding between for
         sub-processes 106–8
      integrated strategy 104–6
   core elements 97
   customer orientation 96–7
   definition 96
   lifecycle 98–9
   objectives 96
   and operational processes 95
   PEMM model for 109
   process innovation as driver of
      projects 93
   selecting method of 99–100
   strategic management connection
      97–8
business process re-engineering (BPR)

196